John Henry Newman

Miscellanies from the Oxford Sermons and Other Writings of John Henry Newman

John Henry Newman

Miscellanies from the Oxford Sermons and Other Writings of John Henry Newman

ISBN/EAN: 9783337084554

Printed in Europe, USA, Canada, Australia, Japan

Cover: Foto ©Lupo / pixelio.de

More available books at **www.hansebooks.com**

MISCELLANIES

*FROM THE OXFORD SERMONS
AND OTHER WRITINGS*

OF

JOHN HENRY NEWMAN, D.D.

STRAHAN & CO., PUBLISHERS
56, LUDGATE HILL, LONDON
1870

LONDON:
PRINTED BY WILLIAM CLOWES AND SONS,
STAMFORD STREET AND CHARING CROSS.

PREFATORY NOTE.

THESE selections have been made, with the author's consent, from his Oxford Sermons, and such other of his Anglican writings as presented short passages calculated to convey some idea of his style and modes of thinking. Dr. Newman's works include a considerable body of abstract theological discussion. This has not been drawn on here, under the idea that those more directly interested in theological studies would prefer to go to the treatises themselves. Besides, these do not readily yield themselves to extract, owing to the texture of the reasoning being invariably so close throughout. The "Apologia" has been untouched from causes somewhat similar. The little volumes on Church History have supplied a few portraits. It is hoped that the passages chosen will, in some degree, contribute to make still better known one of the deepest thinkers and most eloquent writers of the present time.

CONTENTS.

HISTORICAL STUDIES.

THE WORLD'S BENEFACTORS	1
BALAAM	10
SAUL	27
DAVID	43
ST. PAUL	60
ANTONY AND HIS TEMPTATIONS	73
ARIUS	86
CONSTANTINE	92
BASIL AND GREGORY	96
MARTYRDOM	111

MORAL AND PRACTICAL.

THE GREATNESS AND LITTLENESS OF HUMAN LIFE	121
THE MYSTERIOUSNESS OF OUR PRESENT BEING	130
THE IMMORTALITY OF THE SOUL	138
THE INDIVIDUALITY OF THE SOUL	149
THE INVISIBLE WORLD	162
THE LAPSE OF TIME	175
RELIGIOUS PRIVILEGES	182
CURIOSITY A TEMPTATION TO SIN	187
THE PRAISE OF MEN	190
TEMPORAL ADVANTAGES	193
A SOBER MIND	197
MORAL EFFECTS OF COMMUNION WITH GOD	199
THE MIND OF LITTLE CHILDREN	204

CONTENTS.

DOCTRINAL.

	PAGE
THE WORD OF GOD	213
THE THOUGHT OF GOD THE STAY OF THE SOUL	217
BODILY SUFFERING	228
THE MINISTRY OF ANGELS	242
WARFARE THE CONDITION OF VICTORY	251
SECRECY AND SUDDENNESS OF DIVINE VISITATIONS	262
THE VISIBLE TEMPLE	271
THE RESURRECTION OF THE BODY	285
SCRIPTURE A RECORD OF HUMAN SORROW	292
HOLINESS NECESSARY FOR FUTURE BLESSEDNESS	303
WATCHING	315
WAITING FOR CHRIST	325
PRESENT BLESSINGS	338
THE DANGER OF RICHES	346
TEARS OF CHRIST AT THE GRAVE OF LAZARUS	360
A PARTICULAR PROVIDENCE AS REVEALED IN THE GOSPEL	368
TIMES OF PRIVATE PRAYER	382
FORMS OF PRIVATE PRAYER	392

THE WORLD'S BENEFACTORS.

THOSE men are not necessarily the most useful men in their generation, nor the most favoured by God, who make the most noise in the world, and who seem to be principals in the great changes and events recorded in history. On the contrary, even when we are able to point to a certain number of men as the real instruments of any great blessings vouchsafed to mankind, our relative estimate of them, one with another, is often very erroneous; so that on the whole, if we would trace truly the hand of God in human affairs, and pursue His bounty as displayed in the world to its original sources, we must unlearn our admiration of the powerful and distinguished, our reliance on the opinion of society, our respect for the decisions of the learned or the multitude, and turn our eyes to private life, watching in all we read or witness for the true signs of God's presence, the graces of personal holiness manifested in His elect; which, weak as they may seem to mankind, are mighty through God, and have an influence upon the course of His Providence, and bring about great events in the world at large, when the wisdom and strength of the natural man are of no avail.

Now, observe the operation of this law of God's government in respect to the introduction of those temporal blessings which are of the first importance in securing our well-being and comfort in the present life. For example, who was the first cultivator of corn? Who first tamed and domesticated the animals whose strength we use, and whom we make our food? Or who first discovered the medicinal herbs, which from the earliest times have been our resource against disease? If it was mortal man who thus looked through the vegetable and animal worlds, and discriminated between the useful and the worthless, his name is unknown to the millions whom he has thus benefited. It is notorious that those who first suggest the most happy inventions, and open a way to the secret stores of nature; those who weary themselves in the search after truth; strike out momentous principles of action; painfully force upon their contemporaries the adoption of beneficial measures; or, again, are the original cause of the chief events in national history, are commonly supplanted, as regards celebrity and reward, by inferior men. Their works are not called after them, nor the arts and systems which they have given the world. Their schools are usurped by strangers;

and their maxims of wisdom circulate among the children of their people, forming, perhaps, a nation's character, but not embalming in their own immortality the names of their original authors.

Such is the history of the social and political world, and the rule discernible in it is still more clearly established in the world of morals and religion. Who taught the doctors and saints of the Church, who, in their day, or in after times, have been the most illustrious expounders of the precepts of right and wrong, and by word and deed are the guides of our conduct? Did Almighty wisdom speak to them through the operations of their own minds, or rather, did it not subject them to instructors unknown to fame, wiser perhaps even than themselves? Andrew followed John the Baptist, while Simon remained at his nets. Andrew first recognized the Messiah among the inhabitants of despised Nazareth, and he brought his brother to Him. Yet to Andrew, Christ spake no word of commendation, which has been allowed to continue on record; whereas to Simon, even on his first coming, He gave the honourable name by which he is now designated, and afterwards put him forward as the typical foundation of His Church. Nothing indeed can hence be inferred, one way or other, concerning the relative excellence of the two brothers. So far only appears, that in the providential course of events, the one was the secret beginner, and the other the public instrument of a great divine work. St. Paul, again, was honoured with the distinction of a miraculous conversion, and was called to be the chief agent in the propagation of the Gospel among the heathen. Yet to Ananias, an otherwise unknown saint dwelling at Damascus, was committed the high office of conveying the gifts of pardon and the Holy Ghost to the apostle of the Gentiles.

Providence thus acts daily. The early life of all men is private. It is as children, generally, that their characters are formed to good or evil; and those who form them to good, their truest and chief benefactors, are unknown to the world. It has been remarked that some of the most eminent Christians have been blessed with religious mothers, and have in after life referred their own graces to the instrumentality of their teaching. Augustine has preserved to the Church the history of his mother, Monica; but in the case of others, even the name is denied to us of our great benefactress, whosoever she was, and sometimes, doubtless, the circumstance of her service altogether.

When we look at the history of inspiration, the same rule still holds. Consider the Old Testament, which "makes us wise unto salvation." How great a part of it is written by authors unknown. The Book of Judges, the Second of Samuel, the Book of Kings, Chronicles, Esther, and Job, and great part of the Book of Psalms. The last instance is the most remarkable of these. " Profitable " beyond words as is the instruction conveyed to us in every page of Scripture, yet the Psalms have been the most directly and visibly useful part of the whole volume, having been the Prayer Book of the Church ever since they were written; and have done more (as far as we dare judge) to prepare souls for heaven than any of the inspired books, except the Gospels. Yet the authors of a large portion of them are altogether unknown. And so with the Liturgies, which have been the possession of the Christian Church from the beginning. Who were those matured and exalted saints who left them to us? Nay, in the whole system of our worship, who are the authors of each decorous provision and each edifying custom? Who found out the musical tunes in which our praises are offered up to God, and in which resides so wondrous a persuasion "to worship and fall down, and kneel before the Lord our Maker?" Who were those religious men, our spiritual fathers in the "Catholic faith," who raised of old time the excellent fabrics all over the country in which we worship, though with less of grateful reverence for their memory than we might piously express? Of these greatest men in every age there is "no memorial." They "are perished as though they had never been, and become as though they had never been born."

Now I know that reflections of this kind are apt to sadden and vex us, and such of us particularly as are gifted with ardent and enthusiastic minds, with a generous love of what is great and good, and a noble hatred of injustice. These men find it difficult to reconcile themselves to the notion that the triumph of the truth in all its forms is postponed to the next world. They would fain anticipate the coming of the Righteous Judge. Nay, perhaps they are somewhat too favourably disposed towards the present world, to acquiesce without resistance in a doctrine which testifies to the corruption of its decisions and the worthlessness of its honours. But that it is a truth has already been shown almost as matter of fact, putting the evidence of Scripture out of consideration.

Why indeed should we shrink from this gracious law of God's present providence in our own case or in the case of those we love, when our subjection to it does but associate us with the best and noblest of our race, or with beings of nature and condition superior to our own? Andrew is scarcely known, except by name, while Peter has ever held the place of honour all over the Church; yet Andrew brought Peter to Christ. And are not the blessed angels unknown to the world? And is not God Himself, the Author of all good, hid from mankind at large, partially manifested and poorly glorified in a few scattered servants here and there? And His Spirit—do we know whence It cometh and whither It goeth? And though He has taught men whatever there has been of wisdom among them from the beginning, yet when He came on earth in visible form, even then it was said of Him, "The world knew Him not." His marvellous providence works beneath a veil which speaks but an untrue language; and to see Him who is the Truth and the Life, we must stoop underneath it, and so in one sense hide ourselves from the world. They who present themselves at kings' courts pass on to the inner chambers, where the gaze of the rude multitude cannot pierce; and we, if we would see the King of kings in His glory, must be content to disappear from things that are seen. Hid are the saints of God. If they are known to men, it is accidentally, in their temporal offices, as holding some high earthly station, or effecting some mere civil work, not as saints. St. Peter has a place in history far more as a chief instrument of a strange revolution in human affairs than in his true character as a self-denying follower of his Lord, to whom truths were revealed which flesh and blood could not discern.

BALAAM.

WE all profess to revere the Old Testament; yet, for some reason or other, at least one considerable part of it—the historical—is regarded by the mass, even of men who think about religion, as merely historical, as a relation of facts, as antiquities; not in its divine characters, not in its practical bearings, not in reference to themselves. The notion that God speaks in it to them personally; the question, "What does He say?" "What must I do?" does not occur to them. They consider that the Old Testament regards them only so far as it can be made typical of one or two of the great Christian doctrines; they do not consider it in its fulness and in its literal sense as a collection of deep moral lessons, such as are not vouchsafed in the New, though St. Paul expressly says that it is profitable for instruction in righteousness.

If the Old Testament history, generally, be intended

as a permanent instruction to the Church, much more, one would think, must such prominent and remarkable passages in it as the history of Balaam. Yet I suspect a very great number of readers carry off little more from it than the impression of the miracle which occurs in it —the speaking of his ass. And not unfrequently they talk more lightly on the subject than is expedient. Yet I think some very startling and solemn lessons may be drawn from the history, some of which I shall now attempt to set before you.

What is it which the chapters in question set before us? The first and most general account of Balaam would be this: that he was a very eminent person in his age and country, that he was courted and gained by the enemies of Israel, and that he promoted a wicked cause in a very wicked way; that when he could do nothing else for it, he counselled his employers to employ their women as means of seducing the chosen people into idolatry, and that he fell in battle in the war which ensued. These are the chief points, the prominent features of his history as viewed at a distance—and repulsive indeed they are. He took on him the office of a tempter, which is especially the devil's office. But Satan himself does not seem so hateful near as at a distance; and when we look into Balaam's history closely, we shall find points of character which may well interest those who do not consider his beginning and his end. Let us then approach him more nearly, and forget, for a moment, the summary account of him which I have just been giving.

Now, first, he was blessed with God's especial favour. You will ask at once, How could so bad a man be in God's favour? But I wish you to put aside reasonings, and contemplate facts. I say he was especially favoured by God. God has a store of favours in His treasure-house, and of various kinds—some for a time, some for ever; some implying His approbation, others not. He showers favours even on the bad. He makes His sun to rise on the unjust as well as on the just. He willeth not the death of a sinner. He is said to have loved the young ruler, whose heart, notwithstanding, was upon the world. His loving mercy extends over all His works. How He separates, in His own divine thought, kindness from approbation, time from eternity, what He does from what He foresees, we know not, and need not inquire. At present He is loving to all men, as if He did not foresee that some are to be saints, others reprobates, to all eternity. He dispenses His favours variously—gifts, graces, rewards, faculties, circumstances, being indefinitely diversified, nor admitting of discrimination or numbering on our part. Balaam, I say, was in His favour; not indeed for his holiness' sake, not for ever;

but in a certain sense, according to His inscrutable purpose who chooses whom He will choose, and exalts whom He will exalt, without destroying man's secret responsibilities, or His own governance, and the triumph of truth and holiness, and His own strict impartiality in the end. Balaam was favoured in an especial way above the mere heathen. Not only had he the grant of inspiration, and the knowledge of God's will, an insight into the truths of morality, clear and enlarged, such as we Christians even cannot surpass, but he was even admitted to conscious intercourse with God, such as even Christians have not.

But, again, Balaam was, in the ordinary and commonly-received sense of the word, without straining its meaning at all, a very conscientious man. That this is so, will be plain from some parts of his conduct and some speeches of his, of which I proceed to remind you, and which will show also his enlightened and admirable view of moral and religious obligation. When Balak sent to him to call him to curse Israel, he did not make up his mind for himself, as many a man might do, or according to the suggestions of avarice and ambition. No; he brought the matter before God in prayer. He prayed before he did what he did, as a religious man ought to do. Next, when God forbade his going, he at once, as he ought, positively refused to go. "Get you into your land," he said, "for the Lord refuseth to give me leave to go with you." Balak sent again a more pressing message and more lucrative offers, and Balaam was even more decided than before. "If Balak," he said, "would give me his house full of silver and gold, I cannot go beyond the word of the Lord my God, to do less or more." Afterwards God gave him leave to go. "If the men come to call thee, rise up and go with them." Then, and not till then, he went.

Almighty God added, "Yet the word that I shall say unto thee, that shalt thou do." Now, in the next place, observe how strictly he obeyed this command. When he first met Balak, he said, in the words of the text, "Lo, I am come unto thee; have I now any power at all to say anything? The word that God putteth in my mouth, that shall I speak." Again, when he was about to prophesy, he said, "Whatsoever He showeth me I will tell thee;" and he did so, in spite of Balak's disappointment and mortification to hear him bless Israel. When Balak showed his impatience he only replied, calmly, "Must I not take heed to speak that which the Lord hath put in my mouth?" Again he prophesied, and again it was a blessing; again Balak was angered, and again the prophet firmly and serenely answered, "Told not I thee, saying, All that the Lord speaketh, that I must do?" A third time he prophesied blessing; and now Balak's anger was kindled, and he smote his hands together and bade him depart to his place. But Balaam was not thereby moved from his duty. "The wrath of a king is as messengers of death." Balak might have instantly revenged himself upon the prophet; but Balaam, not satisfied with blessing Israel, proceeded, as a prophet should, to deliver himself of what remained of the prophetic burthen, by foretelling, more pointedly than before, destruction to Moab and the other enemies of the chosen people. He prefaced his prophecy with these unacceptable words: "Spake I not also unto thy messengers which thou sentest unto me, saying, If Balak would give me his house full of silver and gold, I cannot go beyond the commandment of the Lord, to do either good or bad of mine own mind, but what the Lord saith, that will I speak? And now, behold, I go unto my people; come, therefore, and I will advertise thee what this people shall do to thy people in the latter days." After delivering his conscience, he "rose up, and went and returned to his place."

All this surely expresses the conduct and the feelings of a high-principled, honourable, conscientious man. Balaam, I say, was certainly such in that very sense in which we commonly use those words. He said, and he did; he professed, and he acted according to his professions; there is no inconsistency in word and deed. He obeys as well as talks about religion; and this being the case, we shall feel more intimately the value of the following noble sentiments which he lets drop from time to time, and which, if he had shown less firmness in his conduct, might have passed for mere words, the words of a maker of speeches, a sophist, moralist, or orator. "Let me die the death of the righteous, and let my last end be like his." "God is not a man, that He should lie; neither the Son of Man, that He should repent. . . . Behold, I have received commandment to bless; and He hath blessed, and I cannot reverse it." "I shall see Him, but not now; I shall behold Him, but not nigh." It is remarkable that these declarations are great and lofty in their mode of expression; and the saying of his recorded by the prophet Micah is of the same kind. Balak asked what sacrifices were acceptable to God. Balaam answered, "He hath showed thee, O man, what is good; and what doth the Lord require of thee, but to do justly, and to love mercy, and to walk humbly with thy God?"

Viewing then the inspired notices concerning Balaam in all their parts, we cannot deny to him the praise which, if those notices have a plain meaning, they certainly do convey, that he was an honourable and religious man, with a great deal of what was good and noble about him; a man whom any one of us at first sight would have trusted, sought out in our difficulties, perhaps made the head of a party, and, anyhow, spoken of with great respect. We may indeed, if we please, say that he fell away afterwards from all this excellence; though, after all, there is something shocking in such a notion. Nay, it is not natural even that ordinary honourable men should suddenly change; but however this *may* be said, it may be said he fell away; but I presume it *cannot* be said he was other than a high-principled man (in the language of the world) when he so spake and acted.

But now the strange thing is, that at this very time, *while* he so spake and acted, he seems as in one sense to be in God's favour, so in another and higher to be under His displeasure. If this be so, the supposition that he fell away will not be in point, the difficulty it proposes to solve will remain; for it will turn out that he was displeasing to God. Amid his many excellences, the passage I have in mind is this, as you will easily suppose : " God's anger was kindled, because he went " with the princes of Moab ; " and the angel of the Lord stood in the way for an adversary against him." Afterwards, when God opened his eyes, " he saw the angel of the Lord standing in the way, and his sword drawn in his hand." " And Balaam said, I have *sinned*, for I knew not that thou stoodest in the way against me ; now, therefore, if it displease thee, I will get me back again."

You observe, Balaam said, "I have sinned," *though* he avers he did not *know* that God was his adversary. What makes the whole transaction more strange is this, that Almighty God had said before, " If the men come to call thee, rise up and go with them ;" and that when Balaam offered to go back again, the angel repeated, " Go with the men." And afterwards we find, in the midst of his heathen enchantments, " God met Balaam," and "put a word in his mouth;" and afterwards " the Spirit of God came unto him."

Summing up then what has been said, we seem, in Balaam's history, to have the following remarkable case, that is, remarkable according to our customary judgment of things : a man divinely favoured, visited, influenced, guided, protected, eminently honoured, illuminated, a man possessed of an enlightened sense of duty, and of moral and religious acquirements, educated, high-minded, conscientious, honourable, firm, and yet on the side of God's enemies, personally under God's displeasure, and in the end (if we go to that) the direct instrument of Satan, and having his portion with the unbelievers. I do not think I have materially overstated any part of this description ; but if it be correct only in substance, it certainly is most fearful, after allowing for incidental exaggeration, most fearful to every one of us, the more fearful the more we are conscious to ourselves in the main of purity of intention in what we do, and conscientious adherence to our sense of duty.

And now it is natural to ask, What is the *meaning* of this startling exhibition of God's ways? Is it really possible that a conscientious and religious man should be found among the enemies of God; nay, should be personally displeasing to Him, and that at the very time God was visiting him with extraordinary favour? What a mystery is this! Surely, if this be so, revelation has added to our perplexities, not relieved them. What instruction, what profit, what correction, what doctrine is there in such portions of inspired Scripture?

In answering this difficulty, I observe, in the first place, that it certainly is impossible—quite impossible—that a really conscientious man should be displeasing to God; at the same time, it is possible to be *generally* conscientious, or what the world calls honourable and high-principled, yet to be destitute of that religious fear and strictness which God calls conscientiousness, but which the world calls superstition or narrowness of mind. And, bearing this in mind, we shall, perhaps, have a solution of our perplexities concerning Balaam.

Balaam obeyed God from a sense of its being *right* to do so, but not from a *desire to please Him*, from *fear and love*. He had other ends, aims, wishes of his own, distinct from God's will and purpose, and he would have effected these if he could. His endeavour was, not to please God, but to please self without displeasing God; to pursue his own ends *as far* as was consistent with duty. In a word, he did not give his heart to God, but obeyed Him, as a man may obey human law, or observe the usages of society or his country, as something external to himself, because he knows he ought to do so, from a sort of rational sense, a conviction of its propriety, expediency, or comfort, as the case may be.

You will observe he *wished* to go with Balak's messengers, only he felt he *ought not* to go; and the problem which he attempted to solve was, *how* to go and yet not offend God. He was quite resolved he would, anyhow, act religiously and conscientiously; he was too honourable a man to break any of his engagements; if he had given his word, it was sacred; if he had duties, they were imperative; he had a character to maintain, and an inward sense of propriety to satisfy; but he would have given the world to have got rid of his duties; and the question was, *how* to do so without violence; and he did not care about walking on the very brink of transgression, so that he could keep from falling over. Accordingly, he was not content with *ascertaining* God's will, but he attempted to *change* it. He inquired of Him a *second time*, and this was to tempt Him. Hence, while

God bade him go, His anger was kindled against him because he went.

This surely is no uncommon character; rather, it is the common case even with the more respectable and praiseworthy portion of the community. I say plainly, and without fear of contradiction, though it is a serious thing to say, that the aim of most men esteemed conscientious and religious, or who are what is called honourable, upright men, is, to all appearance, not how to please God, but how to please themselves without displeasing Him. This surely is so plain that it is scarcely necessary to enlarge upon it. Men do not take for the object towards which they act, God's will, but certain maxims, rules, or measures, right perhaps as far as they go, but defective because they admit of being subjected to certain other ultimate ends, which are not religious. Men are just, honest, upright, trustworthy; but all this, not from the love and fear of God, but from a mere feeling of obligation to be so, and in subjection to certain worldly objects. And thus they are what is popularly called moral, without being religious. Such was Balaam. He was, in a popular sense, a strictly moral, honourable, conscientious man: that he was not so in a heavenly and true sense is plain, if not from the considerations here insisted on, at least from his after history, which (we may presume) brought to light his secret defect, in whatever it consisted. His defect lay in this, that he had not a single eye towards God's will, but was ruled by other objects.

Why did Almighty God give Balaam leave to go to Balak, and then was angry with him for going? I suppose for this reason, because his asking twice was tempting God. God is a jealous God. Sinners as we are—nay, as creatures of His hands—we may not safely intrude upon Him, and make free with Him. We may not dare to do that which we should not dare to do with an earthly superior, which we should be punished, for instance, for attempting in the case of a king or noble of this world. To rush into His presence, to address Him familiarly, to urge Him, to strive to make our duty lie in one direction when it lies in another, to handle rudely and practise upon His holy word, to trifle with truth, to treat conscience lightly, to take liberties (as it may be called) with anything that is God's; all irreverence, profaneness, unscrupulousness, wantonness, is represented in Scripture, not only as a sin, but as felt, noticed, quickly returned on God's part (if I may dare use such human words of the Almighty and All-holy God, without transgressing the rule I am myself laying down—but He vouchsafes in Scripture to represent Himself to us in that only way in which we can attain to the knowledge of Him)—I say, all irreverence towards God is represented as being jealously, and instantly, and fearfully noticed and visited, as friend or stranger among men might resent an insult shown him. This should be carefully considered. We are apt to act towards God and the things of God as towards a mere system, a law, a name, a religion, a principle; not as against a Person, a living, watchful, present, prompt, and powerful eye and arm. That all this is a great error, is plain to all who study Scripture; as is sufficiently shown by the death of 50,070 persons for looking into the Ark—the death of the prophet by the lion, who was sent to Jeroboam from Judah, and did not minutely obey his instructions—the slaughter of the children at Bethel by the bears, for mocking Elisha—the exclusion of Moses from the Promised Land for smiting the rock twice—and the judgment on Ananias and Sapphira.

Now Balaam's fault seems to have been of this nature. God told him distinctly not to go to Balak. He was rash enough to ask a second time, and God as a punishment gave him leave to ally himself to His enemies, and to take part against His people. With this presumptuousness and love of self in his innermost heart, his prudence, firmness, wisdom, illumination, and general conscientiousness, availed him nothing.

A number of reflections crowd upon the mind on the review of this awful history, as I may well call it. First, we see how little we can depend, in judging of right and wrong, on the apparent excellence and high character of individuals. There *is* a right and wrong in matters of conduct, in spite of the world; but it is the world's aim and Satan's aim to take our minds off from the indelible distinctions of things, and to fix our thoughts upon man; to make us dependent on his opinion, his patronage, his honour, his smiles, and his frowns. But if Scripture is to be our guide, it is plain that the most conscientious, religious, high-principled, honourable men (I use the words in their ordinary, not in their Scriptural sense), may be on the side of evil, may be Satan's instruments in cursing—if that were possible—or at least in seducing and enfeebling the people of God. For in the world's judgment, even when most refined, a person is conscientious and consistent who acts up to his standard. This is the world's highest flight; but in its ordinary judgment, a man is conscientious and consistent who is only inconsistent and goes against conscience in any extremity, when hardly beset, and when he must cut the knot or remain in present difficulties. That is, he is thought to obey conscience who only disobeys it when it is a praise and merit to obey it. This, alas! is the way with some of the most honourable of mere men of the world; nay, of the mass of (so called) respectable men.

A second reflection which rises in the mind has relation to the wonderful secret providence of God, while all things seem to go on according to the course of this world. Balaam did not see the angel, yet the angel went out against him as an adversary. He had no open denunciation of God's wrath directed against him. He had sinned, and nothing happened outwardly, but wrath was abroad, and in his path. This, again, is a very serious and awful thought. God's arm is not shortened. What happened to Balaam is as if it took place yesterday. God is what he ever was; we sin as man has ever sinned. We sin without being aware of it. God is our enemy without our being aware of it; and when the blow falls, we turn our thoughts to the creature, we ill treat our ass, we lay the blame on circumstances of this world, instead of turning to Him. " Lord, when Thy hand is lifted up, they will not see; but they shall see "—in the next world, if not here—"and be ashamed for their envy of the people. Yea, the fire of Thine enemies shall devour them."

Here, too, is a serious reflection, that when we have begun an evil course we cannot retrace our steps. Balaam was forced to go with the men; he offered to draw back—he was not allowed—yet God's wrath followed him. This is what comes of committing ourselves to an evil line of conduct; and we see daily instances of it in our experience of life. Men get entangled, and are bound hand and foot in dangerous courses. They make imprudent marriages or connections; they place themselves in dangerous situations; they engage in unprofitable or shameful undertakings. Too often, indeed, they do not discern their evil plight; but when they do they cannot draw back. God seems to say, "Go with the men." They are in bondage, and they must make the best of it; being the slave of the creature, without ceasing to be the responsible servants of God; under His displeasure, yet bound to act as if they could please Him. All this is very fearful.

Lastly, God gives us warnings now and then, but does not repeat them. Balaam's sin consisted in not acting on what was told him *once for all*. Let us beware of trifling with conscience. It is often said that second thoughts are best; so they are in matters of judgment, but not in matters of conscience. In matters of duty first thoughts are commonly best—they have more in them of the voice of God.

SAUL.

THE Israelites seem to have asked for a king from an unthankful caprice and waywardness. The ill conduct, indeed, of Samuel's sons was the occasion of the sin, but "an evil heart of unbelief," to use Scripture language, was the real cause of it. They had ever been restless and dissatisfied, asking for flesh when they had manna, fretful for water, impatient of the wilderness, bent on returning to Egypt, fearing their enemies, murmuring against Moses. They had miracles even to satiety, and then for a change they wished a king, like the nations. This was the chief reason of their sinful demand. And further, they were dazzled with the pomp and splendour of the heathen monarchs around them, and they desired some one to fight their battles, some visible succour to depend on, instead of having to wait for an invisible Providence, which came in its own way and time, little by little, being dispensed silently, or tardily, or (as they might consider) unsuitably. Their carnal hearts did not love the neighbourhood of heaven, and like the inhabitants of Gadara afterwards, they prayed that Almighty God would depart from their coasts.

Such were some of the feelings under which they desired a king like the nations; and God at length granted their request. To punish them He gave them a king *after their own heart*, Saul, the son of Kish, a Benjamite, of whom the Bible speaks in these terms: "I gave them a king in mine anger, and took him away in my wrath."

There is in true religion a sameness, an absence of hue and brilliancy, in the eyes of the natural man; a plainness, austereness, and (what he considers) sadness. It is like the heavenly manna of which the Israelites complained, insipid, and at length wearisome, "like wafers made with honey." They complained that "their soul was dried away." "There is nothing at all," they said, "beside this manna before our eyes. . . . . . We remember the fish which we did eat in Egypt freely; the cucumbers, and the melons, and the leeks, and the onions, and the garlick" (Numbers xi. 5; Exodus xvi.). Such were the dainty meats in which their soul delighted, and for the same reason they desired a king. Samuel had too much of primitive simplicity about him to please them; they felt they were behind the world, and clamoured to be put on a level with the heathen.

Saul, the king whom God gave them, had much to recommend him to minds thus greedy of the dust of the earth. He was brave, daring, resolute, gifted, too, with strength of body as well as of mind—a circumstance which seems to have attracted their admiration. He is described in person as if one of those sons of Anak, before whose giant-forms the spies of the Israelites in the wilderness were as grasshoppers. "A choice young man, and a goodly. There was not among the children of Israel a goodlier person than he; from his shoulders and upward he was higher than any of the people." Both his virtues and his faults were such as became an eastern monarch, and were adapted to secure the fear and submission of his subjects. Pride, haughtiness, obstinacy, reserve, jealousy, caprice—these in their way were not unbecoming qualities in the king after whom their imagination roved. On the other hand, the better parts of his character were of an excellence sufficient to engage the affection of Samuel himself.

As to Samuel, his conduct is far above human praise. Though injuriously treated by his countrymen, who cast him off after he had served them faithfully till he was "old and grey-headed," and who resolved on setting over them a king against his earnest entreaties; yet we find no trace of coldness or jealousy in his behaviour towards Saul. On his first meeting of him he addressed him in the words of loyalty. "On whom is all the desire of Israel? Is it not on thee and on all thy father's house?" Afterwards, when he anointed him king, he "kissed him and said, Is it not because the Lord hath anointed thee to be king over His inheritance?" When he announced him to the people as their king, he said, "See ye him whom the Lord hath chosen, that there is none like him among all the people." And some time after, when Saul had irrecoverably lost God's favour, we are told "Samuel came no more to see Saul until the day of his death; *nevertheless Samuel mourned for Saul.*" In the next chapter he is thus rebuked for immoderate grief: "How long wilt thou mourn for Saul, seeing I have rejected him from reigning over Israel" (1 Sam. ix. 20; x. 1, 24; xv. 35)? Such sorrow speaks favourably for Saul as well as for Samuel. It is not only the grief of a loyal subject and a zealous prophet, but, moreover, of an attached friend; and, indeed, instances are recorded, in the first years of his reign, of forbearance, generosity, and neglect of self, which sufficiently account for the feelings with which Samuel regarded him. David, under very different circumstances, seems to have felt for him a similar affection.

The higher points of his character are brought out in instances such as the following. The first announcement of his elevation came upon him suddenly, but apparently without unsettling him. He kept it secret, leaving it to Samuel, who had made it to him, to publish it. "Saul said unto his uncle, He (that is, Samuel) told us plainly that the asses were found; but of the matter of the kingdom, whereof Samuel spake, *he told him not.*" Nay, it would even seem he was averse to the dignity intended for him; for when the divine lot fell upon him he hid himself, and was not discovered by the people without recourse to divine assistance. The appointment was at first unpopular. "The children of Belial said, How shall this man save us? They despised him, and brought him no presents; *but he held his peace.*" Soon the Ammonites invaded the country beyond Jordan, with the avowed intention of subjugating it. They sent to Saul for relief almost in despair, and the panic spread in the interior as well as among those whose country was immediately threatened. The sacred writer proceeds: "*Behold, Saul came after the herd out of the field;* and Saul said, What aileth the people, that they weep? and they told him the tidings of the men of Jabesh. And the Spirit of God came upon Saul, and his anger was kindled greatly." His order for an immediate gathering throughout Israel was obeyed with the alacrity with which the multitude serve the strong-minded in times of danger. A decisive victory over the enemy followed. Then the popular cry became, "Who is he that said, Shall

Saul reign over us? Bring the men, that we may put them to death. And Saul said, *There shall not a man be put to death this day;* for to-day the Lord hath wrought salvation in Israel" (1 Sam. x., xi.).

Such was Saul's character and success: his character faulty, yet not without promise; his success in arms as great as his carnal subjects could have desired. Yet in spite of Samuel's private liking for him, and in spite of the good fortune which actually attended him, we find that from the beginning the prophet's voice is raised both against people and king in warnings and rebukes, which are omens of his destined destruction. According to the text, "I gave them a king in mine anger, and took him away in my wrath." At the very time that Saul was publicly received as king, Samuel protested, "Ye have this day rejected your God, who Himself saved you out of all your adversities and your tribulations." In a subsequent assembly of the people, in which he testified his uprightness, he says, "Is it not wheat-harvest to-day? I will call unto the Lord, and He shall send thunder and rain, that ye *may perceive and see that your wickedness is great* in asking you a king." Again, "If ye shall still do wickedly, ye shall be consumed, both ye and your king" (1 Sam. xii. 17, 25). And after this, on the first instance of disobedience, and at first sight no very heinous sin, the sentence of rejection is passed upon him: "Thy kingdom shall not continue; the Lord hath sought Him a man after His own heart."

Here, then, a question may be raised. Why was Saul thus marked for vengeance from the beginning? Why these presages of misfortune which from the first hung over him, gathered, fell in storm and tempest, and at length overwhelmed him? Is his character so essentially faulty that it must be thus distinguished for reprobation above all the anointed kings after him? Why, while David is called a man after God's own heart, should Saul be put aside as worthless?

This question leads us to a deeper inspection of his character. Now we know the first duty of every man is the fear of God—a reverence for His word, a love towards Him, a desire to obey Him; and besides, it was peculiarly incumbent on the King of Israel, as God's vicegerent, by virtue of his office, to promote His glory whom his subjects had rejected.

Now Saul "lacked this one thing." His character, indeed, is obscure, and we must be cautious while considering it. Still, as Scripture is given us for our instruction, it is surely right to make the most of what we find there, and to form our judgment by such lights as we possess. It would appear, then, that Saul was never under the abiding sense of religion, or, in Scripture language, "the fear of God," however he might be at times moved and softened. Some men are inconsistent in their conduct, as Samson, or as Eli, in a different way; and yet may have lived by faith, though a weak faith. Others have sudden falls, as David had. Others are corrupted by prosperity, as Solomon. But as to Saul, there is no proof that he had any deep-seated religious principle at all. Rather it is to be feared that his history is a lesson to us, that the "heart of unbelief" may exist in the very sight of God, may rule a man in spite of many natural advantages of character, in the midst of much that is virtuous, amiable, and commendable.

Saul, it would seem, was naturally brave, active, generous, and patient; and what Nature made him such he remained, that is, without improvement, with virtues which had no value, because they required no effort and implied the influence of no principle. On the other hand, when we look for evidence of his faith, that is, his practical sense of things unseen, we discover instead a deadness to all considerations not connected with this present world. It is his habit to treat prophet and priest with a coldness, to say the least, which seems to argue some great internal defect. It would not be inconsistent with the Scripture account of him, even should the real fact be, that (with some general notions concerning the being and providence of God) he doubted of the divinity of the dispensation of which he was an instrument.

The circumstance which first introduces him to the inspired history is not in his favour. While in search of his father's asses, which were lost, he came to the city where Samuel was; and though Samuel was now an old man, and from childhood known as the especial minister and prophet of the God of Israel, Saul seems to have considered him as a mere diviner, such as might be found among the heathen, who, for "the fourth part of a shekel of silver," would tell him his way.

The narrative goes on to mention, that after his leaving Samuel, "God gave him another heart;" and on meeting a company of prophets, "the Spirit of God came upon him, and he prophesied among them." Upon this, "all that knew him beforetime" said, "What is this that is come unto the son of Kish? is Saul also among the prophets? .... therefore it became a proverb." From this narrative we gather that his carelessness and coldness in religious matters were so notorious, that in the eyes of his acquaintance there was a certain strangeness and incongruity which at once struck the mind in associating him with a school of the prophets.

Nor have we any reason to believe, from the after history, that the divine gift, then first imparted, left any religious effect upon his mind. At a later period of his life we find him suddenly brought under the same sacred influence on his entering the school where Samuel taught;

but instead of softening him, its effect upon his outward conduct did but testify the fruitlessness of Divine Grace when acting upon a will obstinately set upon evil.

The immediate occasion of his rejection was his failing under a specific trial of his obedience, set before him at the very time he was anointed. He had collected with difficulty an army against the Philistines: while waiting for Samuel to offer the sacrifice, his people became dispirited, and began to fall off and return home. Here he was doubtless exposed to the temptation of taking unlawful measures to put a stop to their defection. But when we consider that the act to which he was persuaded was no less than that of his offering sacrifice, he being neither priest nor prophet, nor having any commission thus to interfere with the Mosaic ritual, it is plain "his *forcing himself*" to do so (as he tenderly described his sin) was a direct profaneness—a profaneness which implied that he was careless about forms, which in this world will ever be essential to things supernatural, and thought it mattered little whether he acted in God's way or in his own.

After this, he seems to have separated himself from Samuel, whom he found unwilling to become his instrument, and to have had recourse to the priesthood instead. Ahijah, or Ahimelech (as he is afterwards called), the high priest, followed his camp; and the ark too, in spite of the warning conveyed by the disasters which attended the presumptuous use of it in the time of Eli. "And Saul said unto Ahijah, Bring hither the ark of God." While it was brought, a tumult which was heard in the camp of the Philistines increased. On this interruption, Saul irreverently put the ark aside, and went out to the battle.

It will be observed that there was no professed or intentional irreverence in Saul's conduct; he was still on the whole the same he had ever been. He outwardly respected the Mosaic ritual. About this time he built his first altar to the Lord, and in a certain sense seemed to acknowledge God's authority (1 Sam. xiv. 35). But nothing shows he considered there was any vast distinction between Israel and the nations around them. He was *indifferent*, and cared for none of these things. The chosen people desired a king like the nations, and such a one they received.

After this he was commanded to "go and smite the sinners, the Amalekites, and utterly destroy them and their cattle." This was a judgment on them which God had long decreed, though He had delayed it; and He now made Saul the minister of His vengeance. But Saul performed it only so far as fell in with his own inclinations and purposes. He smote, indeed, the Amalekites, and "destroyed all the people with the edge of the sword"—this exploit had its glory. The best of the flocks and herds he spared, and why? To sacrifice therewith to the Lord. But since God had expressly told him to destroy them, what was this but to imply that divine intimations had nothing to do with such matters? What was it but to consider that the established religion was but a useful institution, or a splendid pageant suitable to the dignity of monarchy, but resting on no unseen supernatural sanction? Certainly, he in no sense acted in the fear of God, with the wish to please Him, and the conviction that he was in His sight. One might consider it mere pride and wilfulness in him, acting in his own way because it was his own (which doubtless it was in great measure), except that he appears to have had an eye to the feelings and opinions of men as to his conduct, though not to God's judgment. He "feared the people, and obeyed their voice." Again, he spared Agag, the king of the Amalekites. Doubtless he considered Agag as "his brother," as Ahab afterwards called Benhadad. Agag was a king, and Saul observed towards him that courtesy and clemency which earthly monarchs observe one towards another, and rightly, when no divine command comes in the way. But the God of Israel required a king after his own heart, jealous of idolatry; the people had desired a king like the nations around them.

It is remarkable, however, that while he spared Agag, he attempted to exterminate the Gibeonites with the sword, who were tolerated in Israel by virtue of an oath taken in their favour by Joshua and "the princes of the congregation." This he did "*in his zeal* to the children of Israel and Judah."

From the time of his disobedience in the matter of Amalek, Samuel came no more to see Saul, whose season of probation was over. The evil spirit exerted a more visible influence over him, and God sent Samuel to anoint David privately, as the future king of Israel. I need not trace further the course of moral degradation which is exemplified in Saul's subsequent history. Mere natural virtue wears away when men neglect to deepen it into religious principle. Saul appears in his youth to be unassuming and forbearing: in advanced life he is not only proud and gloomy (as he ever was in a degree), but cruel, resentful, and hard-hearted, which he was not in his youth. His injurious treatment of David is a long history, but his conduct to Ahimelech, the high priest, admits of being mentioned here. Ahimelech assisted David in his escape. Saul resolved on the death of Ahimelech and all his father's house. On his guards refusing to execute his command, Doeg, a man of Edom, one of the nations Saul was raised up to withstand, undertook the atrocious deed. On that day eighty-five priests were slain. Afterwards Nob, the city of the priests, was smitten with the edge of the sword, and all destroyed—"Men and women, children and sucklings, and oxen, and asses, and sheep." That is, Saul executed more complete vengeance on the descendants of Levi, the sacred tribe, than on the sinners, the Amalekites, who laid wait for Israel in the way, on their going up from Egypt.

Last of all, he finishes his bad history by an open act of apostacy from the God of Israel. His last act is like his first, but more significant. He began, as we saw, by consulting Samuel as a diviner : this showed the direction of his mind. It steadily persevered in its evil way—and he ends by consulting a professed sorceress at Endor. The Philistines had assembled their hosts ; Saul's heart trembled greatly ; he had no advisers or comforters ; Samuel was dead ; the priests he had himself slain with the sword. He hoped by magic rites—which he had formerly denounced—to foresee the issue of the approaching battle. God meets him even in the cave of Satanic delusions — but as an antagonist : the reprobate king receives, by the mouth of dead Samuel, who had once anointed him, the news that he is to be "taken away in God's wrath"—that the Lord would deliver Israel, with him, into the hands of the Philistines ; and that on the morrow he and his sons should be numbered with the dead (1 Sam. xxviii. 19).

The next day " the battle went sore against him ; the

archers hit him, and he was sore wounded of the archers." "Anguish came upon him" (2 Sam. i. 9), and he feared to fall into the hands of the uncircumcised. He desired his armour-bearer to draw his sword and thrust him through therewith. On his refusing, he fell upon his own sword, and so came to his end.

Unbelief and wilfulness are the wretched characteristics of Saul's history—an ear deaf to the plainest commands, a heart hardened against the most gracious influences. Do not suppose, because I speak thus strongly, I consider Saul's state of mind to be something very unusual. Let us only reflect on our hardness of heart, and we shall understand something of Saul's ambition when he prophesied. We may be conscious to ourselves of the truth of things sacred as entirely as if we saw them; and yet we often feel in as ordinary and as unconcerned a mood as if we were altogether unbelievers. Again, let us reflect on our callousness after mercies received, or after suffering. We are often in worse case even than this; for to realize the unseen world in our imagination, and feel as if we saw it, may not always be in our power. What makes our insensibility still more alarming is, that it follows the grant of the highest privileges. There is something awful in this, if we understood it; as if that peculiar hardness of heart which we experience, in spite of whatever excellences of character we may otherwise possess—like Saul, in spite of the benevolence, or fairness, or candour, or consideration, which are the virtues of this age—was the characteristic of a soul transgressing after it had "tasted the powers of the world to come," and an earnest of the second death. May this thought rouse us to a deeper seriousness than we have at present, while Christ continues to intercede for us, and grant us time for repentance!

DAVID

WHEN Saul was finally rejected for not destroying the Amalekites, Samuel was bid go to Bethlehem, and anoint, as future king of Israel, one of the sons of Jesse, who should be pointed out to him when he was come there. Samuel accordingly went thither and made a sacrifice; when, at his command, Jesse's seven sons were brought by their father, one by one, before the prophet; but none of them proved to be the choice of Almighty God. David was the youngest and out of the way, and it seemed to Jesse as unlikely that God's choice should fall upon him, as it appeared to Joseph's brethren and to his father, that he and his mother and brethren should, as his dreams foretold, bow down before him. On Samuel's inquiring, Jesse said, "There remaineth yet the youngest, and, behold, he keepeth the sheep." On Samuel's bidding, he was sent for. "Now he was ruddy," the sacred historian proceeds, "and withal of a beautiful countenance, and goodly to look to. And the Lord said, Arise, anoint him, for this is he." After Samuel had anointed him, "the Spirit of the Lord came upon David from that day forward." It is added, "But the Spirit of the Lord departed from Saul."

David's anointing was followed by no other immediate mark of God's favour. He was tried by being sent back again, in spite of the promise, to the care of his sheep, till an unexpected occasion introduced him to Saul's court. The withdrawing of the Spirit of the Lord from Saul was followed by frequent attacks from an evil spirit, as a judgment upon him. His mind was depressed, and a "trouble," as it is called, came upon him, with symptoms very like those which we now refer to derangement. His servants thought that music, such perhaps as was used in the schools of the prophets, might soothe and restore him; and David was recommended by one of them for that purpose in the words of the text: "Behold, I have seen a son of Jesse the Bethlehemite, that is cunning in playing, and a mighty valiant man, and a man of war, and prudent in matters, and a comely person, and the Lord is with him."

David came in the power of that sacred influence whom Saul had grieved and rejected. The Spirit which inspired his tongue guided his hand also, and his sacred songs became a medicine to Saul's diseased mind. "When the evil spirit from God was upon Saul, ...

David took an harp, and played with his hand; so Saul was refreshed, and was well, and the evil spirit departed from him." Thus he is first introduced to us in that character in which he still has praise in the Church, as "the anointed of the God of Jacob, and the sweet psalmist of Israel." (2 Sam. xxiii. 1.)

Saul "loved David greatly, and he became his armour-bearer;" but the first trial of his humility and patience was not over, while many other trials were in store. After a while he was a second time sent back to his sheep; and though there was war with the Philistines, and his three eldest brethren were in the army with Saul, and he had already essayed his strength in defending his father's flocks from wild beasts, and was "a mighty valiant man," yet he contentedly stayed at home as a private person, keeping his promise of greatness to himself, till his father bade him go to his brethren to take them a present from him, and report how they fared. An accident, as it appeared to the world, brought him forward. On his arrival at the army, he heard the challenge of the Philistine champion, Goliath of Gath. I need not relate how he was divinely urged to engage the giant, how he killed him, and how he was in consequence again raised to Saul's favour; who, with an infirmity not inconsistent with the deranged state of his mind, seems to have altogether forgotten him.

From this time began David's public life; but not yet the fulfilment of the promise made to him by Samuel. He had a second and severer trial of patience to endure for many years; the trial of "being still" and doing nothing before God's time, though he had (apparently) the means in his hands of accomplishing the promise for himself. It was to this trial that Jeroboam afterwards showed himself unequal. He too was promised a kingdom, but he was tempted to seize upon it in his own way, and so forfeited God's protection.

David's victory over Goliath so endeared him to Saul, that he would not let him go back to his father's house. Jonathan too, Saul's son, at once felt for him a warm affection, which deepened into a firm friendship. "Saul set him over the men of war; and he was accepted in the sight of all the people, and also in the sight of Saul's servants." (1 Sam. xviii. 5.) This prosperous fortune, however, did not long continue. As Saul passed through the cities from his victory over his enemies, the women of Israel came out to meet him, singing and dancing, and they said, "Saul hath slain his thousands, and David his ten thousands." Immediately the jealous king was "very wroth, and the saying displeased him;" his sullenness returned; he feared David as a rival; and "eyed him from that day and forward." On the morrow, as David was playing before him, as at other times, Saul threw his javelin at him. After this, Saul displaced him from his situation at his court, and sent him to the war, hoping so to rid himself of him by his falling in battle; but by God's blessing David returned victorious.

In a second war with the Philistines, David was successful as before; and Saul, overcome with gloomy and malevolent passions, again cast at him with his javelin, as he played before him, with the hope of killing him.

This repeated attempt on his life drove David from Saul's court; and for some years after, that is, till Saul's death, he was a wanderer upon the earth, persecuted in that country which was afterwards to be his own kingdom. Here, as in his victory over Goliath, Almighty God purposed to show us, that it was *His* hand which set David on the throne of Israel. David conquered his enemy by a sling and stone, in order, as he said at the time, that all . . . . might know "that the Lord saveth not with sword and spear; for the battle is the Lord's." (1 Sam. xvii. 47.) Now again, but in a different way, His guiding providence was displayed. As David slew Goliath without arms, so now he refrained himself and used them not, though he possessed them. Like Abraham he traversed the land of promise "as a strange land" (Heb. xi. 9), waiting for God's good time. Nay, far more exactly, even than to Abraham, was it given to David to act and suffer that life of faith which the Apostle describes, and by which "the elders obtained a good report." By faith he wandered about, "being destitute, afflicted, evil-entreated, in deserts, and in mountains, and in dens, and in caves of the earth." On the other hand, through the same faith, he "subdued kingdoms, wrought righteousness, obtained promises, waxed valiant in fight, turned to flight the armies of the aliens."

On escaping from Saul, he first went to Samuel to ask his advice. With him he dwelt some time. Driven thence by Saul, he went to Bethlehem, his father's city, then to Ahimelech the high-priest, at Nob. Thence he fled, still through fear of Saul, to Achish, the Philistine king of Gath; and finding his life in danger there, he escaped to Adullam, where he was joined by his kindred, and put himself at the head of an irregular band of men, such as, in the unsettled state of the country, might be usefully and lawfully employed against the remnant of the heathen. After this he was driven to Hareth, to Keilah, which he rescued from the Philistines, to the wilderness of Ziph among the mountains, to the wilderness of Maon, to the strongholds of Engedi, to the wilderness of Paran. After a time he again betook himself to Achish, king of Gath, who gave him a city; and there it was that the news was brought him of the death of Saul in battle, which was the occasion of his elevation first to the throne of Judah, afterwards to that of all Israel, according to the promise of God made to him by Samuel.

It need not be denied that, during these years of wandering, we find in David's conduct instances of infirmity and inconsistency, and some things which, without being clearly wrong, are yet strange and startling in so favoured a servant of God. With these we are not concerned, except so far as a lesson may be gained from them for themselves. We are not at all concerned with them as regards our estimate of David's character. That character is ascertained and sealed by the plain word of Scripture, by the praise of Almighty God, and is no subject for our criticism; and if we find in it traits which we cannot fully reconcile with the approbation divinely given to him, we must take it in faith to be what it is said to be, and wait for the future revelations of Him who "overcomes when He is judged." Therefore I dismiss these matters now, when I am engaged in exhibiting the eminent obedience and manifold virtues of David. On the whole, his situation, during these years of trial, was certainly that of a witness for Almighty God, one who does good and suffers for it, nay, suffers on rather than rid himself from suffering by any unlawful act.

Now then let us consider what was, as far as we can

understand, his especial grace, what is his gift; as faith was Abraham's distinguishing virtue, meekness the excellence of Moses, self-mastery the gift especially conspicuous in Joseph.

This question may best be answered by considering the purpose for which he was raised up. When Saul was disobedient, Samuel said to him, "Thy kingdom shall not continue: the Lord hath sought Him *a man after His own heart*, and the Lord hath commanded him to be captain over His people, because thou hast not kept that which the Lord commanded thee." (1 Sam. xiii. 14.) The office to which first Saul and then David were called, was different from that with which other favoured men before them had been intrusted. From the time of Moses, when Israel became a nation, God had been the king of Israel, and His chosen servants, not delegates, but mere organs of His will. Moses did not direct the Israelites by his own wisdom, but he spake to them, as God spake from the pillar of the cloud. Joshua, again, was merely a sword in the hand of God. Samuel was but His minister and interpreter. God acted, the Israelites "stood still and saw" His miracles, then followed. But, when they had rejected Him from being king over them, then their chief ruler was no longer a mere organ of His power and will, but had a certain authority intrusted to him, more or less independent of supernatural direction; and acted, not so much *from* God, as *for* God, and *in the place of* God. David, when taken from the sheepfolds "to feed Jacob His people and Israel His inheritance," "fed them," in the words of the Psalm, "with a faithful and true heart; and ruled them prudently with all his power." (Ps. lxxviii. 71-73.) From this account of his office, it is obvious that his very first duty was that of *fidelity to Almighty God* in the trust committed to him. He had power put into his hands, in a sense in which neither Moses had it, nor Samuel. He was charged with a certain office, which he was bound to administer according to his ability, so as best to promote the interests of Him who appointed him. Saul had neglected his Master's honour; but David, in this an eminent type of Christ, "came to do God's will" as a viceroy in Israel, and, as being tried and found faithful, he is especially called "a man after God's own heart."

David's peculiar excellence then is that of *fidelity to the trust committed to him;* a firm, uncompromising, single-hearted devotion to the cause of his God, and a burning zeal for His honour.

This characteristic virtue is especially illustrated in the early years of his life. He was tried therein and found faithful; before he was put in power, it was proved whether he could obey. Till he came to the throne, he was like Moses or Samuel, an instrument in God's hands, bid do what was told him and nothing more;—having borne this trial of obedience well, in which Saul had failed, then at length he was intrusted with a sort of discretionary power, to use in his Master's service.

Observe how David was tried, and what various high qualities of mind he displayed in the course of the trial. First, the promise of greatness was given him, and Samuel anointed him. Still he stayed in the sheepfolds; and though called away by Saul for a time, yet returned contentedly when Saul released him from attendance. How difficult it is for such as know they have gifts suitable to the Church's need to refrain themselves till God makes a way for their use! and the trial would be the more severe in David's case, in proportion to the ardour and energy of his mind; yet he fainted not under it. Afterwards for seven years, as the time appears to be, he withstood the strong temptation, ever before his eyes, of acting without God's guidance, when he had the means of doing so. Though skilful in arms, popular with his countrymen, successful against the enemy, the king's son-in-law, and on the other hand grievously injured by Saul, who not only continually sought his life, but even suggested to him a traitor's conduct by accusing him of treason, and whose life was several times in his hands, yet he kept his honour pure and unimpeachable. He feared God and honoured the king; and this at a time of life especially exposed to the temptations of ambition.

There is a resemblance between the early history of David and that of Joseph. Both distinguished for piety in youth, the youngest and the despised of their respective brethren, they are raised, after a long trial, to a high station, as ministers of God's Providence. Joseph was tempted to a degrading adultery; David was tempted by ambition. Both were tempted to be traitors to their masters and benefactors. Joseph's trial was brief; but his conduct under it evidenced settled habits of virtue which he could call to his aid at a moment's notice. A long imprisonment followed, the consequence of his obedience, and borne with meekness and patience; but it was no part of his temptation, because, when once incurred, release was out of his power. David's trial, on the other hand, lasted for years, and grew stronger as time went on. His master too, far from "putting all that he had into his hand" (Genesis xxxix. 4), sought his life. Continual opportunity of avenging himself incited his passions; self-defence, and the divine promise, were specious arguments to seduce his reason. Yet he mastered his heart, —he was "still;"—he kept his hands clean and his lips guileless,—he was loyal throughout,—and in due time inherited the promise.

Let us call to mind some of the circumstances of his stedfastness recorded in the history.

He was about twenty-three years old when he slew the Philistine; yet, when placed over Saul's men of war, in the first transport of his victory, we are told he "behaved himself wisely." (1 Sam. xviii. 5-30.) When fortune turned, and Saul became jealous of him, still "David behaved himself wisely in all his ways, and the Lord was with him." How like is this to Joseph under different circumstances! "Wherefore, when Saul saw that he behaved himself very wisely, he was afraid of him; and all Israel and Judah loved David." Again, "And David behaved himself more wisely than all the servants of Saul, so that his name was much set by." Here in shifting fortunes is evidence of that staid, composed frame of mind in his youth, which he himself describes in the one hundred and thirty-first Psalm. "My heart is not haughty, nor mine eyes lofty . . . . . . Surely I have behaved and quieted myself, as a child that is weaned of his mother."

The same modest deportment marks his subsequent conduct. He consistently seeks counsel of God. When he fled from Saul he went to Samuel; afterwards we find him following the directions of the prophet Gad, and afterwards of Abiathar the high priest. (1 Sam. xxii. 5, 20; xxiii. 6.) Here his character is in full contrast to the character of Saul.

Further, consider his behaviour towards Saul when he had him in his power; it displays a most striking and admirable union of simple faith and unblemished loyalty.

Saul, while in pursuit of him, went into a cave in Engedi. David surprised him there, and his companions advised to seize him, if not to take his life. They said, "Behold the day of which the Lord said unto thee." (1 Sam. xxiv. 4.) David, in order to show Saul how entirely his life had been in his power, arose and cut off a part of his robe privately. After he had done it, his "heart smote him" even for this slight freedom, as if it were a disrespect offered towards his king and father. "He said unto his men, The Lord forbid that I should do this thing unto my master, the Lord's anointed, to stretch forth mine hand against him, seeing he is the anointed of the Lord." When Saul left the cave, David followed him and cried, "My Lord the king. And when Saul looked behind him, David stooped with his face to the earth, and bowed himself." He hoped that he could now convince Saul of his integrity. "Wherefore hearest thou men's words," he asked, "saying, Behold, David seeketh thy hurt? Behold, this day thine eyes have seen how that the Lord had delivered thee to-day into mine hand in the cave: and some bade me kill thee .... Moreover, my father, see, yea see the skirt of thy robe in my hand: for in that I cut off the skirt of thy robe, and killed thee not, know thou and see, that there is neither evil nor transgression in mine hand, and I have not sinned against thee: yet thou huntest my soul to take it. The Lord judge between me and thee, and the Lord avenge me of thee: but mine hand shall not be upon thee ...... After whom is the king of Israel come out? after whom dost thou pursue? after a dead dog, after a flea. The Lord therefore judge .... and see, and plead my cause, and deliver me out of thine hand." Saul was for the time overcome; he said, " Is this thy voice, my son David? and Saul lifted up his voice and wept." And he said, " Thou art more righteous than I; for thou hast rewarded me good, whereas I have rewarded thee evil." He added, "And now, behold, I know well that thou shalt surely be king." At another time David surprised Saul in the midst of his camp, and his companion would have killed him; but he said, " Destroy him not, for who can stretch forth his hand against the Lord's anointed and be guiltless?" (1 Sam. xxvi. 9.) Then, as he stood over him, he meditated sorrowfully on his master's future fortunes, while he himself refrained from interfering with God's purposes. " Surely the Lord shall smite him; or his day shall come to die; or he shall descend into battle and perish." David retired from the enemy's camp; and when at a safe distance, roused Saul's guards, and blamed them for their negligent watch, which had allowed a stranger to approach the person of their king. Saul was moved the second time; the miserable man, as if waking from a dream which hung about him, said, "I have sinned; return, my son David . . . . . . behold, I have played the fool, and have erred exceedingly." He added, truth overcoming him, "Blessed be thou, my son David; thou shalt both do great things, and also shalt still prevail."

How beautiful are these passages in the history of the chosen king of Israel! How do they draw our hearts towards him, as one whom in his private character it must have been an extreme privilege and a great delight to know! Surely the blessings of the patriarchs descended in a united flood upon "the lion of the tribe of Judah," the type of the true Redeemer who was to come. He inherits the prompt faith and magnanimity of Abraham; he is simple as Isaac; he is humble as Jacob; he has the youthful wisdom and self-possession, the tenderness, the affectionateness, and the firmness of Joseph. And, as his own especial gift, he has an overflowing thankfulness, an ever-burning devotion, a zealous fidelity to his God, a high unshaken loyalty towards his king, an heroic bearing in all circumstances, such as the multitude of men see to be great, but cannot understand. Be it our blessedness, unless the wish be presumptuous, so to acquit ourselves in troubled times; cheerful amid anxieties, collected in dangers, generous towards enemies, patient in pain and sorrow, subdued in good fortune! How manifold are the ways of the Spirit, how various the graces which He imparts; what depth and width is there in that moral truth and virtue for which we are created! Contrast one with another the Scripture saints! how different are they, yet how alike! how fitted for their respective circumstances, yet how unearthly, how settled and composed in the faith and fear of God! As in the services, so in the patterns of the Church, God has met all our needs, all our frames of mind. "Is any afflicted? let him pray; is any merry? let him sing psalms." (James v. 13.) Is any in joy or in sorrow? there are saints at hand to encourage and guide him. There is Abraham for nobles, Job for men of wealth and merchandise, Moses for patriots, Samuel for rulers, Elijah for reformers, Joseph for those who rise into distinction; there is Daniel for the forlorn, Jeremiah for the persecuted, Hannah for the downcast, Ruth for the friendless, the Shunammite for the matron, Caleb for the soldier, Boaz for the farmer, Mephibosheth for the subject; but none is vouchsafed to us in more varied lights, and with more abundant and more affecting lessons, whether in his history or in his writings, than he who is described as cunning in playing, and a mighty valiant man, and prudent in matters, and comely in person, and favoured by Almighty God.

ST. PAUL.

EVERY season of Paul's life is full of wonders, and admits of a separate commemoration; which indeed we do make whenever we read the Acts of the Apostles or his Epistles.

We cannot well forget the manner of his conversion. He was journeying to Damascus with authority from the chief priests to seize the Christians, and bring them to Jerusalem. He had sided with the persecuting party from their first act of violence, the martyrdom of St. Stephen; and he continued foremost in a bad cause, with blind rage endeavouring to defeat what really was the work of Divine power and wisdom. In the midst of his fury he was struck down by miracle, and converted to the faith he persecuted. Observe the circumstances of the case. When the blood of Stephen was shed, Saul, then a young man, was standing by, "consenting unto his death," and "kept the raiment of them that slew him."

(Acts xxii. 20.) Two speeches are recorded of the Martyr in his last moments; one, in which he prayed that God would pardon his murderers,—the other his witness that he saw the heavens opened, and Jesus on God's right hand. His prayer was wonderfully answered. Stephen saw his Saviour; the next vision of that Saviour to mortal man was vouchsafed to the very young man, even Saul, who shared in his murder and his intercession.

Strange, indeed, it was; and what would have been St. Stephen's thoughts could he have known it! The prayers of righteous men avail much. The first martyr had power with God to raise up the greatest apostle. Such was the honour put upon the first fruits of those sufferings upon which the Church was entering. Thus from the beginning the blood of the martyrs was the seed of the Church. Stephen, one man, was put to death for saying that the Jewish people were to have exclusive privileges no longer; but from his very grave rose the favoured instrument by whom the thousands and ten thousands of the Gentiles were brought to the knowledge of the truth!

Herein then, first, is St. Paul's conversion memorable; that it was a triumph over the enemy. When Almighty God would convert the world, opening the door of faith to the Gentiles, who was the chosen preacher of His mercy? Not one of Christ's first followers. To show

His power, He put forth his hand into the very midst of the persecutors of His Son, and seized upon the most strenuous among them. The prayer of a dying man is the token and occasion of his triumph which He had reserved for Himself. His strength is made perfect in weakness. As of old, He broke the yoke of His people's burden, the staff of their shoulder, the rod of their oppressor. (Isa. ix. 4.) Saul made furiously for Damascus, but the Lord Almighty "knew his abode, and his going out and coming in, and his rage against Him," and "because his rage against Him, and his tumult came up before Him," therefore, as in Sennacherib's case, though in a far different way, He "put His hook in his nose and His bridle in his lips, and turned him back by the way by which he came." (Isa. xxxvii. 28, 29.) "He spoiled principalities and powers, and made a show of them openly" (Col. ii. 15), triumphing over the serpent's head while his heel was wounded. Saul, the persecutor, was converted, and preached Christ in the synagogues.

In the next place, St. Paul's conversion may be considered as a suitable introduction to the office he was called to execute in God's providence. I have said it was a triumph over the enemies of Christ; but it was also an expressive emblem of the nature of God's general dealings with the race of man. What are we all but rebels against God, and enemies of the Truth? What were the Gentiles in particular at that time, but "alienated" from Him, "and enemies in their mind by wicked works?" (Col. i. 21.) Who then could so appropriately fulfil the purpose of Him who came to call sinners to repentance, as one who esteemed himself the least of the apostles, that was not meet to be called an Apostle, because he had persecuted the Church of God? When Almighty God in His infinite mercy purposed to form a people to Himself out of the heathen, as vessels for glory, first He chose the instrument of this His purpose, as a brand from the burning, to be a type of the rest. There is a parallel to this order of Providence in the Old Testament. The Jews were bid to look unto the rock whence they were hewn. (Isa. li. 1.) Who was the especial patriarch of their nation?—Jacob. Abraham himself, indeed, had been called and blessed by God's mere grace. Yet Abraham had remarkable faith. Jacob, however, the immediate and peculiar patriarch of the Jewish race, is represented in the character of a sinner, pardoned and reclaimed by Divine mercy, a wanderer exalted to be the father of a great nation. Now I am not venturing to describe him as he really was, but as he is represented to us; not personally, but in that particular point of view in which the sacred history has placed him; not as an individual, but as he is typically, or in the way of doctrine. There is no mistaking the marks of his character and fortunes in the *history*, designedly (as it would seem) recorded to humble Jewish pride. He makes his own confession as St. Paul afterwards: "I am not worthy of the least of all Thy mercies." (Gen. xxxii. 10.) Every year, too, the Israelites were bid bring their offering, and avow before God that "a Syrian ready to perish was their father." (Deut. xxvi. 5.) Such as was the father, such (it was reasonable to suppose) would be the descendants. None would be "greater than their father Jacob." (John iv. 12.) for whose sake the nation was blest.

In like manner St. Paul is, in one way of viewing the dispensation, the spiritual father of the Gentiles; and in the history of his sin and its most gracious forgiveness, he exemplifies far more than his brother apostles his own Gospel; that we are all guilty before God, and can be saved only by His free bounty. In his own words, "for this cause obtained he mercy, that in him first Jesus Christ might show forth all *long-suffering for a pattern* to them which should hereafter believe on Him to life everlasting." (1 Tim. i. 16.)

And in the next place, St. Paul's previous course of life rendered him, perhaps, after his conversion, more fit an instrument of God's purposes towards the Gentiles, as well as a more striking specimen of it. Here it is necessary to speak with caution. We know that, whatever were St. Paul's successes in the propagation of the Gospel, they were in their source and nature not his, but through "the grace of God which was with him." Still, God makes use of human means, and it is allowable to inquire reverently what these were, and why St. Paul was employed to convert the heathen world rather than St. James the Less, or St. John. Doubtless his intellectual endowments and acquirements were among the circumstances which fitted him for his office. Yet, may it not be supposed that there was something in his previous religious history which especially disciplined him to be "all things to all men?" Nothing is so difficult as to enter into the characters and feelings of men who have been brought up under a system of religion different from our own; and to discern how they may be most forcibly and profitably addressed, in order to win them over to the reception of Divine truths, of which they are at present ignorant. Now St. Paul had had experience in his own case of a state of mind very different from that which belonged to him as an apostle. Though he had never been polluted with heathen immorality and profaneness, he had entertained views and sentiments very far from Christian; and had experienced a conversion to which the other apostles (as far as we know) were

F

strangers. I am far indeed from meaning that there is ought favourable to a man's after religion in an actual unsettling of principle, in lapsing into infidelity, and then returning again to religious belief. This was not St. Paul's case; *he* underwent no radical change of religious principle. Much less would I give countenance to the notion, that a previous immoral life is other than a grievous permanent hindrance and a curse to a man after he has turned to God. Such considerations, however, are out of place in speaking of St. Paul. What I mean is, that his awful rashness and blindness, his self-confident, headstrong, cruel rage, against the worshippers of the true Messiah, then his strange conversion, then the length of time that elapsed before his solemn ordination, during which he was left to meditate in private on all that had happened, and to anticipate the future, all this constituted a peculiar preparation for the office of preaching to a lost world, dead in sin. It gave him an extended insight, on the one hand, into the ways and designs of Providence, and on the other hand into the workings of sin in the human heart, and the various modes of thinking to which the mind may be trained. It taught him not to despair of the worst sinners, to be sharp-sighted in detecting the sparks of faith amid corrupt habits of life, and to enter into the various temptations to which human nature is exposed. It wrought in him a profound humility, which disposed him (if we may say so) to bear meekly the abundance of the revelations given him; and it imparted to him a practical wisdom how to apply them to the conversion of others, so as to be weak with the weak, and strong with the strong, to bear their burdens, to instruct and encourage them, to "strengthen his brethren," to rejoice and weep with them, in a word, to be an earthly *Paraclete*, the comforter, help, and guide of his brethren. It gave him to know in some good measure the *hearts of men;* an attribute (in its fulness) belonging to God alone, and possessed by Him in union with perfect purity from all sin; but which in us can scarcely exist without our own melancholy experience, in some degree, of moral evil in ourselves, since the innocent (it is their privilege) have not eaten of the tree of the knowledge of good and evil.

Lastly, to guard against misconception of these last remarks, I must speak distinctly on a part of the subject only touched upon hitherto, viz., on St. Paul's spiritual state before his conversion. For, in spite of what has been said by way of caution, perhaps I may still be supposed to warrant the maxim sometimes maintained, that the greater sinner makes the greater saint.

Now, observe, I do not allege that St. Paul's previous sins made him a more spiritual Christian afterwards, but rendered him *more fitted for a particular purpose* in God's providence,—more fitted, when converted, to reclaim others; just as a knowledge of languages (whether divinely or humanly acquired) fits a man for the office of missionary, without tending in any degree to make him a better man. I merely say, that if we take two men *equally* advanced in faith and holiness, that one of the two would preach to a variety of men with the greater success who had the greater experience in his own religious history of temptation, the war of flesh and spirit, sin, and victory over sin; though at the same time, at first sight it is of course unlikely that he who had experienced all these changes of mind *should* be equal in faith and obedience to the other who had served God from a child.

But, in the next place, let us observe, how very far St. Paul's conversion is, in matter of fact, from holding out any encouragement to those who live in sin, or any self-satisfaction to those who have lived in it; as if their present or former disobedience could be a gain to them.

Why was mercy shown to Saul the persecutor? He himself gives us the reason, which we may safely make use of. "I obtained mercy, because I did it ignorantly in unbelief." (1 Tim. i. 12, 13.) And why was he "enabled" to preach the Gospel? "Because Christ counted him faithful." We have here the reason more clearly stated even than in Abraham's case, who was honoured with special Divine revelations, and promised a name on the earth, because God "knew him, that he would command his children and his household after him, to keep the way of the Lord, to do justice and judgment." (Gen. xviii. 19.) Saul was ever faithful, according to his notion of "the way of the Lord." Doubtless he sinned deeply and grievously in persecuting the followers of Christ. Had he known the Holy Scriptures, he never would have done so; he would have recognized Jesus to be the promised Saviour, as Simeon and Anna had, from the first. But he was bred up in a human school, and paid more attention to the writings of men than to the word of God. Still, observe, he differed from other enemies of Christ in this, that he kept a clear conscience, and habitually obeyed God according to his knowledge. God speaks to us in two ways, in our hearts and in His word. The latter and clearer of these informants St. Paul knew little of; the former he could not but know in his measure (for it was within him), and he obeyed it. That inward voice was but feeble, mixed up and obscured with human feelings and human traditions; so that what his conscience told him to do, was but partially true, and in part was wrong. Yet still, believing it to speak God's will, he deferred to it, acting as he did afterwards when he "was not disobedient to the heavenly vision," which informed him Jesus was the Christ. (Acts xxvi. 19.) Hear his own account of himself:

"I have lived in all good conscience before God until this day." "After the most straitest sect of our religion, I lived a Pharisee." "Touching the righteousness which is in the Law, blameless." (Acts xxiii. 1 ; xxvi. 5. Phil. iii. 6.) Here is no ease, no self-indulgent habits, no wilful sin against the light,—nay, I will say no pride. That is, though he was doubtless influenced by much sinful self-confidence, in his violent and bigoted hatred of the Christians, and though (as well as even the best of us) he was doubtless liable to the occasional temptations and defilements of pride, yet, taking pride to mean open rebellion against God, warring against God's authority, setting up reason against God, this he had not. He "verily thought within himself that he ought to do many things contrary to the name of Jesus of Nazareth." Turn to the case of Jews and Gentiles who remained unconverted, and you will see the difference between them and him. Think of the hypocritical Pharisees, who professed to be saints, and were sinners ; "full of extortion, excess, and uncleanness (Matt. xxiii. 25, 27) ;" believing Jesus to be the Christ, but not confessing Him, as "loving the praise of men more than the praise of God." (John xii. 43.) St. Paul himself gives us an account of them in the second chapter of his Epistle to the Romans. Can it be made to apply to his own previous state? Was the name of God blasphemed among the

Gentiles through him?—On the other hand, the Gentile reasoners sought a vain wisdom. (1 Cor. i. 22.) These were they who despised religion and practical morality as common matters, unworthy the occupation of a refined and cultivated intellect. " Some mocked, others said, We will hear thee again of this matter." (Acts xvii. 32.) They prided themselves on being above vulgar prejudices,—in being indifferent to the traditions afloat in the world about another life,—in regarding all religions as equally true and equally false. Such a hard, vain-glorious temper our Lord solemnly condemns, when he says to the Church at Laodicea, "I would thou wert cold or hot."

The Pharisees, then, were breakers of the Law; the Gentile reasoners and statesmen were infidels. Both were proud, both despised the voice of conscience. We see, then, from this review, the kind of sin which God pities and pardons. All sin, indeed, when repented of, He will put away; but pride hardens the heart against repentance and sensuality debases it to a brutal nature. The Holy Spirit is quenched by open transgressions of conscience and contempt of His authority. But, when men err in ignorance, following closely their own notions of right and wrong, though these notions are mistaken,—great as is their sin, if they might have possessed themselves of truer notions—(and very great as was St. Paul's sin, because he certainly might have learned from the Old Testament far clearer and diviner doctrine than the tradition of the Pharisees), yet such men are not left by the God of all grace. God leads them on to the light, in spite of their errors in faith, if they continue strictly to obey what they believe to be His will. And, to declare this comfortable truth to us, St. Paul was thus carried on by the Providence of God, and brought into the light by miracle, that we may learn, by a memorable instance of His grace, what He ever does, though He does not in ordinary cases thus declare it openly to the world.

ANTONY AND HIS TEMPTATIONS.

A HERMIT'S life—that is, a strictly monastic or solitary life—may be called unnatural, and is not sanctioned by the Gospel. Christ sent His Apostles by two and two; and surely He knew what was in man from the day that He said, "It is not good for him to be alone." So far, then, Antony's manner of life may be said to have no claim upon our admiration; but this part of his pattern did not extend to his imitators, who by their numbers were soon led to the formation of monastic societies, and who, after a while, entangled even Antony himself in the tie of becoming in a certain sense their religious head and teacher. Monachism consisting, not in solitariness, but in austerities, prayers, retirement, and obedience, had nothing in it, so far, but what was perfectly Christian, and, under circumstances, exemplary; especially when viewed in its connection with the relative duties, which were soon afterwards appropriated to it, of being almoner to the poor, educating the clergy, and defending the faith as delivered to us. Monachism became, in a little time, nothing else than a peculiar department of the Christian ministry—a ministry not of the sacraments, or clerical, but especially of the word and doctrine; not indeed by any formal ordination to it, for it was as yet a lay profession, but by the common right, or rather duty, which attaches to all of us to avow, propagate, and defend the truth, especially when our devotion to it has the countenance and encouragement of Church authorities.

St. Antony's life, written by his friend the great Athanasius, has come down to us. Some critics, indeed, doubt its genuineness, and consider it interpolated. I conceive no question can be raised about its *substantial* accuracy; and on rising from the perusal of it, we are able to pronounce Antony an extraordinary man. Enthusiastic he certainly must be accounted; had he lived in this day and in this country, he would have been exposed to a considerable (though of course not insuperable) temptation to become a sectarian. Panting after some higher rule of life than that which the ordinary forms of society admit of, and finding our present lines too rigidly drawn to include any style of mind that is out-of-the-way, any rule that is not "gentlemanlike," "comfortable," and "established," he might possibly have broken what he could not bend. The question is not whether he would have been justified in so doing (of course not); nor whether the most angelic temper of all is not that which settles down content with what is everyday (as Abraham's heavenly guests eat of the calf which he had dressed, and as our Saviour went down to Nazareth, and was subject to his parents); but whether such resignation to worldly comforts is not quite as often at least the characteristic of a grovelling mind also, —whether there are not minds between the lowest and the highest of ardent feelings, keen imaginations, and undisciplined tempers, who are under a strong irritation prompting them to run wild,—whether it is not our duty (so to speak) to play with such, carefully letting out line lest they snap it; and whether our established system is as indulgent and as wise as is desirable in its treatment of such persons, inasmuch as it provides no occupation for them, does not understand how to turn them to account, lets them run to waste, tempts them to schism, loses them, and is weakened by the loss. For instance, had we some regular missionary seminary, such an institution would in one way supply the deficiency I speak of.

As for Antony: did I see him before me, I might be tempted to consider him somewhat of an enthusiast; but what I desire to point out to the reader is the subdued and Christian form which his enthusiasm took. It was not vulgar, bustling, imbecile, unstable, undutiful; it was calm and composed, manly, intrepid, magnanimous, full of affectionate loyalty to the Church and to the Truth.

Antony was born A.D. 251, while Origen was still alive; while Cyprian was Bishop of Carthage; Dionysius, Bishop of Alexandria; and Gregory Thaumaturgus, of Neocæsarea: he lived till A.D. 335, to the age of 105, nine years after the birth of St. Chrysostom, and two years after that of St. Augustine. He was an Egyptian by birth, and the son of noble, opulent, and Christian parents. He was brought up as a Christian, and from his boyhood showed a strong disposition towards a solitary life. Shrinking from the society of his equals, and despising the external world in comparison of the world within him, he set himself against what is considered a liberal education—that is, the acquisition of foreign languages. At the same time he was very dutiful to his parents, simple and self-denying in his habits, and attentive to the sacred services and readings of the Church.

Before he arrived at man's estate, he had lost both his parents, and was left with a sister, who was a child, and an ample inheritance. His mind at this time was earnestly set upon imitating the Apostles and their converts, who gave up their possessions and followed Christ. One day, about six months after his parents' death, as he went to church, as usual, the subject pressed seriously upon him. The gospel of the day happened to contain the text, "If thou wilt be perfect, go sell all that thou hast," &c. Antony applied it to himself, and acted upon it. He had three hundred acres, of especial fertility even in Egypt; these he at once made over to the use of the poor of his own neighbourhood. Next, he turned into money all his personal property, and reserving a portion for his sister's use, gave the rest to the poor. After which he was struck by hearing in church the text— "Take no thought for the morrow;" and, considering he had not yet fully satisfied the evangelical precept, he gave away what he had reserved, placing his sister in the care of some trustworthy female acquaintances, who had devoted themselves to a single life.

He commenced his ascetic life, according to the custom hitherto observed, by retiring to a place not far from his own home. Here he remained for a while, to steady and fix his mind in his new habits, and to gain what advice he could towards the formation of them, from such as had already engaged in them. This is a remarkable trait, as Athanasius records it as showing how little he was influenced by self-will or sectarian spirit in what he was doing; how ardently he pursued an ascetic life as in itself good, and how willing he was to become the servant of any who might give him directions in his pursuit.

After a while, our youth's enthusiasm began to take its usual course. His spirits fell, his courage flagged; a reaction followed, and the temptations of this world assaulted him with a violence which showed that as yet he scarcely understood the true meaning of his profession. Had he been nothing more than an enthusiast, he would have gone back to the world. His abandoned property, the guardianship of his sister, his family connections, the conveniences of wealth, worldly reputation, disgust of the sameness and coarseness of his food, bodily infirmity, the tediousness of his mode of living, and the painfulness of idleness, became instruments of temptation. And other and fiercer assaults arose. However, his faith rose above them all, or rather as Athanasius says: "not himself, but the grace of God that was in him."

Such a life Antony lived for about fifteen years. At the end of this time, being now thirty-five, he betook himself to the desert, having first spent some days in prayers and holy exercises in the tombs. There, however, we are necessarily introduced to another subject—his alleged conflicts with the evil spirits.

It is quite certain that Antony believed himself to be subjected to sensible and visible conflicts with evil spirits. It is far from my desire to rescue him from the imputation of enthusiasm; the very drift of my account of him being to show how enthusiasm is sobered and refined by being submitted to the discipline of the Church, instead of being allowed to run wild externally to it. If he were not an enthusiast, or in danger of being such, we should lose one chief instruction his life conveys. This admission, however, does not settle the question to which the narrative of his spiritual conflicts gives rise. The following is the account of his visit to the tombs :—

"Thus bracing himself after the pattern of Elias, he set off to the tombs, which were some distance from his village ; and, giving directions to an acquaintance to bring him bread after some days' interval, he entered into one of them, suffered himself to be shut in, and remained there by himself. This the enemy not enduring, yea rather dreading, lest before long he should engross the desert also with his holy exercise, assaulted him one night with a host of spirits, and so lashed him, that he lay speechless on the ground from the torture, which he declared was far more severe than from strokes which man could inflict. But, by God's providence, who does not overlook those who hope in Him, on the next day his acquaintance came with the bread, and, on opening the door, saw him lying on the ground, as if dead. Whereupon he carried him to the village church, and laid him on the ground; and many of his relations and the villagers took their places by the body, as if he were already dead. However, about midnight his senses returned, and, collecting himself, he observed that they were all asleep except his aforesaid acquaintance; whereupon he beckoned him to his side, and asked him, without waking any of them, to carry him back again to the tombs.

"The man took him back; and when he was shut in, as before, by himself, being unable to stand from his wounds, he lay down and began to pray. Then he cried out loudly, 'Here am I, Antony; I do not shun your blows. Though ye add to them, yet nothing shall separate me from the love of Christ.' And then he began to sing, 'Though a host should encamp against me, yet shall not my heart be afraid.' The devil has no trouble in devising divers shapes of evil. During the night, therefore, the Evil One made so great a tumult that the whole place seemed to be shaken, and, as if they broke down the four walls of the building, they seemed to rush in, in the form of wild beasts and reptiles. . . . . But Antony, though scourged and pierced, felt indeed his bodily pain, but the rather kept vigil in his soul. So, as he lay groaning in body, yet a watcher in his mind, he spoke in taunt, 'Had ye any power, one of you would be enough to assail me; you try, if possible, to frighten me with your number, because the Lord has spoiled you of your strength. Those pretended forms are the proof of your impotence. Our seal and wall of defence is faith in the Lord.' After many attempts, then, they gnashed their teeth at him, because they were rather making themselves a sport than him. But the Lord a second time remembered the conflict of Antony, and came to his help. Raising his eyes, he saw the roof as if opening, and a beam of light descending towards him; suddenly the devils vanished, his pain ceased, and the building was whole again. Upon this Antony said, 'Where art thou, Lord? Why didst thou not appear at the first, to ease my pain?' A voice answered, 'Antony, I was here, but waited to see thy bearing of the contest. Since, then, thou hast sustained and not been worsted, I will be to thee an aid for ever, and will make thy name famous in every place.'"

After this preliminary vigil, Antony made for the desert, where he spent the next twenty years in solitude. To enter into the state of opinion and feeling which the accounts of his life there imply, it is necessary to observe, that as regards the Church's warfare with the devil, the primitive Christians considered themselves to be similarly circumstanced with the Apostles. They did not draw a line between the condition of the Church in their day and in the first age, but believed that what it had been, such it was still in its trials and in its powers; that the open assaults of Satan, and their own means of repelling them, were such as they are described in the Gospels. Exorcism was a sacred function in the primitive Church, and the energumen took his place with catechumens and penitents, as in the number of those who had the especial prayers, and were allowed some of the privileges of the Christian body. Our Saviour speaks of the power of exorcising as depending on fasting and prayer, in certain special cases, and thus seems to countenance the notion of a direct conflict between the Christian athlete and the powers of evil, a conflict carried on by definite weapons, for definite ends, and not that indirect warfare merely which the religious conduct of life implies. "This kind can come forth by nothing but by prayer and fasting." Surely none of Christ's words are chance words: He spoke *with a purpose*, and the Holy Spirit guided the Evangelists in their selection of them, *with a purpose;* and if so, this text is a rule and an admonition, and was acted upon as such by the primitive Christians, whether from their received principles of interpretation, or the traditional practice of the Church.

In like manner, whether from their mode of interpreting Scripture or from the opinions and practices which came down to them, they conceived the devil to have that power over certain brute animals which Scripture sometimes assigns to him. He is known on one memorable occasion to have taken the form of a serpent; at another time, a legion of devils possessed a herd of swine. These instances may, for what we know, be revealed *specimens* of a whole side of the Divine dispensation, viz., the interference of spiritual agencies, good or bad, with the course of the world, under which, perhaps, the speaking of Balaam's ass falls; and the early Christians, whether so understanding Scripture, or from their traditionary system, acted as if they were so. They considered that brute nature was widely subject to the power of spirits; as, on the other hand, there had been a time when even the Creator Spirit had condescended to manifest Himself in the bodily form of a dove. Their notions concerning local demoniacal influences in oracles and idols, in which they were sanctioned by Scripture, confirmed this belief. . . . . . When, then, we read of Antony's sensible contests with the powers of evil, the abstract possibility of these is to be decided by the existence, in his day, of such parallel *facts* as demoniacal possessions, which certainly *are* witnessed unanimously by his contemporaries; and the really superhuman character of what seemed like natural occurrences is to be estimated, not by the mere circumstance that they may be brought under natural laws, as demoniacal possessions also may be by the physician, but by the known actual presence of unseen agents to which they may be referred. Antony's conflict in the tombs may be solved into a dream, or an attack from jackals; yet this only removes the real agent a step further back. Satan may still have been the real agent at bottom, and have been discerned by Antony through the shadow of things sensible.

These things being considered, I judge of Antony's life thus: there may be enthusiasm here; there may be, at times, exaggerations and misconceptions of what, as they really happened, meant nothing. And still it may be true that that conflict begun by our Lord, when He was interrogated and assaulted by Satan, was continued in the experience of Antony, who lived not so very long after Him. How far the evil spirit acted, how far he was present in natural objects, how far was dream, how far fancy, is little to the purpose. I see, anyhow, the root of a great truth here, and think that those are wiser who admit something than those who deny all. I see Satan frightened at the invasions of the Church upon his kingdom; I see him retreating step by step; I see him dispossessed by fasting and prayer, as was predicted; and I see him doing his utmost in whatever way to resist. Nor is there anything uncongenial to the Gospel system that so direct a war should be waged upon him; a war without the ordinary duties of life and of society for its subject-matter and instruments. Our Saviour Himself was forty days in the wilderness, and St. Paul in prison,

St. Peter at Joppa, and St. John at Patmos, show that social duties may be providentially suspended under the Gospel, and a direct intercourse with the next world be imposed upon the Christian. And if so much be allowed, certainly there is nothing in Antony's life to make us suspicious of him personally. His doctrine was pure and unimpeachable; and his temper is high and heavenly —without cowardice, without gloom, without formality, and without self-complacency. Superstition is abject and crouching, it is full of thoughts of guilt; it distrusts God, and dreads the powers of evil. Antony at least has nothing of this, being full of holy confidence, divine peace, cheerfulness and valorousness, be he (as some men may judge) ever so much an enthusiast.

ARIUS.

ARIUS first published his heresy about the year 319. It is said that on the death of Achillas, he had aspired to the primacy of the Egyptian Church; and, according to Philostorgios, the historian of his party, a writer of little credit, he had generously resigned his claims in favour of Alexander, who was elected. His ambitious character renders it not improbable that he was a candidate for the vacant dignity; but the difference of age between himself and Alexander, which must have been considerable, at once accounts for the elevation of the latter, and it is an evidence of the indecency of Arius in becoming a competitor at all. His first attack on the Catholic doctrine was conducted with an openness which, considering the general duplicity of his party, is the most honourable trait in his character. In a public meeting of the clergy of Alexandria, he accused his diocesan of Sabellianism; an insult which Alexander, from deference to the talents and learning of the objector, sustained with somewhat too little of the dignity befitting the "Ruler of the People." The mischief which ensued from his misplaced weakness, was considerable. Arius was one of the public preachers of Alexandria; and, as some suppose, Master of the Catechetical School. Others of the city Presbyters were stimulated by his example to similar irregularities. Colluthus, Carponas, and Sarmatas, began to form each his own party, in a church which Meletius had already troubled; and Colluthus went so far as to promulgate an heretical doctrine and to found a sect. Still hoping to settle these disorders without the exercise of his episcopal power, Alexander summoned a meeting of his clergy, in which Arius was allowed to state his doctrines freely, and to argue in their defence; and, whether from a desire not to overbear the discussion, or from distrust in his own power of accurately expressing the truth, and anxiety about the charge of heresy brought against himself, the primate, though in nowise a man of feeble mind, is said to have refrained from committing himself on the controverted subject, "applauding," as Sozomen says, "sometimes one party and sometimes the other." At length the error of Arius appeared to be of that serious and confirmed nature, that countenance of it became sinful. The heresy began to spread beyond the Alexandrian Church; the indecision of Alexander excited the murmurs of the

Catholics; till, at last, called unwillingly to the discharge of a severe duty, he gave public evidence of his real indignation against the blasphemies which he had so long endured, and excommunicated Arius with his followers.

This proceeding, obligatory as it was on a Christian bishop, and ratified by the concurrence of a provincial council, and expedient even for the immediate interests of Christianity, had other churches been equally honest in their allegiance to the true faith, had the effect of increasing the influence of Arius, by throwing him upon his fellow Lucianists of the rival dioceses of the East, and giving notoriety to his name and tenets. In Egypt, indeed, he had already been supported by the Meletian faction; which, in spite of its profession of orthodoxy, continued in alliance with him, through jealousy to the Church, even after he had fallen into heresy. But the countenance of these schismatics was of small consideration, compared with the powerful aid frankly tendered him, on his excommunication, by the leading men in the great Catholic communities of Asia Minor and the East. Palestine was the first to afford him a retreat from Alexandrian orthodoxy, where he received a cordial reception from the learned Eusebius, Metropolitan of Cæsarea, Athanasius of Anazarbus, and others; who, in letters in his behalf, did not hesitate to declare their concurrence with him in the full extent of his heresy. Eusebius even declared that Christ was not very God (ἀληθινὸς θεός); and his associate Athanasius asserted, that He was in the number of the hundred sheep of the parable, *i.e.*, the creatures of God.

Yet, in spite of the countenance of these and other eminent men, Arius found it difficult to maintain his ground against the general indignation which his heresy excited. He was resolutely opposed by Philogonius, patriarch of Antioch, and Macarius of Jerusalem; who promptly answered the call made upon them by Alexander, in his circulars addressed to the Syrian Churches. In the meanwhile Eusebius of Nicomedia, the early friend of Arius, and the ecclesiastical adviser of Constantia, the Emperor's sister, declared in his favour; and offered him a refuge, which he readily accepted, from the growing unpopularity which attended him in Palestine. Supported by the patronage of so powerful a prelate, Arius was now scarcely to be considered in the position of a schismatic or an outcast. He assumed in consequence a more calm and respectful demeanour towards Alexander; imitated the courteous language of his friend; and addressed his diocesan with an affectation of humility, and deferred or appealed to previous statements made by Alexander himself on the doctrine in dispute. At this time also he seems to have corrected and com pleted his system. George, afterwards Bishop of Laodicea, taught him an evasion for the orthodox test ἐκθεοῦ, by a reference to 1 Cor. xi. 12. Asterius, a sophist of Cappadocia, supported the secondary sense of the word *Logos* as applied to Christ by a reference to such passages as Joel ii. 25; and, in order to explain away the force of the μόνογενης, maintained, that to Christ alone out of all creatures it had been given to be fashioned under the immediate presence and perilous weight of the Divine hand. Now, too, as it appears, the title of ἀληθινὸς θεός was ascribed to him; the ἀλλοιωτὸν was withdrawn; and an admission of His *actual* indefectibility substituted for it. The heresy being thus placed on a less exceptionable basis, the influence of Eusebius was exerted in Councils both in Bithynia and Palestine; in which Arius was acknowledged, and more urgent solicitations addressed to Alexander, in order to effect his readmission into the Church.

This was the history of the controversy for the first four or five years of its existence; *i. e.*, till the era of the Battle of Hadrianople (A.D. 323), by the issue of which Constantine, becoming master of the Roman world, was at liberty to turn his thoughts to the state of Christianity in the eastern province of the Empire. From this date it is connected with civil history; a consequence natural, and indeed necessary, under the existing circumstances, though it was the occasion of subjecting Christianity to fresh persecutions, in place of those which its nominal triumph had terminated. When a heresy, condemned to excommunication by one Church, was taken up by another, and independent Christian bodies then stood in open opposition, nothing was left to those who desired peace, to say nothing of orthodoxy, but to bring the question under the notice of a General Council. But as a previous step, the leave of the civil power was plainly necessary for so public a display of that wide-spreading association, of which the faith of the Gospel was the uniting and animating principle. Thus the Church could not meet together in one, without entering into a sort of negotiation with the powers that be; whose jealousy it is the duty of Christians, both as individuals and as a body, if possible, to dispel. On the other hand, the Roman Emperor, as a professed disciple of the truth, was, of course, bound to protect its interests, and to afford every facility for its establishment in purity and efficacy. It was under these circumstances that the Nicene Council was convoked.

CONSTANTINE.

IT is an ungrateful task to discuss the private opinions and motives of an Emperor who was the first to profess himself the Protector of the Church, and to relieve it from the abject and suffering condition in which it had lain for three centuries. Constantine is our benefactor; inasmuch as we, who now live, may be considered to have received the gift of Christianity by means of the increased influence which he gave to the Church. And, were it not that in conferring his benefaction, he burdened it with the bequest of an heresy, which outlived his age by many centuries, and still exists in its effects in the divisions of the East, nothing would here be said, from mere grateful recollection of him, by way of analysing the state of mind in which he viewed the benefit which he has conveyed to us. But his conduct as it discovers itself in the subsequent history, natural as it was in his case, yet has somewhat of a warning in it, which must not be neglected in after times.

It is of course impossible accurately to describe the various feelings with which one in Constantine's peculiar position was likely to regard Christianity; yet the joint effect of them all may be gathered from his actual conduct, and the state of the civilized world at the time. He found his empire distracted with civil and religious dissensions, which tended to the dissolution of Society; at a time, too, when the barbarians without were pressing upon it with a vigour, formidable in itself, but far more menacing in consequence of the decay of the ancient spirit of Rome. He perceived the power of its old polytheism, from whatever cause, exhausted, and a newly risen philosophy vainly endeavouring to resuscitate a mythology which had done its work, and now, like all things of earth, was fast returning to the dust from which it was taken. He heard the same philosophy inculcating the principles of that more exalted and refined religion which a civilized age will always require; and he witnessed the same substantial teaching, as he would consider it, embodied in the precepts, and enforced by the energetic discipline, the union, and the example of the Christian Church. Here his thoughts would rest, as in a natural solution of the investigation to which the state of his empire gave rise; and, without knowing enough of the internal characters of Christianity to care to instruct himself in them, he would discern, on the face of it, a doctrine more real than that of philosophy, and a rule of life more self-denying than that of the Republic. The Gospel seemed to be the fit instrument of a civil reformation, being but a new form of the old wisdom which had existed in the world at large from the beginning. Revering, nay, in one sense, honestly submitting to its faith, yet he acknowledged it rather as a system than joined it as an institution; and, by refraining from the sacrament of baptism till his last illness, he acted in the spirit of men of the world in every age, who dislike to pledge themselves to engagements which they still intend to fulfil, and to descend from the position of judges to that of disciples of the truth.

Peace is so eminently a perfection of the Christian temper, conduct, and discipline, and it had been so wonderfully exemplified in the previous history of the Church, that it was almost unavoidable in a heathen soldier and statesman to regard it as the sole precept of the Gospel. It required a far more refined moral perception to detect and to approve the principle on which this peace is founded in Scripture; to submit to the dictation of truth, as such, as a primary authority in matters of political and private conduct; to understand how belief in a certain creed was a condition of divine favour; how the social union was intended to result from a unity of opinions; the love of man to spring from the love of God;

and zeal to be prior in the succession of Christian graces to benevolence. It had been predicted by Him who came to offer peace to the world, that, in matter of fact, that gift would be changed into the sword of discord; mankind being alienated from the doctrine, more than they were won over by the amiableness, of Christianity. But He alone was able thus to discern through what a succession of difficulties divine truth advances to its final victory; shallow minds anticipate the end apart from the course which leads to it. Especially they who receive scarcely more of His teaching than the instinct of civilization recognizes (and Constantine must, on the whole, be classed among such), view the religious dissensions of the Church as simply evil, and (as they would fain prove) contrary to His own precepts; whereas, in fact, they are but the history of truth in its first stage of trial, when it aims at being "pure" before it is "peaceable;" and are reprehensible so far, as baser passions mix themselves with that true loyalty towards God which desires His own glory in the first place, and only in the second place the tranquillity and good order of society.

BASIL AND GREGORY.

IT often happens that men of very dissimilar talents and tastes are attracted together by their very dissimilitude. They live in intimacy for a time, perhaps a long time, till their circumstances alter, or some sudden event comes to try them. Then the peculiarities of their respective minds are brought out into action; and quarrels ensue, which end in coolness or separation. Such are the two main characters which are found in the Church—high energy and sweetness of temper; far from incompatible of course, united in Apostles, though in different relative proportions, yet only partially combined in ordinary Christians, and often altogether parted from each other.

This contrast of character, leading first to intimacy, then to difference, is interestingly displayed, though painfully, in one passage of the history of Basil and Gregory. Gregory the affectionate, the tender-hearted, the man of quick feelings, the accomplished, the eloquent preacher—and Basil, the man of firm resolve and hard deeds, the high-minded ruler of Christ's flock, the diligent labourer in the field of ecclesiastical politics. Thus they differed; yet not as if they had not much in common still: both had the blessing and discomfort of a sensitive mind; both were devoted to an ascetic life; both were men of classical tastes; but both were special champions of the orthodox creed; both were skilled in argument, and successful in their use of it; both were in highest place in the Church, the one Exarch of Cæsarea, the other Patriarch of Constantinople.

Basil and Gregory were both natives of Cappadocia; but here, again, under different circumstances. Basil was born of a good family, and with Christian ancestors; Gregory was the son of a Bishop of Nazianzus, who had been brought up an idolater, or rather an Hypsistarian, a mongrel sort of religionist, part Jew, part Pagan. He was brought over to Christianity by the efforts of his wife Nonna, and at Nazianzus admitted by baptism into the Church. In process of time he was made bishop of that city; but, not having very clear doctrinal views, he was betrayed in 360 into signing the Arian creed, which caused him much trouble, and from which at length his son rescued him. Cæsarea being at no insurmountable distance from Nazianzus, the two friends had known each other in their own country; but their intimacy began at Athens, whither they separately repaired for the purposes

H

of education. This was about A.D. 351, when each of them was twenty-two years of age. Gregory came to the seat of learning shortly before Basil, and thus was able to be his host and guide on his arrival; but fame had reported Basil's merits before he came, and he seems to have made his way, in a place of all others most difficult to a stranger, with a facility peculiar to himself. He soon found himself admired and respected by his fellow-students; but Gregory was his only friend, and shared with him the reputation for talent and attainments. They remained at Athens four or five years; and, at the end of the time, made the acquaintance of Julian, since of evil name in history as the Apostate.

The friends had been educated for rhetoricians, and their oratorical powers were such, that they seemed to have every prize in prospect which a secular ambition could desire. Their names were known far and wide, their attainments acknowledged by enemies, and they themselves personally popular in their circle of acquaintance. It was under these circumstances that they took the extraordinary resolution of quitting the world together; extraordinary the world calls it, utterly perplexed to find that any conceivable objects can, by any sane person, be accounted better than its own gifts and favours. They resolved to seek baptism of the Church, and to consecrate their gifts to the service of the Giver. With characters of mind very different—the one grave, the other lively; the one desponding, the other sanguine; the one with deep feelings, the other with acute and warm, they agreed together in holding that the things that are seen are not to be compared to the things that are not seen. They quitted the world, while it entreated them to stay. What passed when they were about to leave Athens, represents as in a figure the parting which they and the world took of each other. When the day of valediction arrived, their companions and equals, nay, some of their tutors came about them, and resisted their departure by entreaties, arguments, and even by violence. This occasion showed, also, their respective dispositions; for the firm Basil persevered and went; the tender-hearted Gregory was softened, and stayed a while longer. Basil, indeed, in spite of the reputation which attended him, had, from the first, felt disappointment with the celebrated abode of philosophy and literature, and seems to have given up the world from a conviction of its emptiness. .... Yet Gregory had inducements of his own to leave the world, not to insist on his love of Basil's company. His mother had devoted him to God both before and after his birth; and when he was a child he had a remarkable dream which made a great impression upon him. .... The impression, indeed, was as "a spark of heavenly fire," or "a taste of divine milk and honey."

As far then as these descriptions go, one might say that Gregory's abandonment of the world arose from an early passion, as it might be called, for a purity higher than his own nature; and Basil's from a profound sense of the world's nothingness and the world's defilements. Both seem to have viewed it as a sort of penitential exercise, as well as a means towards perfection.

When they had once resolved to devote themselves to the service of religion, the question arose, how they might best improve and employ the talents committed to them. Somehow, the idea of marrying and taking orders, or taking orders and marrying, building or improving their parsonage, and showing forth the charities and the humanities and the gentilities of a family man, did not suggest itself to their minds. They fancied that they must give up wife, children, property, if they could be perfect; and, this being taken for granted, that their choice did but lie between two modes of life, both of which they regarded as extreme. Here, then, for a time, they were in some perplexity. Gregory speaks of two ascetic disciplines, that of the solitary and that of the secular; one of which, he says, profits a man's self, the other his neighbour. Midway, however, between these lay the cenobite, or what we commonly call the monastic; removed from the world yet acting in a certain circle. And this was the rule which the friends at length determined to adopt, withdrawing from mixed society in order to be of greater service to it.

Not many years passed after their leaving Athens, when Basil put his resolution into practice; and, having fixed upon Pontus for his retirement, wrote to Gregory to remind him of his promise. Gregory hesitated. Then he wrote to expostulate with him. Gregory's answer was as follows:—

"I have not stood to my word, I own it; having protested, ever since Athens and our friendship and union of heart there, that I would be your companion, and follow a strict life with you. Yet I act against my wish, duty annulled by duty, the duty of friendship by the duty of filial reverence. . . . . However, I still shall be able to perform my promise in a measure, if you will accept thus much. I will come to you for a time, if, in turn, you will give me your company here; thus we shall be quits in friendly service, while we have all things common. And thus I shall avoid distressing my parents, without losing you."

When we bear in mind what has been already mentioned about Gregory's father, we may well believe that there really were very urgent reasons against the son leaving him, when it came to the point, over and above the ties which would keep him with a father and mother, both advanced in years. Basil, however, was disappointed;

and instead of retiring to Pontus, devoted a year to visiting the monastic institutions of Syria and Egypt. On his return, his thoughts again settled on his friend Gregory; and he attempted to overcome the obstacle in the way of their old project, by placing himself in a district called Tiberius, near Gregory's own home. Finding, however, the spot cold and damp, he gave up the idea of it. On one occasion, while he was yet living in Cæsarea, where for a time he had taught rhetoric, Gregory wrote to him a familiar letter, as from a countryman to an inhabitant of a town.

Meanwhile Basil had chosen for his retreat a spot near Neocæsarea, in Pontus, close by the village where lay his father's property, where he had been brought up in childhood by his grandmother, Macrina, and whither his mother and sister had retired for a monastic life after his father's death. The river Iris ran between the two places. Within a mile of their monastery was the Church of the Forty Martyrs, where father, mother, and sister were successively buried. On settling there, he again wrote to Gregory, urging him to come.

Gregory answered this letter by one which is still extant, in which he satirizes, point by point, the picture of the Pontine solitude which Basil had drawn to allure him; perhaps from distaste for it, perhaps in the temper of one who studiously disparages what, if he had admitted the thought, might prove too great a temptation for him. He ends thus: "This is longer, perhaps, than a letter, but shorter than a comedy. For yourself it will be good of you to take this castigation well; but if you do not, I will give you some more of it." Basil *did* take the castigation well; but this did not save him from the infliction of the concluding threat; for Gregory, after paying him a visit, continued in the same bantering strain in a later epistle.

* * * * * *

The next kindly intercourse between Basil and Gregory took place on occasion of the difference between Basil and his bishop, Eusebius, when Gregory interfered successfully to reconcile them. And the next arose out of circumstances which followed the death of Gregory's brother, Cæsarius. On his death-bed he had left all his goods to the poor; a bequest which was interfered with, first by servants and others about him, who carried off at once all the valuables on which they could lay hands; and after Gregory had come into possession of the residue, by the fraud of certain pretended creditors, who appealed to the law on his refusing to satisfy them. Basil, on this occasion, gained him the interest of the Prefect of Constantinople, and another, whose influence was great at court.

We now come to the election of Basil to the Exarchate of Cappadocia, which was owing in no small degree to the exertions of Gregory and his father in his favour. The event, which was attended with considerable hazard of defeat from the strength of the civil party, and an episcopal faction opposed to Basil, doubtless was at the moment a cause of increased affection between the friends, though it was soon the occasion of the difference and coolness which I have already spoken of. Gregory, as I have said, was of an amiable temper, fond of retirement and literary pursuits, and cultivating Christianity in its domestic and friendly aspect, rather than amid the toils of ecclesiastical warfare. I have also said enough to show that I have no thoughts whatever of accusing him of any approach to self-indulgence; and his subsequent conduct at Constantinople made it clear how well he could undergo and fight up against persecution in the quarrel of the Gospel. But such scenes of commotion were real sufferings to him, even independently of the personal danger of them; he was unequal to the task of ruling, and Basil in vain endeavoured to engage him as his coadjutor and comrade in the government of his Exarchate.

At length Gregory came to Cæsarea, where Basil showed him all marks of affection and respect; and when Gregory declined any public attentions, from a fear of the jealousy it might occasion, his friend let him do as he would, regardless, as Gregory observes, of the charge which might fall on himself, of neglecting Gregory, from those who were ignorant of the circumstances. However, Basil could not detain him long in the metropolitan city.

* * * * * *

About two years after Basil's elevation, a dispute arose between him and Anthimus, Bishop of Tyana. Cappadocia had been divided by the civil power into two parts; and Anthimus contended that an ecclesiastical division must necessarily follow the civil, and that, in consequence, he himself, as holding the chief see in the second Cappadocia, was the rightful metropolitan of the province. The justice of the case was with Basil, but he was opposed by the party of bishops who were secretly Arianizers, and had already opposed themselves to his election. Accordingly, having might on his side, Anthimus began to alienate the monks from Basil, to appropriate the revenues of the Church of Cæsarea, which lay in his province, and to expel or gain over the presbyters, giving, as an excuse, that respect and offerings ought not to be paid to heterodox persons.

Gregory at once offered his assistance to his friend, hinting to him, at the same time, that some of those about him had some share of blame in the dispute. It happened unfortunately for their intimacy that they were respectively connected with distinct parties in the Church. Basil knew and valued and gained over many of the semi-Arians, who dissented from the orthodox doctrine more from over subtlety or want of clearness of mind, than from unbelief. Gregory was in habits of intimacy with the religious brethren of Nazianzus, his father's see, and these were eager for orthodoxy almost as a badge of party. Basil, in one of his letters, had reflected on these monks; and, on this occasion, Gregory warned him against Eustathius and his friends, whose orthodoxy was suspicious, and who, being ill-disposed towards Anthimus, were likely to increase the difference between the latter and Basil.

Gregory's offer of assistance to Basil was frankly made, and seems to have been as frankly accepted. "I will come if you wish me," he had said, "if so be, to advise with you, if the sea wants water, or you a counsellor; at all events, to gain benefit, and to act the philosopher by bearing ill-usage in your company." Accordingly they set out together for Mount Taurus, in the second Cappadocia, where there was an estate or Church dedicated to St. Orestes, the property of the see of Cæsarea. On their return with the produce of the farm, they were encountered by the retainers of Anthimus, who blocked up the pass, and attacked their company. This warfare between Christian bishops was obviously a great scandal to the Church, and Basil adopted a measure which he considered would put an end to it. He increased the number of bishopricks in that district, considering that residents might be able to secure the produce of the estate without disturbance, and to quiet and gain over the minds of those who had encouraged Anthimus in his opposition. Sasima was a village in this neighbourhood, and here he determined to place his friend Gregory, doubtless considering that he could not show him a greater mark of confidence than to commit to him the management of the quarrel, or confer on him a post, to his own high spirit more desirable, than the place of risk and responsibility.

Gregory had been unwilling even to be made a priest, but he shrunk with fear from the office of a bishop. He had on his mind that overpowering sense of the awfulness of the ministerial commission which then prevailed in more serious minds. "I feel myself to be unequal to this warfare," he had said on his ordination, "and therefore have hid my face, and slunk away. And I ought to sit down in solitude, being filled with bitterness, and to keep silence, from a conviction that the days were evil, since God's beloved have kicked against the truth, and we have become revolting children. And besides this, there is the internal warfare with one's passions, which my body of humiliation wages with me night and day, part hidden, part open—and the tossing to and fro and whirling through the senses and the delights of life ;

and the deep mire in which I stick fast; and the law of sin warring against the law of the spirit, and striving to efface the royal image in us, and whatever of a divine effluence has been vested in us. Before one has subdued with all one's might the principle which drags one down, and has cleansed the mind duly, and has surpassed others much in approach to God, I consider it unsafe either to undertake cure of souls, or mediatorship between God and man, for some such thing is a priest." With these admirable feelings the weakness of man mingled itself: at the urgent command of his father he submitted to be consecrated; but the reluctance which he had felt to undertake the office was now transferred to his occupying the see to which he had been appointed. An ascetic, like Gregory, ought not to have complained of the country as deficient in beauty and interest, even though he might be allowed to feel the responsibility of a situation which made him a neighbour of Anthimus. Yet such was his infirmity; and he repelled the accusations of his mind against himself by charging Basil with unkindness in placing him at Sasima. On the other hand, it is possible that Basil, in his eagerness for the settlement of the Exarchate, too little consulted the character and taste of Gregory; and, above all, the feelings of duty which bound him to Nazianzus. This is the latter's account of the matter, in a letter which displays much heat and even resentment against Basil :—" Give me," he says, "peace and quiet above all things. Why should I be fighting for sucklings and birds which are not mine, as if in a matter of souls and church rules? Well, play the man, be strong, turn everything to your own glory, as rivers suck up the mountain rill, thinking little of friendship or intimacy, compared with high aims and piety, and disregarding what the world will think of you for all this, being the property of the Spirit alone; while, on my part, so much shall I gain from this your friendship, not to trust in friends, nor to put anything above God."

In the beginning of the same letter, he throws the blame upon Basil's episcopal throne, which suddenly made him higher than himself. Elsewhere he accuses him of ambition, and desire of aggrandising himself. Basil, on the other hand, seems to have accused him of indolence and want of spirit.

Such was the melancholy crisis of an estrangement which had been for some time in preparation. Henceforth no letters, which are preserved, passed between the two friends; nor are any acts of intercourse discoverable in their history. Anthimus appointed a rival bishop to Sasima; and Gregory, refusing to contest the see with him, returned to Nazianzus. Basil laboured by himself. Gregory retained his feeling of Basil's unkindness even after his death; though he revered and admired him not less, or even more than before, and attributed his conduct to a sense of duty. In his commemorative oration, after praising his erection of new sees, he says: "Into this measure I myself was brought in by the way. I do not seem bound to use a soft phrase. For admiring as I do all he did, more than I can say, this one thing I cannot praise, for I will confess my feeling, which is otherwise not unknown to the world, his extraordinary and unfriendly conduct towards me, of which time has not removed the pain. For to this I trace all the irregularity and confusion of my life, and my not being able, or not seeming, to command my feelings, though the latter of the two is a small matter; unless, indeed, I may be suffered to make this excuse for him, that, having views beyond this earth, and having departed hence before life was over, he viewed everything as the Spirit's; and knowing how to reverence friendship, then only slighted it, when it was a duty to prefer God, and to make more account of the things hoped for, than things perishable."

This lamentable occurrence took place eight or nine years before Basil's death; he had before and after it many trials, many sorrows; but this probably was the greatest of all.

MARTYRDOM.

THE word martyr properly means "a witness," but is used to denote exclusively one who has suffered death for the Christian faith. Those who have witnessed for Christ without suffering death are called confessors; a title which the early martyrs often made their own, before their last solemn confession unto death, or martyrdom. Our Lord Jesus Christ is the chief and most glorious of martyrs, as having before Pontius Pilate witnessed a good confession; but we do not call Him a martyr, as being much more than a martyr. True it is He died for the truth, but that was not the chief purpose of His death. He died to save us sinners from the wrath of God. He was not only a martyr, He was an atoning sacrifice.

He is the supreme object of our love, gratitude, and reverence. Next to Him, we honour the noble army of martyrs; not, indeed, comparing them with Him, "who is above all, God blessed for ever;" or as if they in suffering had any part in the work of reconciliation; but because they have approached most closely to His pattern of all His servants. They have shed their blood for the Church, fulfilling the text: "He laid down His life for us, and we ought to lay down our lives for the brethren." They have followed His steps, and claim our grateful remembrance. Had St. Stephen shrunk from the trial put upon him, and recanted to save his life, no one can estimate the consequences of such a defection. Perhaps (humanly speaking) the cause of the Gospel would have been lost; the Church might have perished; and, though Christ had died for the world, the world might not have received the knowledge or the benefits of His death. The channels of grace might have been destroyed, the sacraments withdrawn from the feeble and corrupt race which has such need of them.

Now, it may be said that many men suffer pain, as great as martyrdom, from disease and in other ways: again, that it does not follow that those who happened to be martyred were always the most useful and active defenders of the faith; and therefore, that in honouring the martyrs we are honouring with especial honour those to whom indeed we *may* be peculiarly indebted (as in the case of the apostles), but nevertheless who may have been but ordinary men, who happened to stand in the most exposed place, in the way of persecution, and were slain as if by chance, because the sword met them first. But this, it is feared, would be a strange way of reasoning in any parallel case. We are grateful to those who have done us favours, rather than to those who might or would, if it had so happened. We have no concern with the question whether the martyrs were the best of men or not, or whether others would have been martyrs too, had it been allowed them. We are grateful to those who were such, from the plain matter of fact that they were, such, that they did go through much suffering in order that the world might gain an inestimable benefit, the light of the Gospel.

But in truth, if we could view the matter considerately, we shall find that (as far as human judgment can decide on such a point) the martyrs of the primitive times were, as such, men of a very elevated faith, not only our benefactors, but far our superiors. Let us consider what it was then to be a martyr.

First, it was to be a voluntary sufferer. Men, perhaps, suffer in various diseases more than the martyrs did, but they cannot help themselves. Again, it has frequently happened that men have been persecuted for their religion without having expected it, or being able to avert it. These in one sense indeed are martyrs, and we naturally think affectionately of those who have suffered in our cause, whether voluntarily or not. But this was not the case with the primitive martyrs. They knew beforehand clearly enough the consequences of preaching the Gospel; they had frequent warnings brought home to them of the sufferings in store for them if they persevered in their labours of brotherly love. Their Lord and Master had suffered before them; and besides suffering Himself, had expressly foretold their sufferings. "If they have persecuted Me, they will also persecute you." They were repeatedly warned and strictly charged by the chief priests and rulers not to preach Christ's name. They had experience of lesser punishments from their adversaries in earnest of the greater; and at length they saw their brethren one by one slain for persevering in their faithfulness to Christ. Yet they continued to keep the faith, though they might be victims of their obedience any day.

All this must be considered when we speak of their sufferings. They lived under a continual trial, a daily exercise of faith, which we, living in peaceable times, can scarcely understand. Christ had said to His apostles, "Satan hath desired to have you, that he may sift you as wheat." Consider what is meant by sifting, which is a continued agitation, a shaking about to separate the mass of corn into two parts. Such was the early discipline inflicted on the Church. No mere sudden stroke came upon it; but it was solicited day by day, in all its members, by every argument of hope and fear, by threats and inducements, to desert Christ. This was the lot of the martyrs. Death, their final suffering, was but a confirmation of a life of anticipated death. Consider how distressing anxiety is—how irritating and wearying it is to be in a state of constant excitement, with the duty of maintaining calmness and steadiness in the midst of it, and how especially inviting any prospect of tranquillity would appear in such circumstances, and then we shall have some notion of a Christian's condition under a persecuting heathen government. I put aside for the present the peculiar reproach and contempt which was the lot of the primitive Church, and their actual privations. Let us merely consider them as harassed, shaken as wheat in a sieve. Under such circumstances, the stoutest hearts are in danger of failing. They could steel themselves against certain definite sufferings, or prepare themselves to meet one expected crisis; but they yield to the incessant annoyance which the apprehension of persecution and importunity of friends inflict on them. They sigh for peace; they gradually come to believe that the world is not so wrong as some men say it is, and that it is possible to be over strict and over nice. They learn to temporise and be double-minded. First one falls, and then another; and such instances come as an additional argument for concession to those that remain firm as yet, who of course feel dispirited, lonely, and begin to doubt the correctness of their own judgment; while on the other hand, those who have fallen, in self-defence become their tempters. Thus the Church is sifted, the cowardly falling off, the faithful continuing firm, though in dejection and perplexity. Among these latter are the martyrs; not accidental victims taken at random, but the picked and choice ones, the elect remnant, a sacrifice well pleasing to God, because a costly gift, the finest wheat-flour of the Church; men who have been warned what to expect from their profession, and have had many opportunities of relinquishing it, but have "borne and had patience, and for Christ's name sake have laboured and have not fainted." Such was St. Stephen, not entrapped into a confession and slain (as it were) in ambuscade, but boldly confronting his persecutors, and, in spite of circumstances that foreboded death, awaiting their fury. And if martyrdom in early times was not the chance and unexpected death of those who happened to profess the Christian faith, much less is it to be compared to the sufferings of disease, be they greater or not. No one is maintaining that the mere undergoing pain is a great thing. A man cannot help himself when in pain; he cannot escape from it, be he as desirous to do so as he may. The devils bear pain against their will. But to be a martyr is to feel the storm coming, and willingly to endure it at the call of duty, for Christ's sake and for the good of the brethren; and this is a kind of firmness which we have no means of displaying at the present day, though our deficiency may be, and is continually evidenced, as often as we yield (which is not seldom) to inferior and ordinary temptations.

But, in the next place, the suffering itself of martyrdom was in some respects peculiar It was a death cruel in itself, publicly inflicted, and heightened by the fierce exultation of a malevolent populace. When we are in pain, we can lie in peace by ourselves; we receive the sympathy and kind services of those about us; and, if we like it, we can retire altogether from the sight of others, and suffer without a witness to interrupt us. But the sufferings of martyrdom were for the most part public, attended with every circumstance of ignominy and popular triumph, as well as with torture. Criminals, indeed, are put to death without kindly thoughts from the bystanders; still, for the most part, even criminals receive commiseration and a sort of respect. But the early Christians had to endure "the shame" after their Master's pattern. They had to die in the midst of enemies who reviled them, and in mockery bid them (as in Christ's case) come down from the cross. They were supported on no easy couch, soothed by no attentive friends; and considering how much the depressing power of pain depends upon the imagination, this circumstance alone at once separates their sufferings widely from all instances of pain in disease. The unseen God alone was their comforter, and this invests the scene of their suffering with supernatural majesty, and awes us when we think of them. "Yea, though I walk through the valley of the shadow of death, I will fear no evil; for Thou art with me." A martyrdom is a season of God's especial power in the eye of faith, as great as if a miracle were visibly wrought.

MORAL AND PRACTICAL.

THE GREATNESS AND LITTLENESS
OF HUMAN LIFE.

"The days of the years of my pilgrimage are an hundred and thirty years: few and evil have the days of the years of my life been, and have not attained unto the days of the years of the life of my fathers in the days of their pilgrimage."—GEN. xlvii. 9.

WHY did the aged patriarch call his days few, who had lived twice as long as men now live, when he spoke? Why did he call them evil, seeing he had on the whole lived in riches and honour, and, what is more, in God's favour? Yet he described his time as short, his days as evil, and his life as but a pilgrimage. Or if we allow that his afflictions were such as to make him reasonably think cheaply of his life, in spite of the blessings which attended it, yet that he should call it short, considering he had so much more time for the highest purposes of his being than we have, is at first sight surprising. He alludes indeed to the longer life which had been granted to his fathers, and perhaps felt a decrepitude greater than theirs had been; yet this difference between him and them could hardly be the real ground of his complaint in the text, or more than a confirmation or occasion of it. It was not because Abraham had lived one hundred and seventy-five years, and Isaac one hundred and eighty, and he himself, whose life was not yet finished, but one hundred and thirty, that he made this mournful speech. For it matters not when time is gone what length it has been; and this doubtless was the real cause why the patriarch spoke as he did, not because his life was shorter than his father's, but because it was well-nigh over. When life is past, it is all one whether it has lasted two hundred years or fifty. And it is this characteristic, stamped on human life in the day of its birth, viz., that it is mortal, which makes it under all circumstances and in every form equally feeble and despicable. All the points in which men differ, health and strength, high and low estate, happiness or misery, vanish before this common lot, mortality. Pass a few years, and the longest lived will be gone. Nor will what is past profit him then, except in its consequences.

And this sense of the nothingness of life, impressed on us by the very fact that it comes to an end, is much deepened when we contrast it with the capabilities of us who live it. Had Jacob lived to Methusaleh's age, he would have called it short. This is what we all feel, though at first sight it seems a contradiction, that even though the days as they go be slow, and be laden with many events, or with sorrows, or dreariness, lengthening them out and making them tedious, yet the year passes quick though the hours tarry, and time bygone is as a dream, though we thought it would never go while it was going. And the reason seems to be this; that when we contemplate human life in itself, in however small a portion of it, we see implied in it the presence of a soul, the energy of a spiritual existence, of an accountable being: consciousness tells us this concerning it every moment. But when we look back on it in memory, we view it but externally as a mere lapse of time, as a mere earthly history. And the longest duration of this external world is as dust, and weighs nothing against one moment's life of the world within. Thus we are ever expecting great things from life, from our internal consciousness, every moment of our having souls; and we are ever being disappointed on considering what we have gained from time past, and can hope from time to come. And life is ever promising and never fulfilling; and hence, however long it be, our days are few and evil.

Our earthly life then gives promise of what it does not accomplish. It promises immortality, yet it is mortal; it contains life in death, and eternity in time; and it attracts us by beginnings which faith alone brings to an end. I mean, when we take into account the powers with which our souls are gifted as Christians, the very consciousness of these fills us with a certainty that they must last beyond this life. That is in the case of good and holy men, whose present state, I say, is to them who know them well an earnest of immortality. The greatness of their gifts, contrasted with their scanty time for exercising them, forces the mind forward to the thought of another life as almost the necessary counterpart and consequence of this life, and certainly implied in this life, provided there be a righteous governor of the world who does not make man for nought. . . . . And if this earthly life is short, even when longest, from the great disproportion between it and the powers of regenerate man, still more is this the case, of course, where it is cut short and death comes prematurely. Men there are, who in a single moment of their lives have shown a superhuman height and majesty of mind which it would take ages for them to employ on its proper objects, and, as it were, to exhaust; and who by such passing flashes, like rays of the sun and the darting of lightning, give token of their immortality, give token to us that they are but angels in disguise, the elect of God, sealed for eternal life, and destined to judge the world and to reign with Christ for ever. Yet they are suddenly taken away, and we have hardly recognized them when we lose them.

Can we believe that they are not removed for higher things elsewhere? This is sometimes said with reference to our intellectual powers, but it is still more true of our moral nature. There is something in moral truth and goodness, in faith, in firmness, in heavenly-mindedness, in meekness, in courage, in lovingkindness, to which this world's circumstances are quite unequal, for which the longest life is insufficient, which makes the highest opportunities of this world disappointing, which must burst the prison of this world to have its appropriate range. So that when a good man dies, one is led to say, "He has not half showed himself, he has had nothing to exercise him; his days are gone like a shadow, and he is withered like grass."

I say the word "disappointing" is the only word to express our feelings on the death of God's saints. Unless our faith be very active, so as to pierce beyond the grave and realize the future, we feel depressed at what seems like a failure of great things. And from this very feeling surely, by a sort of contradiction, we may fairly take hope; for if this life be so disappointing, so unfinished, surely it is not the whole. This feeling of disappointment will often come upon us in an especial way, on happening to hear of or to witness the deathbeds of holy men. The hour of death seems to be a season, of which, in the hands of Providence, much might be *made*, if I may use the term ; much might be done for the glory of God, the good of man, and the manifestation of the person dying. And beforehand friends will perhaps look forward, and expect that great things are then to take place, which they shall never forget. Yet, "How dieth the wise man? as the fool." Such is the preacher's experience, and our own bears witness to it. King Josiah, the zealous servant of the living God, died the death of wicked Ahab, the worshipper of Baal. True Christians die as other men. One dies by a sudden accident, another in battle, another without friends to see how he dies, a fourth is insensible, or not himself. Thus the opportunity seems thrown away, and we are forcibly reminded that "the manifestation of the sons of God" is hereafter; that "the earnest expectation of the creature" is but waiting for it; that this life is unequal to the burthen of so great an office as the due exhibition of those secret ones who shall one day "shine forth as the sun in the kingdom of their Father."

But further (if it be allowable to speculate), one can conceive even the same kind of feeling, and a most transporting one, to come over the soul of the faithful Christian when just separated from the body, and conscious that his trial is once for all over. Though his life has been a long and painful discipline, yet when it is over we may suppose him to feel at the moment the same sort of surprise at its being ended as generally follows any exertion in this life when the object is gained and the anticipation over—when we have wound up our minds for any point of time, any great event, an interview with strangers, or the sight of some wonder, or the occasion of some unusual trial. When it comes, and is gone, we have a strange reverse of feeling from our changed circumstances. Such, but without any mixture of pain, without any lassitude, dulness, or disappointment, may be the happy contemplation of the disembodied spirit : as if it said to itself, "So all is now over; this is what I have so long waited for, for which I have nerved myself, against which I have prepared, fasted, prayed, and wrought righteousness. Death is come and gone—it is over. Ah! is it possible? What an easy trial, what a cheap price for eternal glory! A few sharp sicknesses, or some acute pain a while, or some few and evil years, or some struggles of mind, dreary desolateness for a season, fightings and fears, afflicting bereavements, or the scorn and ill-usage of the world—how they fretted me, how much I thought of them! Yet how little really they are! How contemptible a thing is human life, contemptible in itself, yet in its effects invaluable! for it has been to me like a small seed of easy purchase, germinating and ripening into bliss everlasting."

Such being the unprofitableness of this life viewed in itself, it is plain how we should regard it while we go through it. We should remember that it is scarcely more than an accident of our being; that it is no part of ourselves, who are immortal; that we are immortal spirits, independent of time and space; and that this life is but a sort of outward stage, on which we act for a time, and which is only sufficient and only intended to answer the purpose of trying whether we will serve God or no. We should consider ourselves to be in this world in no fuller sense than players of any game are in the game; and life to be a sort of dream, as detached and as different from our real eternal existence, as a dream differs from waking; a serious dream, indeed, as affording a means of judging us, yet in itself a kind of shadow without substance, a scene set before us, in which we seem to be, and in which it is our duty to act just as if all we saw had a truth and reality, because all that meets us influences us and our destiny. . . . .

Let us then thus account of our present state. It is precious, as revealing to us, amid shadows and figures, the existence and attributes of Almighty God and His elect people. It is precious, because it enables us to hold intercourse with immortal souls who are on their trial as we are. It is momentous as being the scene and means of our trial; but beyond this it has no claims upon us. "Vanity of vanities, says the preacher, all is vanity." We may be poor or rich, young or old, honoured or slighted, and it ought to affect us no more, neither to elate us nor depress us, than if we were actors in a play, who know that the characters that they represent are not their own, and that though they may appear to be superior one to another, to be kings or to be peasants, they are in reality all on a level.

THE MYSTERIOUSNESS OF OUR PRESENT BEING.

"I will praise Thee, for I am fearfully and wonderfully made, marvellous are Thy works, and that my soul knoweth right well."—PSALM cxxxix. 14.

IN the very impressive Psalm from which these words are taken, this is worth noticing among other things. That the inspired writer finds, in the mysteries without and within him, a source of admiration and praise. "I will *praise* Thee, *for* I am fearfully and wonderfully made : *marvellous* are Thy works." When Nicodemus heard of God's wonderful working, he said : "How can these things be?" But holy David glories in what the natural man stumbles at. It awes his heart and imagination to think that God sees him wherever he is, yet without provoking or irritating his reason. He has no proud thoughts rising against what he cannot understand, and calling for his vigilant control. He does not submit his reason by an effort, but he bursts forth in exultation to think that God is so mysterious. "Such knowledge is too wonderful for me;" he says, "it is high, I cannot attain unto it." This reflection is suitable on this festival (Trinity Sunday), on which our thoughts are especially turned to the great doctrine of the Trinity in Unity. . . . I will endeavour to show that the difficulty which human words have in expressing it, is no greater than we meet with when we would express in human words even those earthly things of which we actually have experience, and which we cannot deny to exist, because we see them. So that our part evidently lies in using the mysteries of religion as David did, simply as a means of impressing on our minds the inscrutableness of Almighty God. Mysteries in religion are measured by the proud according to their own capacity; by the humble, according to the power of God: the humble glorify God for them, the proud exalt themselves against them.

The text speaks of earthly things. "I am fearfully and wonderfully made." Now, let us observe some of the mysteries that are involved in our own nature.

1. First, we are made up of soul and body. Now, if we did not know this so that we cannot deny it, what notion could our minds ever form of such a mixture of natures, and how should we ever succeed in making those who go only by abstract reason take in what we meant? The body is made of matter: this we see; it has a

certain extension, make, form, and solidity. By the soul we mean that invisible principle which thinks. We are conscious we are alive, and are rational. Each man has his own thoughts, feelings, and desires; each man is one to himself, and he knows himself to be one and indivisible—one in such sense, that while he exists, it were an absurdity to suppose he can be any other than himself; one in a sense in which no material body which consists of parts can be one. He is sure that he is distinct from the body, though joined to it, because he is one, and the body is not one, but a collection of many things. He feels, moreover, that he is distinct from it because he uses it; for what a man can use he is superior to. No one can by any possibility mistake his body for himself. It is *his*, it is not he. This principle, then, which thinks and acts in the body, and which each person feels to be himself, we call the soul. We do not know what it is : it cannot be reached by any of the senses : we cannot see it or touch it. It has nothing in common with extension or form. To ask what shape the soul is, would be as absurd as to ask what is the shape of a thought, or a wish, or a regret, or a hope. And hence we call the soul spiritual and immaterial, and say that it has no parts, and is of no size at all. All this seems undeniable. Yet observe, if all this be true, what is meant by saying that it is *in* the body, any more than saying that a thought or a hope is in a stone or a tree? How is it joined to the body? what keeps it one with the body? what keeps it in the body? what prevents it any moment from separating from the body? When two things which we see are united, they are united by some connexion which we can understand. A chain or cable keeps a ship in its place. We lay a foundation of a building in the earth, and the building endures. But what is it that unites soul and body? how do they touch? how do they keep together? how is it that we do not wander to the stars, or to the depths of the sea, or to and fro as chance may carry us, while our body remains where it was on the earth? So far from its being wonderful that the body one day dies, how is it that it is made to live and move at all? how is it that it keeps from dying a single hour? Certainly it is as incomprehensible as any thing can be, how soul and body can make up one man ; and unless we had the instance before our eyes, we should seem in saying so, to be using words without meaning. For instance, would it not be extravagant and idle to speak of time as deep or high, or of space as quick or slow. Not less idle, surely, it perhaps seems to some races of spirits, to say that thought and mind have a body, which in the case of man they have according to God's marvellous will. It is certain, then, that experience outstrips reason in its capacity of knowledge : why then should reason circumscribe faith, when it cannot compass sight?

2. Again: the soul is not only one, and without parts, but moreover, as if by a great contradiction given in terms, it is in every part of the body. It is nowhere, yet everywhere. It may be said, indeed, that it is especially in the brain; but granting this, for argument's sake, yet it is quite certain, since every part of his body belongs to him, that a man's self is in every part of his body. No part of a man's body is like a mere instrument, as a knife or a crutch might be, which he takes up and may lay down. Every part of it is part of himself; it is connected into one by his soul, which is one. Supposing we take stones and raise a house, the building is not really one; it is composed of a number of separate parts, which, viewed as collected together, we call one, but which are not one, except in our notion of them. But the hands and feet, the head and trunk, form one body under the presence of the soul within them. Unless the soul were in every part, they would not form one body; so that the soul is in every part, uniting it with every other, though it consists of no part at all. I do not, of course, mean that there is any real contradiction in these opposite truths—indeed, we know that there is not and cannot be, because they *are* true—because human nature is a fact before us. But the state of the case is a contradiction *when put into*

words; we cannot so express it as not to involve an apparent contradiction: and then, if we discriminate our terms, and make distinctions, and balance phrases, and so on, we shall seem to be technical, and artificial, and speculative, and to use words without meaning. Now this is precisely our case as regards the doctrine of the ever-blessed Trinity. We have never been in heaven. God, as He is in Himself, is hid from us. We are informed concerning Him by those who were inspired by Him for the purpose, nay, by His co-eternal Son Himself, who "knoweth the Father," when He came on earth. And in the message they delivered to us from above are declarations concerning His nature, which seem to run counter the one to the other. He is revealed to us as one God, the Father, one indivisible Spirit. Yet there is said to exist in Him from everlasting His only-begotten Son, the same as He is, and yet distinct, and from and in Them both from everlasting, and indivisibly, exists the co-equal Spirit. All this, put into words, seems a contradiction in terms: men have urged it as such; then Christians, lest they should seem to be unduly and harshly insisting upon words which clash with each other, and so should dishonour the truth of God, and cause hearers to stumble, have limited their words, and classified them; and then, for doing this, they have been accused of speculating and theorizing. The same result doubtless would take place in the parallel case already mentioned. Had we no bodies, and were a revelation made us that there was a race who had bodies as well as souls, what a number of powerful objections should we seem to possess against that revelation! We might plausibly say, that the words used in conveying it were arbitrary and unmeaning. What (we should ask) was the meaning of saying that the soul had no parts, yet was in every part of the body? What was meant by saying it was everywhere, and nowhere? How could it be one, and yet repeated, as it were, ten thousand times over every atom and pore of the body, which it was said to exist in? How could it be confined to the body at all? How did it act upon the body? How happened it, as was pretended, that, when the soul did but will, the arm moved or the feet walked? How can a spirit, which cannot touch anything, yet avail to move so large a mass of matter, and so easily, as the human body? These are some of the questions which might be asked, partly on the ground that the alleged fact was impossible, partly that the idea was self-contradictory. And these are just the kind of questions with which arrogant and profane minds do assail the revealed doctrine of the Holy Trinity.

3. Further consider what a strange state we are in when we dream, and how difficult it would be to convey to a person who had never dreamed what was meant by

dreaming. *His* vocabulary would contain no words to express any middle idea between perfect possession and entire suspension of the mind's powers. He would acknowledge what it was to be awake, what it was to be insensible; but a state between the two he would neither have words to describe, nor, if he were self-confident and arrogant, inclination to believe, however well it was attested by those who ought to know. . . . . . .

Now if we have mysteries even about ourselves, which we cannot even put into words accurately, much more may we suppose, even were we not told it, that there are mysteries in the nature of Almighty God; and, so far from its being improbable that there should be mysteries, the declaration that there are, even adds some probability to the revelation which declareth them. On the other hand, still more unreasonable is disbelief, if grounded on the mysteriousness of the revelation, because if we cannot put into consistent human language human things, much less is there to surprise us if human words are insufficient to describe heavenly things.

THE IMMORTALITY OF THE SOUL.

"What shall a man give in exchange for his soul?"—MATT. xvi. 26.

I SUPPOSE there is no tolerably-informed Christian but considers he has a correct notion of the difference between our religion and the paganism it supplanted. Every one, if asked what it is we have gained by the Gospel, will promptly answer that we have gained the knowledge of our immortality, of our having souls which will live for ever; that the heathen did not know this, but that Christ taught it, and that His disciples know it. Every one will say, and say truly, that this was the great and solemn doctrine which gave the Gospel a claim to be heard when first preached, which arrested the thoughtless multitudes who were busied in the pleasures and pursuits of this life, awed them with the vision of the life to come, and sobered them till they turned to God with a true heart. It will be said, and said truly, that this doctrine of a future life was the doctrine which broke the power and the fascination of paganism. The poor benighted heathen were engaged in all the frivolities and absurdities of a false ritual which had obscured the light of nature. They knew God, but they forsook Him for the inventions of man; they made protectors and guardians for themselves; and had "gods many, and lords many." They had their profane worship, their gaudy processions, their indulgent creed, their easy observances, their sensual festivities, their childish extravagances, such as might suitably be the religion of beings who were to live for seventy or eighty years, and then die once for all, never to live again. "Let us eat and drink, for to-morrow we die," was their doctrine and their rule of life. "To-morrow we die." This the holy apostles admitted. They taught so far as the heathen, "To-morrow we die;" but then they added, "And after death the judgment"—judgment upon the eternal soul, which lives in spite of the death of the body. And this was the truth which awakened men to the necessity of having a better and deeper religion than that which had spread over the earth, when Christ came—which so wrought upon them that they left that old false worship of theirs, and it fell. Yes! though throned in all the power of the world, a sight such as eye had never before seen; though supported by the great and the many, the magnificence of kings and the stubbornness of people, it fell. Its ruins remain scattered over the face of the earth—the shattered works of its great upholder, that fierce enemy of God, the pagan Roman Empire. Those ruins are found even among ourselves, and show how marvellously great was its power, and therefore how much more powerful was that which broke its power; and this was the doctrine of the immortality of the soul. So entire is the revolution which is produced among men wherever this high truth is really received.

I have said that every one of us is able fluently to speak of this doctrine, and is aware that the knowledge of it forms the fundamental difference between our state and that of the heathen. And yet, in spite of our being able to speak about it, and our "form of knowledge" (as St. Paul terms it, Rom. ii. 20), there seems scarcely room to doubt that the greater number of those who are called Christians in no true sense realize it in their own minds at all. Indeed it is a very difficult thing to bring home to us, and to feel that we have souls; and there cannot be a more fatal mistake than to suppose we see what the doctrine means as soon as we can use the words which signify it. So great a thing is it to understand that we have souls, that the knowing it, taken in connexion with its results, is all one with *being serious*, *i.e.*, truly religious. To discern our immortality, is necessarily connected with fear, and trembling, and repentance, in the case of every Christian. Who is there but would be sobered by an actual sight of the flames of hell-fire and the souls therein hopelessly enclosed? Would not all his thoughts be drawn to that awful sight, so that he would stand still gazing fixedly upon it, and forgetting everything else, seeing nothing else, hearing nothing, engrossed with the contemplation of it; and when the sight was withdrawn, still having it fixed in his memory, so that he would be henceforth dead to the pleasures and employments of this world considered in themselves, thinking of them only in reference to that fearful vision? This would be the overpowering effect of such a disclosure, whether it actually led a man to repentance or not. And thus absorbed in the thought of the life to come are those who really and heartily receive the words of Christ and His apostles. Yet to this state of mind, and therefore to this true knowledge, the multitude of men called Christians are certainly strangers. A thick veil is drawn over their eyes; and, in spite of their being able to talk of the doctrine, they are as if they had never heard of it. They go on just as the heathen did of old; they eat, they drink; or they amuse themselves in vanities, and live in the world, without fear and without sorrow, just as if God had not declared that their conduct in this life would decide their destiny in the next; just as if they either had no souls, or had nothing or little to do with the saving of them, which was the creed of the heathen.

Now let us consider what it is to bring home to ourselves that we have souls, and in what the especial difficulty of it lies; for this may be of use to us in our attempt to realize this awful truth.

We are from our birth apparently dependent upon things about us. We see and feel that we could not live or go forward without the aid of man. To a child, this world is everything; he seems to himself a part of this world—a part of this world in the same sense in which a branch is part of a tree; he has little notion of his own separate existence; that is, he has no just idea he has a soul. And if he goes through life with his notions unchanged, he has no just notion even to the end of life that he has a soul. He views himself merely in his connection with this world, which is his all; he looks to this world for his good, as to an idol; and when he has to look beyond this life, he is able to discern nothing in prospect, because he has no idea of anything, nor can fancy anything but this life. And if he is obliged to fancy something, he fancies this life over again; just as the heathen, when they reflected on those traditions of another life which were floating among them, could but fancy the happiness of the blessed to consist in the enjoyment of the sun, and the sky, and the earth, as before, only as if these were to be more splendid than they are now.

To understand that we have souls, is to feel our separation from things visible, our independence of them, our distinct existence in ourselves, our individuality, our power of acting for ourselves, this way or that way, our accountableness for what we do. These are the great truths which lie wrapped up indeed even in a child's mind, and which God's grace can unfold there, in spite of the influence of the external world; but at first this outward world prevails. We look off from self to the things around us, and forget ourselves in them. Such is our state—a depending for support on the reeds which are no stay, and overlooking our real strength—at the time when God begins His process of reclaiming us to a truer view of our place in His great system of providence. And when He visits us, then in a little while there is a stirring within us. The unprofitableness and feebleness of the things of this world are forced upon our minds; they promise, but cannot perform; they disappoint us. Or, if they do perform what they promise, still (so it is) they do not satisfy us. We still crave for something, we do not well know what; but we are sure it is something which this world has not given us. And then its changes are so many, so sudden, so silent, so continual. It never leaves changing; it goes on to change till we are quite sick at heart: then it is that our reliance on it is broken. It is plain we cannot continue to depend upon it unless we keep pace with it, and go on changing too; but this we cannot do. We feel that while it changes we are one and the same; and thus under God's blessing we come to have some glimpse of the meaning of our independence of things temporal, and our immortality. And should it so happen that misfortunes come upon us (as they often do), then still more are we led to understand the nothingness of this world; then still more are we led to distrust it, and are weaned from the love of it, till at length it floats before our eyes merely as some idle veil, which, notwithstanding its many tints, cannot hide the view of what is beyond it; and we begin by degrees to perceive that there are but two beings in the whole universe, our own soul, and the God who made it.

Sublime, unlooked-for doctrine, yet most true! To every one of us there are but two beings in the whole world, himself and God; for, as to this outward scene, its pleasures and pursuits, its honours and cares, its contrivances, its personages, its kingdoms, its multitude of busy slaves—what are they to us? Nothing—no more than a show. "The world passeth away, and the lust thereof." And as to those others nearer us, who are not to be classed with the vain world, I mean our friends and relations, whom we are right in loving, these too, after all, are nothing to us here. They cannot really help or profit us; we see them and they act upon us, only (as it were) at a distance, through the medium of sense. They cannot get at our souls; they cannot enter into our thoughts or really be companions to us. In the next world it will, through God's mercy, be otherwise; but here we enjoy not their presence, but the anticipation of what one day shall be; so that, after all, they vanish before the clear vision we have, first of our own existence, next of the presence of the great God in us and over us, as our Governor and Judge, who dwells in us by our conscience, which is His representative.

And now consider what a revolution will take place in the mind that is not utterly reprobate, in proportion as it realizes this relation between itself and the most high God. We never in this life can fully understand what is meant by living for ever; but we can understand what is meant by this world's *not* living for ever, by its dying never to rise again. And learning this we learn that we owe it no service, no allegiance; it has no claim over us, and can do us no material good or harm. On the other hand, the law of God written on our hearts bids us serve Him, and Scripture completes the precepts which Nature began. And both Scripture and conscience tell us we are answerable for what we do, and that God is a righteous judge; and above all, our Saviour, as our visible Lord God, takes the place of the world as the only-begotten of the Father, having shown Himself openly that we may not say that God is hidden. And thus a man is drawn forward by all sorts of powerful influences to turn from things temporal to things eternal, to deny himself, and to take up his cross and follow Christ. For there are Christ's awful threats and warnings to make him serious, His precepts to attract and elevate him, His promises to cheer Him, His gracious deeds and sufferings to humble him to the dust, and to bind his heart once and for ever in gratitude to Him who is so surpassing in mercy. All these things act upon him; and as truly as St. Matthew rose from the receipt of custom when Christ called, heedless what bystanders would say of him, so they who through grace obey the secret voice of God, move onward contrary to the world's ways, and careless what mankind may say of them, as understanding that they have souls, which is the one thing they have to care about. . . . . .

Let us then seriously question ourselves, and beg of God grace to do so honestly, whether we are loosened from the world, or whether, living as dependent on it, and not on the Eternal Author of our being, we are in fact taking our portion with this perishing outward scene, and ignorant of our having souls. Let it be well understood, that to realize our own individual accountableness and immortality is not required of a person all at once. I never said a person was not in a hopeful way who did

IMMORTALITY OF THE SOUL. 147

not thus fully discern the world's vanity and the worth of his soul. But a man is truly in a very desperate way who does not wish, who does not try to discern and feel all this. I want a man, on the one hand, to confess his immortality with his lips, and on the other, to live as if he tried to understand his own words, and then he is in the way of salvation; he is in the way towards heaven, even though he has not yet fully emancipated himself from the fetters of this world. Indeed, none of us (of course) are entirely loosened from this world. We all use words in speaking of our duties, higher and fuller than we really understand.

Oh, that there were such a heart in us, to put aside this visible world, to desire to look at it as a mere screen between us and God, and think of Him who has entered in beyond the veil, and who is watching us, trying us yet, and blessing, and influencing, and encouraging us towards good, day by day. And oh! what a blessed discovery it is to those who make it, that this world is but vanity, and without substance, and that really they are ever in their Saviour's presence. He knows his blessedness, and needs not another to tell it him. He knows in whom he has believed; and in the hour of danger or trouble he knows what is meant by that peace which Christ did not explain when He gave it to His apostles, but merely said it was not as the world could give.

"Thou wilt keep him in perfect peace whose mind is stayed on Thee, because he trusteth in Thee. Trust ye in the Lord for ever, for in the Lord Jehovah is everlasting strength" (Isaiah xxvi. 3, 4).

THE INDIVIDUALITY OF THE SOUL.

"The spirit shall return unto God, who gave it."—ECCLES. xii. 7.

HERE we are told that upon death the spirit of man returns to God. The sacred writer is not speaking of good men only, or of God's chosen people, but of men generally. In the case of all men, the soul, when severed from the body, returns to God. God gave it; He made it; He sent it into the body, and He upholds it there. He upholds it in distinct existence wherever it is. It animates the body while life lasts; it returns again—it relapses into the unseen state upon death. Let us steadily contemplate this truth, which at first sight we may fancy we altogether enter into. The point to be considered is this: that every soul of man, which is or has been on earth, has a separate existence; and that in eternity, not in time merely—in the unseen world, not merely in this—not only during its mortal life, but even from the hour of its creation, whether joined to a body of flesh or not.

Nothing is more difficult than to realise that every man has a distinct soul—that every one of all the millions who live or have lived, is as whole and independent a being in himself as if there were no one else in the whole world but he. To explain what I mean. Do you think that a commander of an army realises it when he sends a body of men on some dangerous service? I am not speaking as if he were wrong in so sending them; I only ask, in matter of fact, does he, think you, commonly understand that each of those poor men has a soul, as dear to himself, as precious in its nature, as his own? Or does he not rather look on the body of men collectively, as one mass, as parts of a whole, as but the wheels or springs of some great machine to which he assigns the individuality, not to each soul that goes to make it up?

This instance will show what I mean, and how open we all lie to the remark that we do not understand the doctrine of the distinct individuality of the human soul. We class men in masses, as we might connect the stones of a building. Consider our common way of regarding history, politics, commerce, and the like, and you will own that I speak truly. We generalize and lay down laws, and then contemplate these creations of our own minds, and act upon and towards them as if they were real beings, dropping what are more truly such. Take another instance. When we talk of national greatness, what does it mean? Why, it really means that a certain distinct definite number of immortal individual beings happen for a few years to be in circumstances to act together and one upon another in such a way as to be able to act upon the world at large, to gain an ascendancy over the world, to gain power and wealth, and to look like one, and to be talked of and to be looked up to as one. They seem for a short time to be some one thing; and we, from our habit of living by sight, regard them as one, and drop the notion of their being anything else. And when this one dies, and that one dies, we forget that it is the passage of separate immortal beings into an unseen state, that the whole which appears is but appearance, and that the component parts are the realities. No, we think nothing of this; but though fresh and fresh men die, and fresh and fresh men are born, so that the whole is ever shifting, yet we forget all that drop away, and are insensible to all that are added; and we still think that this whole, which we call the nation, is one and the same, and that the individuals which come and go exist only in it and for it, and are but as the grains of a husk or the leaves of a tree.

Or, again, survey some populous town. Crowds are pouring through the streets, some on foot, some in carriages; while the shops are full, and the houses, too, could we see into them. Every part of it is full of life. Hence we gain a general idea of splendour, magnificence, opulence, and energy. But what is the truth? Why, that every being in that great concourse is his own centre, and all things about him are but shades, but a "vain shadow," in which he "walketh and disquieteth himself in vain." He has his own hopes and fears, desires, judgments, and aims; he is everything to himself, and no one else is really anything. No one outside of him can really touch him—can touch his soul, his immortality; he must live with himself for ever. He has a depth within him unfathomable, an infinite abyss of existence, and the scene in which he bears part for the moment is but like a gleam of sunshine upon its surface.

Again: when we read history, we meet with accounts of great slaughters and massacres, great pestilences, famines, conflagrations, and so on; and here again we are accustomed in an especial way to regard collections of people as single individuals. We cannot understand that a multitude is a collection of immortal souls.

I say immortal souls. Each of those multitudes not only *had*, while he was upon earth, but has a soul, which did in its own time but return to God who gave it, and not perish, and which now lives unto Him. All those millions upon millions of human beings who ever trod the earth, and saw the sun successively, are at this moment in existence all together. This, I think, you will grant we do not duly realize. All those Canaanites whom the children of Israel slew, every one of them is somewhere in the universe now at this moment, where God has assigned him a place. We read: " They utterly destroyed all that was in Jericho, young and old." Again, as to Ai: "So it was, that all that fell that day, both of men and women, were twelve thousand." Again: "Joshua took Makkedah, Libnah, Lachish, Eglon, Hebron, Debir, and smote them with the edge of the sword, and utterly destroyed all the souls that were therein." Every one of those souls still lives. They had their separate thoughts and feelings when on earth; they have them now. They had their likings and pursuits, they gained what they thought good, and enjoyed it; and they still somewhere or other live, and what they then did in the flesh surely has its influence upon their present destiny. They live, reserved for a day which is to come, when all nations shall stand before God.

But why should I speak of the devoted nations of Canaan, when Scripture speaks of a wider, more comprehensive judgment, and in one place appears to hint at the present state of awful waiting in which they are who were involved in it? What an overwhelming judgment was the Flood! All human beings on the earth but eight were cut off by it. That old world of souls still lives, though its material tabernacle was drowned. Scripture, I say, signifies this; obscurely indeed, yet still, as it appears, certainly. St. Peter speaks of "the spirits in prison," that is, then in prison, who had been "disobedient," "when once the long-suffering of God waited in the days of Noah." Those many, many souls, who were violently expelled from their bodies by the waters of the deluge, were alive two thousand years afterwards, when St. Peter wrote. Surely they are alive still. And so of all the other multitudes we may read of. All the Jews who perished in the siege of Jerusalem still live. Sennacherib's army still lives; Sennacherib himself still lives; all the persecutors of the Church that ever were are still alive. The kings of Babylon are still alive; they are still as they are described by the prophet; weak indeed now, and in "hell beneath," but having an account to give, and waiting for the day of summons. All who have ever gained a name in the world, all the mighty men of war that ever were, all the scheming aspirants, all the reckless adventurers, all the covetous traders, all the proud voluptuaries, are still in being, though helpless and unprofitable. Balaam, Saul, Joab, Ahithophel, good and bad, wise and ignorant, rich and poor, each has his separate place, each dwells by himself in that sphere of light or darkness which he has provided for himself here

What a view this sheds upon history! We are accustomed to read it as a tale of fiction, and we forget that it concerns immortal beings, who cannot be swept away, who are what they were, however this earth may change.

And so again, all the names we see written on monuments in churches or churchyards. All the writers whose name and works we see in libraries; all the workmen who raised the great buildings, far and near, which are the wonder of the world, they are all in God's remembrance—they all live.

It is the same with those whom we ourselves have seen, who are now departed. I do not now speak of those whom we have known and loved. These we cannot forget, we cannot rid our memory of them; but I speak of all whom we have ever seen: it is also true that they live; where, we know not, but live they do. We may recollect when children, perhaps, once seeing a person; and it is almost like a dream to us now that we did. It seems like an accident, which goes and is all over, like some creature of the moment, which has no existence beyond it. The rain falls, and the wind blows, and showers and storms have no existence beyond the time when we felt them; they are nothing in themselves. But if we have but once seen any child of Adam, we have seen an immortal soul. It has not passed away as a breeze or sunshine, but it lives; it lives at this moment in one of those many places, whether of bliss or misery, in which all souls are reserved unto the end.

Or, again, let us call to mind those whom we knew a little better, though not intimately; all who died suddenly or before their time; all whom we have seen in high health and spirits; all whom we have seen in circumstances which, in any way, brought out their characters and gave them some place in our memories. They are gone from our sight, but they all live still, each with his own thoughts; they are but waiting for the judgment.

I think we shall say that these thoughts concerning others are not familiar to us, yet no one can say they are not just. And I think, too, that the thoughts concerning others, which *are* familiar to us, are not those which become believers in the Gospel; whereas these which I have been tracing do become us, as tending to make us think less of this world, with its hopes and fears, its plans, successes, and enjoyments.

Moreover, every one of all the souls which have ever been on earth, is, as I have already implied, in one of two spiritual states, so distinct from one another, that one is the subject of God's favour, and the other under His wrath; the one in the way to eternal happiness, the other to eternal misery. This is true of the dead, and is true of the living also. All are tending one way or the other; there is no middle or neutral state for any one, though as far as the sight of the external world goes, all men seem to be in a middle state common to one and all. Yet, much as men look the same, and impossible as it is for us to say where each man stands in God's sight, there are two, and but two, classes of men, and these have characters and destinies as far apart in their tendencies as light and darkness. This is the case even of those who are in the body, and it is much more true of those who have passed into the unseen state.

No thought, of course, is more overpowering than that every one who lives or has lived is destined for endless bliss or torment. It is far too vast for us to realize. But what especially increases the mind's confusion, when it attempts to do so, is just this very thing which I have been mentioning, that there are but these two states, that every individual among us is either in one or the other. It is certainly quite beyond our understandings, that all men should now be living together as relatives, friends, associates, neighbours; that we should be familiar or intimate with each other; that there should be among us a general intercourse, circulation of thought, interchange of good offices, the action of mind upon mind, and will upon will, and conduct upon conduct; and yet, after all, that there should be a bottomless gulf between us, running among us invisibly, and cutting us off into two parties; not, indeed, a gulf impassable here, God be praised!—

not impassable till we pass into the next world—still really existing, so that every person we meet is in God's unerring eye either on the one side or the other; and did He please to take him hence at once, would find himself either in Paradise or in the place of torment. Our Lord observes this concerning the Day of Judgment: "Two women shall be grinding at the mill; the one shall be taken, and the other left. Two men shall be in the field; the one shall be taken, and the other left."

What makes this thought still more solemn is that we have reason to suppose that souls on the wrong side of the line are far more numerous than those on the right. It is wrong to speculate, but it is safe to be alarmed. This much we know, that Christ says expressly, "Many are called, few are chosen." "Broad is the way that leadeth to destruction, and many there be who go in thereat;" whereas, "Narrow is the way that leadeth to life, and few there be who find it."

If, then, it is difficult, as I have said it is, to realize that all who ever lived still live, it is as difficult, at least, to believe that they are in a state either of eternal rest or eternal woe; that all whom we have known, and who are gone, are, and that we who still live, were we now to die, should then at once be either in the one state or the other. Nay, I will say more. When we think seriously on the subject, it is almost impossible to comprehend, I do not say that a great number, but that any person whom we see before us, however unsatisfactory appearances may be, is really under God's displeasure, and in a state of reprobation. So hard is it to live by faith ! . . . . . How blessed would it be if we really understood this ! what a change it would produce in our thoughts, unless we were utterly reprobate, to understand what and where we are—accountable beings on their trial, with God for their friend and the devil for their enemy, and advanced a certain way on their road either to heaven or to hell ! No truths, indeed, ever so awful, ever so fully brought home to the mind, will change it, if the love of God and of holiness be not there; but none among us, as we may humbly trust, is in this reprobate state. One wishes to think that no one has so done despite to the Spirit of grace, and so sinned against the blood of the covenant, as to have nothing of his regenerate nature left to him; no one among us, but if he shut his eyes to the external world, and opened them to the world within him, contemplated his real state and prospects, and called to mind his past life, would be brought to repentance and amendment.

Endeavour then, my brethren, to realize that you have souls, and pray God to enable you to do so. Endeavour to disengage your thoughts and opinions from the things that are seen ; look at things as God looks at them, and judge of them as He judges. Pass a very few years, and you will actually experience what as yet you are called on to believe. There will be no need of the effort of mind to which I invite you. When you have passed into the unseen state, there will be no need of shutting your eyes to this world, when this world has vanished from you, and you have nothing before you but the throne of God, and the slow but continual movements about it in preparation of the Judgment. In that interval, when you are in that vast receptacle of disembodied souls, what will be your thoughts about the world which you have left? How poor will then seem to you its highest aims, how faint its keenest pleasures, compared with the infinite aims, the infinite pleasures, of which you will at length feel your souls to be capable! O, my brethren! let the thought be upon you day by day, especially when you are tempted to sin. Avoid sin as a serpent; it looks and promises well; it bites afterwards. It is dreadful in memory, dreadful even on earth; but in that awful period, when the fever of life is over, and you are waiting in silence for the Judgment, with nothing to distract your thoughts, who can say how dreadful may be the memory of sins done in the body? Then the very apprehension of their punishment, when Christ shall suddenly visit, will doubtless outweigh a thousandfold their gratification, such as it was, which you felt in committing them; and if so, what will be the proportion between it and that punishment, if, after all, it be actually inflicted? Let us lay to heart our Saviour's own most merciful words. "Be not afraid," He says, "of them that kill the body, and after that have no more that they can do. But I will forewarn you whom ye shall fear. Fear Him which, after He hath killed, hath power to cast into hell. Yea, I say unto you, fear Him."

THE INVISIBLE WORLD.

"While we look not at the things which are seen, but at the things which are not seen: for the things which are seen are temporal; but the things which are not seen are eternal."—2 COR. iv. 18.

THERE are two worlds, "the visible and the invisible," as the Creed speaks—the world we see, and the world we do not see; and the world we do not see as really exists as the world we do see. It really exists, though we see it not. The world we see we know to exist, *because* we see it. We have but to lift up our eyes and look around us, and we have proof of it: our eyes tell us. We see the sun, moon, and stars, earth and sky, hills and valleys, woods and plains, seas and rivers. And again, we see men, and the works of men; we see cities and stately buildings, and their inhabitants, men running to and fro, and busying themselves to provide for themselves and their families, or to accomplish great designs, or for the very business' sake. All that meets our eyes forms one world. It is an immense world; it reaches to the stars. Thousands on thousands of years might we speed up to the sky, and, though we were swifter than the light itself, we should not reach them all. They are at distances from us greater than any that is assignable. So high, so wide, so deep is the world; and yet it also comes near and close to us. It is everywhere; and it seems to have no room for any other world.

And yet, in spite of this universal world which we see, there is another world quite as far-spreading, quite as close to us, and more wonderful; another world all around us, though we see it not, and more wonderful than the world we see, for this reason, if for no other, that we do not see it. All around us are numberless objects, coming and going, watching, working, or waiting, which we see not. This is that other world, which the eyes reach not unto, but faith only.

Let us dwell upon this thought. We are born into a world of sense; that is, of the real things which lie round about us one great department comes to us, accosts us through our bodily organs, and eyes, ears, and fingers. We feel, hear, and see them; and we know they exist because we do thus perceive them. Things innumerable lie about us, animate and inanimate; but one particular class of these innumerable things is thus brought home to us through our senses. Only, moreover, while they act upon us, they make their presence known. We are sensible of them at the time, or are conscious that we perceive them. We not only see, but know that we see them; we not only hold intercourse, but know that we do. We are among men, and we know that we are. We feel cold and hunger; we know what sensible things remove them. We eat, drink, clothe ourselves, dwell in houses, converse and act with others, and perform the duties of social life; and we feel vividly that we are doing so while we do so. Such is our relation towards one part of the innumerable beings which lie around us. They act upon us, and we know it: we act upon them in turn, and know we do.

But all this does not interfere with the existence of that other world which I speak of acting upon us, yet not impressing us with the consciousness that it does so. It may as really be present and exert an influence as that which reveals itself to us. And that such a world there is, Scripture tells us. Do you ask what it is, and what it contains? I will not say that all that belongs to it is vastly more important than what we see, for among things visible are our fellow-men, and nothing created is more precious and noble than a son of man. But still, taking the things which we see altogether, the world we do not see is on the whole a much higher world than that which we do see. For, first of all, He is there who is above all things, who has created all, before whom they all are as nothing, and with whom nothing can be compared. Almighty God, we know, exists more really and absolutely than any of those fellow-men whose existence is conveyed to us through the senses. Yet we see Him not, hear Him not, we do but "feel after Him," yet without finding Him. It appears, then, that the things which are seen are but a part, but a secondary part of the beings around us, were it only on this ground, that Almighty God, the Being of Beings, is not in their number, but among "the things which are not seen." Once, and once only, for three-and-thirty years, has He condescended to become one of the beings which are seen, when the Second Person of the ever-blessed Trinity was, by an unspeakable mercy, born of the Virgin Mary into this sensible world. And then He was seen, heard, handled; He ate, He drank, He slept, He conversed, He went about, He acted as other men; but excepting this brief period His presence has never been perceptible; He has never made us conscious of His existence by means of our senses. He came, and He retired beyond the veil; and to us individually it is as if He had never showed Himself; we have as little sensible experience of His presence. Yet " He liveth evermore."

And in that other world are the souls also of the dead. They, too, when they depart hence, do not cease to exist, but they retire from this visible scene of things, or, in other words, they cease to act towards us and before us *through our senses.* They live as they lived before; but that outward frame, through which they were able to hold communion with other men, is in some way, we know not how, separated from them, and dries away and shrivels up as leaves may drop off a tree. They remain, but without the usual means of approach towards us, and correspondence with us. As when a man loses his voice or hand, he still exists as before, but cannot any longer talk or write, or otherwise hold intercourse with us. So when he loses not voice and hand only, but his whole frame, or is said to die, there is nothing to show that he is gone; but we have lost our means of apprehending him.

Again: angels also are inhabitants of the world invisible, and concerning them much more is told us than concerning the souls of the faithful departed, because the latter "rest from their labours," but the angels are actively employed among us in the Church. They are said to be "ministering spirits, sent forth to minister for them who shall be heirs of salvation." No Christian is so humble but he has angels to attend on him, if he lives by faith and love. Though they are so glorious, so pure, so wonderful, that the very sight of them (if we were allowed to see them) would strike us to the earth, as it did the prophet Daniel, holy and righteous as he was;

yet they are our "fellow-servants," and our fellow-workers, and they carefully watch over and defend even the humblest of us, if we be Christ's. That they form part of our unseen world appears from the vision seen by the patriarch Jacob. We are told that when he fled from his brother Esau, "he lighted upon a certain place, and tarried there all night, because the sun had set; and he took of the stones of that place, and put them for his pillow, and lay down in that place to sleep." How little did he think that there was anything very wonderful in this spot! It looked like any other spot. It was a lone, uncomfortable place; there was no house there; night was coming on; and he had to sleep upon the bare rock. Yet how different was the truth! He saw but the world that is seen; he saw not the world that is not seen; yet the world that is not seen was there. It was there, though it did not at once make known its presence, but needed to be supernaturally displayed to him. He saw it in his sleep. "He dreamed, and behold, a ladder set up on the earth, and the top of it reached up to heaven: and behold, the angels of God ascending and descending on it. And behold, the Lord stood above it." This was the other world. Now let this be observed. Persons commonly speak as if the other world did not exist now, but would after death. No; it exists now, though we see it not. It is among us and around us. Jacob was *shown* this in his dream. Angels were all about him, though he knew it not. And what Jacob saw in his sleep, that Elisha's servant saw as if with his eyes; and the shepherds, at the time of the Nativity, not only saw, but heard. They heard the voices of those blessed spirits who praise God night and day, whom we, in our lower state of being, are allowed to copy and assist.

We are, then, in a world of spirits, as well as in a world of sense, and we hold communion with it, and take part in it, though we are not conscious of doing so. If this seems strange to any one, let him reflect that we are undeniably taking part in a third world, which we do indeed see, but about which we do not know more than about the angelic hosts—the world of brute animals. Can anything be more marvellous or startling, unless we were used to it, than that we should have a race of beings about us whom we do see, and as little know their state, or can describe their interests or their destiny, as we can tell of the inhabitants of the sun and moon? It is, indeed, a very overpowering thought, when we get to fix our minds on it, that we familiarly use—I may say, hold intercourse with—creatures who are as much strangers to us, as mysterious, as if they were the fabulous, unearthly beings, more powerful than man, and yet his slaves, which eastern superstitions have invented. We have more real knowledge about the angels than about the brutes. They have, apparently, passions, habits, and a certain accountableness; but all is mystery about them. We do not know whether they can sin or not, whether they are under punishment, whether they are to live after this life. We inflict very great sufferings on a portion of them, and they, in turn, every now and then seem to retaliate upon us, as if by a wonderful law. We depend on them in various important ways; we use their labour, we eat their flesh. This, however, relates to such of them as come near us. Cast your thoughts abroad on the whole number of them, large and small, in vast forests, or in the water, or in the air; and then say whether the presence of such countless multitudes, so various in their natures, so strange and wild in their shapes, living on the earth without ascertainable object, is not as mysterious as anything which Scripture says about angels? Is it not plain to our senses that there is a world inferior to us in the scale of beings, with which we are connected, without understanding what it is? And is it difficult to faith to admit the word of Scripture concerning our connection with a world superior to us? . . .

Men think they are lords of this world, and may do as they will. They think this earth their property, and its movements in their power; whereas it has other lords besides them, and is the scene of a higher conflict than they are capable of conceiving. It contains Christ's little ones, whom they despise, and His angels, whom they disbelieve; and these at length shall take possession of it, and be manifested. At present, "all things," to appearance, "continue as they were from the beginning of the creation;" and scoffers ask, "Where is the promise of His coming?" but at the appointed time there will be a "manifestation of the sons of God," and the hidden saints "shall shine out as the sun in the kingdom of their Father." When the angels appeared to the shepherds it was a sudden appearance—"Suddenly there was with the angel a multitude of the heavenly host." How wonderful a sight! The night had before that seemed just like any other night, as the evening on which Jacob saw the vision seemed like any other evening. They were keeping watch over their sheep; they were watching the night as it passed. The stars moved on. It was midnight. They had no idea of such a thing when the angel appeared. Such are the power and virtue hidden in things which are seen, and at God's will they are manifested. They were manifested for a moment to Jacob, for a moment to Elisha's servant, for a moment to the shepherds. They will be manifested for ever when Christ comes at the Last Day, "in the glory of His Father, with the holy angels;" then this world will fade away, and the other world will shine forth.

Let these be your thoughts, my brethren, especially in

the spring season, when the whole face of Nature is so rich and beautiful. Once only in the year, yet once, does the world which we see show forth its hidden powers, and in a manner manifest itself. Then the leaves come out, and the blossoms on the fruit trees and flowers, and the grass and corn spring up. There is a sudden rush and burst outwardly of that hidden life which God has lodged in the material world.

Well, that shows, as by a sample, what it can do at God's command, when He gives the word. This earth, which now buds forth in leaves and blossoms, will one day burst forth into a new world of light and glory, in which we shall see saints and angels dwelling. Who would think, except from his experience of former springs all through his life—who could conceive two or three months before, that it was possible that the face of Nature, which then seemed so lifeless, should become so splendid and varied? How different is a tree, how different is a prospect, when leaves are on it and off it! How unlikely it would seem, before the event, that the dry and naked branches should suddenly be clothed with what is so bright and so refreshing! Yet in God's good time leaves come on the trees. The season may delay, but come it will at last. So it is with the coming of that eternal spring for which all Christians are waiting. Come it will, though it delay; yet, though it tarry, let us wait for it, " because it will surely come, it will not tarry." Therefore we say day by day, "Thy kingdom come," which means: O Lord, show Thyself; manifest Thyself; Thou that sittest between the cherubim, show Thyself; stir up Thy strength, and come and help us! The earth that we see does not satisfy us; it is but a beginning; it is but a promise of something beyond it—even when it is gayest, with all its blossoms on, and shows most touchingly what lies in it; yet it is not enough. We know much more lies hid in it than we see. A world of saints and angels, a glorious world, the palace of God, the mountain of the Lord of Hosts, the heavenly Jerusalem, the throne of God and Christ—all these wonders, everlasting, all-precious, mysterious, and incomprehensible, lie hid in what we see. What we see is the outward shell of an eternal kingdom; and on that kingdom we fix the eyes of our faith. Shine forth, O Lord, as when on Thy Nativity Thine angels visited the shepherds: let Thy glory blossom forth as bloom and foliage on the trees. Change with Thy mighty power this visible world into that diviner world, which as yet we see not. Destroy what we see, that it may pass and be transformed into what we believe. Bright as is the sun, and the sky, and the clouds; green as are the leaves and the fields; sweet as is the singing of the birds, we know that they are not all; and we will not take up with a part for the whole. They proceed from a centre of love and goodness, which is God Himself; but they are not His fulness; they speak of heaven, but they are not heaven; they are but as stray beams and dim reflections of His image; they are but crumbs from the table. We are looking for the coming of the day of God, when all the outward world, fair though it be, shall perish; when the heavens shall be burnt, and the earth melt away. We can bear the loss, for we know it will be but the removal of an evil. We know that to remove the world which is seen will be the manifestation of the world which is not seen. We know that what we see is as a screen hiding from us God and Christ, and His saints and angels. And we earnestly desire and pray for the dissolution of all that we see, from our longing after that which we do not see.

O blessed they, indeed, who are destined for a sight of those wonders in which they now stand, at which they now look, but which they do not recognize. Those wonderful things of the new world are even now as they shall be then. They are immortal and eternal; and the souls who shall then be made conscious of them will see them in their calmness and their majesty where they ever have been. But who can express the surprise and rapture which will come upon those who, having died in faith, wake up to enjoyment. The life then begun we know will last for ever: yet surely if memory be to us then what it is now, that will be a day much to be observed unto the Lord through all the ages of eternity. We may increase indeed for ever in knowledge and in love; still that first waking from the dead, the day at once of our birth and our espousals, will ever be endeared and hallowed in our thoughts. When we find ourselves after long rest gifted with fresh powers; vigorous with the seed of eternal life within us; able to love God as we wish; conscious that all trouble, sorrow, pain, anxiety, and bereavement, is over for ever; blessed in the full affection of those earthly friends whom we loved so poorly and could protect so feebly, while they were with us in the flesh; and above all, visited by the immediate, visible, ineffable presence of God Almighty, with His only begotten Son our Lord Jesus Christ, and His co-equal, co-eternal Spirit, that great sight in which is the fulness of joy and pleasure for evermore; what deep, incommunicable, unimaginable thoughts will be then upon us! What depths will be stirred up within us! What secret harmonies awakened, of which human nature seemed incapable! Earthly words are indeed all worthless to minister to such high anticipations. Let us close our eyes and keep silence. "All flesh is grass, and all the goodliness thereof is as the flower of the field. The grass withereth, the flower fadeth, because the spirit of the Lord bloweth upon it. Surely the people is grass; the grass withereth, the flower fadeth, but the word of our God shall stand for ever."

THE LAPSE OF TIME.

WE naturally shrink from the thought of death, and of its attendant circumstances; but all that is hateful about it will be fulfilled in our case, one by one. But all this is nothing compared with the consequences implied in it. Death stops us; it stops our race. Men are engaged about their work, or about their pleasure; they are in the city, or the field; anyhow they are stopped; their deeds are suddenly gathered in—a reckoning is made—all is sealed up till the great day. What a change is this! In the words used familiarly in speaking of the dead, they are no more. They were full of schemes and projects; whether in a greater or humbler rank, they had their hopes and fears, their prospects, their pursuits, their rivalries; all these are now come to an end. One builds a house, and its roof is not finished; another buys merchandize, and yet it is not sold. And all their virtues and pleasing qualities which endeared them to their friends are, as far as this world is concerned, vanished. Where are they who were so active, so sanguine, so generous? the amiable, the modest, the kind? We are told they are dead; they suddenly disappeared; that is all we know about it. They were silently taken from us; they are not met in the seat of the elders, nor in the assemblies of the people; in the mixed concourse of men, nor in the domestic retirement which they prized. As Scripture describes it, "The wind has passed over them, and they are gone, and their place shall know them no more." And they have burst the many ties which held them; they were parents, brothers, sisters, children, and friends; but the bond of kindred is broken, and the silver cord of love is loosed. They have been followed by the vehement grief of tears, and the long sorrow of aching hearts; but they make no return, they answer not; they do not even satisfy our wish to know that they sorrow for us as we for them. We talk about them thenceforth as if they were persons we do not know; we talk about them as third persons; whereas they used to be always with us, and every other thought which was within us was shared by them. Or perhaps, if our grief is too deep, we do not mention their names at all. And their possessions, too, all fall to others. The world goes on without them; it forgets them. Yes, so it is; the world contrives to forget that men have souls, it looks upon them all as mere parts of some great visible system. This continues to move on; to this the world ascribes a sort of life and personality. When one or other of its members die, it considers them only as falling out of the system, and as come to nought. For a minute, perhaps, it thinks of them in sorrow, then leaves them—leaves them for ever. It keeps its eye on things seen and temporal. Truly whenever a man dies, rich or poor, an immortal soul passes to judgment; but somehow we read of the deaths of persons we have seen or heard of, and this reflection never comes across us. Thus does the world really cast off men's souls, and recognizing only their bodies, it makes it appear as if "that which befalleth the sons of men befalleth beasts, even one thing befalleth them; as the one dieth so dieth the other; yea, they have all one breath, so that a man hath no pre-eminence over a beast, for all is vanity."

But let us follow the course of a soul thus casting off the world, and cast off by it. It goes forth as a stranger on a journey. Man seems to die and to be no more, when he is but quitting us, and is really beginning to live. Then he sees sights which before it did not even enter into his mind to conceive, and the world is even less to him than he to the world. Just now he was lying on the bed of sickness, but in that moment of death what an awful change has come over him! What a crisis for him! There is stillness in the room that lately held him;

nothing is doing there, for he is gone, he now belongs to others; he now belongs entirely to the Lord who bought him; to Him he returns; but whether to be lodged safely in His place of hope, or to be imprisoned against the great Day, that is another matter, that depends on the deeds done in the body, whether good or evil. And now what are his thoughts? How infinitely important now appears the value of time, now when it is nothing to him! Nothing; for though he spend centuries waiting for Christ, he cannot now alter his state from bad to good, or from good to bad. What he dieth that he must be for ever; as the tree falleth so must it lie. This is the comfort of the true servant of God, and the misery of the transgressor. His lot is cast once and for all, and he can but wait in hope or in dread. Men on their death-beds have declared that no one could form a right idea of the value of time till he came to die; but if this has truth in it, how much more truly can it be said after death! What an estimate shall we form of time while we are waiting for judgment! Yes, it is we—all this, I repeat, belongs to us most intimately. It is not to be looked at as a picture, as a man might read a light book in a leisure hour. *We* must die, the youngest, the healthiest, the most thoughtless; *we* must be thus unnaturally torn in two, soul from body; and only united again to be made more thoroughly happy or to be miserable for ever.

Such is death considered in its inevitable necessity, and its unspeakable importance—nor can we ensure to ourselves any certain interval before its coming. The time may be long; but it may also be short. It is plain a man may die any day; all we can say is, that it is unlikely he will die. But of this, at least, we are certain, that, come it sooner or later, death is continually on the move towards us. We are ever nearer and nearer to it. Every morning we rise we are nearer that grave in which there is no work, nor device, than we were. Thus life is ever crumbling away under us. What should we say to a man, who was placed on some precipitous ground, which was ever crumbling under his feet, and affording less and less secure footing, yet was careless about it? Or what should we say to one who suffered some precious liquor to run from its receptacle into the thoroughfares of men, without a thought to stop it? who carelessly looked on and saw the waste of it becoming greater and greater every minute? But what treasure can equal time? It is the seed of eternity : yet we suffer ourselves to go on, year after year, hardly using it at all in God's service, or thinking it enough to give Him at most a tithe or a seventh of it, while we strenuously and heartily sow to the flesh, that from the flesh we may reap corruption. We try how little we can safely give to religion, instead of having the grace to give abundantly.

"Rivers of water run down mine eyes, because men keep not Thy law;" so says the Psalmist. Doubtless an inspired prophet saw far more clearly than we can see, the madness of men in squandering their treasure upon sin, which is meant to buy their chief good; but if so, what must this madness appear in God's sight! What an inveterate, malignant evil is it in the hearts of the sons of men, that this leads them to sit down to eat, and drink, and rise up to play, when time is hurrying on and judgment coming? We have been told what He thinks of man's unbelief, though we cannot enter into the depth of His thoughts. He showed it to us in act and deed, as far as we could receive it, when He even sent His only-begotten Son into the world as at this time, to redeem us from the world,—which, most surely, was not lightly done; and we also learn His thoughts about it from the words of that most merciful Son,—which most surely were not lightly spoken. "The wicked," He says, "shall go into everlasting punishment."

Oh that there were such a heart in us that we would fear God, and keep His commandments always! But it is of no use to speak; men know their duty—they will not do it. They say they do not need or wish to be told it, that it is an intrusion, and a rudeness, to tell them of death and judgment. So it must be,—and we, who have to speak to them, must submit to them. Speak we must, as an act of duty to God, whether they will hear, or not, and then must leave our words as a witness. Other means for rousing them we have none. We speak from Christ our gracious Lord, their Redeemer, who has already pardoned them freely, yet they will not follow Him with a true heart; and what can be done more?

RELIGIOUS PRIVILEGES.

CHRISTIANITY, considered as a moral system, is made up of two elements, beauty and severity; whenever either is indulged to the loss or disparagement of the other, evil ensues. In heathen times, Greek and Barbarian in some sense divided these two between them; the latter were the slaves of dreary and cruel superstitions, and the former abandoned themselves to a joyous polytheism. And so again in these latter times, the two chief forms of heresy into which opposition to primitive truth has developed, were remarkable, at least in their origin, three hundred years ago, and at times since, the one for an unrefined and self-indulgent religiousness, the other for a stern, dark, cruel spirit, very unamiable, yet still inspiring more respect than the other.

Even the Jews, to whom this earth was especially given, and who might be supposed to be at liberty without offence to satiate themselves in its gifts, were not allowed to enjoy it without restraint. Even the paschal lamb, their great typical feast, was eaten "with bitter herbs" (Exod. xii. 8). And, as time went on, the Prophets were given, who were more or less moulded after the pattern of Elijah, in "suffering affliction and in patience," and were typical of the one great Prophet of the Church who was to come. Much more are Christians to recollect, and to rejoice, that "the brother of low degree" is to be "exalted," and "the rich" to be "made low;" and that the Apostles, whose steps we are to follow, hungered and thirsted, and were naked, and were buffeted, and had no certain dwelling-place, and were accounted the filth of the world and the offscouring of all things.

Let us thus enter upon the rich and happy months which lie before us, when the earth puts forth all her excellence, and robes herself in her bright garments, and scatters her most precious gifts. Thus let us hallow Rogation Sunday, which is to-day, suitably to the Church's intention, which has made these days of abstinence attend upon it, by way of warning us that we must not enjoy our Father's temporal blessings without reserve. "He visiteth the earth and blesseth it; He maketh it very plenteous. . . He provideth for the earth; He watereth her furrows. He crowneth the year with His goodness, and His clouds drop fatness" (Psalm lxv. 9-12). And we acknowledge His bountifulness, we commemorate His providence, we enter upon His gifts, by abstaining from them. As the Israelites brought the first-fruits of their land in a basket (Deut. xxvi. 1-11) and left it in the priest's hand before the altar of the Lord their God, so do we in another way, but in the same spirit, begin our thankful use of God's blessings by a prudent delay and a lowly prayer. We deprecate wrath, we intreat mercy; as Job sacrificed for his sons, so we for ourselves. We remind ourselves, that though "every creature of God is good," we ourselves, God's creatures, are the one exception to that rule; that though His gifts are holy and innocent, our hearts are frail and wayward; that they are good in the sending, yet dangerous in the taking—good in the use, but harmful in the enjoyment. As before meat, day by day, we say a grace and then begin, so now do we ask a blessing on the whole year, by pausing ere we enter upon it.

This is to feed ourselves *with* fear. Thus let us proceed in the use of all our privileges, and all will be benefits. Let us not keep festivals without keeping vigils; let us not keep Eastertide without observing Lent; let us not approach the Sunday feast without keeping the Friday abstinence; let us not adorn churches without studying personal simplicity and austereness; let us not cultivate the accomplishments of taste and literature without the corrective of personal discomfort; let us not attempt to advance the power of the Church, to enthrone her rulers, to rear her palaces, and to ennoble her name, without recollecting that she must be mortified within while she is in honour in the world, and wear the Baptist's hair shirt and leathern girdle under the purple ephod and the jewelled breastplate.

And let us beware, on the other hand, of dishonouring and rudely rejecting God's gifts, out of gloominess or sternness; let us beware of fearing without feasting. "Every creature of God is good, and nothing to be refused." Let us beware, though it must be a sad perversion of mind which admits of it,—let us beware of afflicting ourselves for sin, without first coming to the Gospel for strength to do so. And let us not so plunge ourselves in the sense of our offences, as not withal to take delight in the contemplation of our privileges. Let us rejoice while we mourn. Let us look up to our Lord and Saviour the more we shrink from the sight of ourselves; let us have the more faith and love the more we exercise repentance. Let us, in our penitence, not substitute the Law *for* the Gospel, but add the Law *to* the Gospel. Those who do despite to baptismal grace fall under the Law; but they do not fall *from* the Gospel, if they are repentant; they fall under the Law without the Gospel, if they continue in sin; they receive the Law with the Gospel, if they return. The Law which once introduced the Gospel, in such cases becomes its instrument. They fall indeed under bondage, but they have the power of Christ's grace to enable them to bear it.

And in like manner, as they must not defraud themselves of Christian privileges, neither need they give up God's temporal blessings. All the beauty of nature, the kind influences of the seasons, the gifts of sun and moon, and the fruits of the earth, the advantages of civilized life, and the presence of friends and intimates; all these good things are but one extended and wonderful type of God's benefits in the Gospel. Those who aim at perfection will not reject the gift, but add a corrective; they will add the bitter herbs to the fatted calf and the music and dancing; they will not refuse the flowers of earth, but they will toil in plucking up the weeds. Or if they refrain from one temporal blessing, it will be to reserve another; for this is one great mercy of God, that while He allows us a discretionary use of His temporal gifts, He allows a discretionary abstinence also; and He almost enjoins upon us the use of some, lest we should forget that this earth is His creation, and not of the evil one.

CURIOSITY A TEMPTATION TO SIN.

ONE chief cause of the wickedness which is everywhere seen in the world, and in which, alas! each of us has more or less his share, is our curiosity to have some fellowship with darkness, some experience of sin, to know what the pleasures of sin are like. I believe it is even thought unmanly by many persons (though they may not like to say so in plain words), unmanly and a thing to be ashamed of, to have no knowledge of sin by personal experience, as if it argued a strange seclusion from the world, a childish ignorance of life, a singleness and narrowness of mind, and a superstitious, slavish fear. Not to know sin by experience brings upon a man the laughter and jest of his companions: nor is it wonderful this should be the case in the descendants of that guilty pair to whom Satan in the beginning held out admittance into a strange world of knowledge and enjoyment, as the reward of disobedience to God's commandment. "When the woman saw that the tree was good for food, and that it was pleasant to the eyes, and a tree to be desired to make one wise, she took of the fruit thereof, and did eat, and gave unto her husband with her, and he did eat." A discontent with the abundance of blessings which were given, because something was withheld, was the sin of our first parents: in like manner, a wanton roving after things forbidden, a curiosity to know what it was to be as the heathen, was the chief source of the idolatries of the Jews; and we at this day inherit with them a like nature from Adam.

I say curiosity strangely moves us to disobedience, in order that we may have experience of the pleasure of disobedience. Thus we "rejoice in our youth, and let our hearts cheer us in the days of our youth, and walk in the ways of our heart, and in the sight of our eyes." And we thus intrude into things forbidden, in various ways; in reading what we should not read, in hearing what we should not hear, in seeing what we should not see, in going into company whither we should not go, in presumptuous reasonings and arguings when we should have faith, in acting as if we were our own masters when we should obey. We indulge our reason, we indulge our passions, we indulge our ambition, our vanity, our love of power; we throw ourselves into the society of bad, worldly, or careless men; and all the while we think that, after having acquired this miserable knowledge of good and evil, we can return to our duty, and continue where we left off; merely going aside a moment to shake ourselves, as Samson did, and with an ignorance like his, that our true heavenly strength is departed from us.

Now this delusion arises from Satan's craft, the father of lies, who knows well that if he can get us once to sin, he can easily make us sin twice and thrice, till at length we are taken captive at his will. He sees that curiosity is man's great and first snare, as it was in Paradise; and he knows that if he can but force a way into his heart by this chief and exciting temptation, those temptations of other kinds, which follow in life, will easily prevail over us; and, on the other hand, that if we resist the beginnings of sin, there is every prospect through God's grace that we shall continue in a religious way. His plan of action, then, lies plain before him—to tempt us violently, while the world is new to us, and our hopes and feelings are eager and restless. Hence is seen the Divine wisdom, as well as the merciful consideration of the advice contained in so many parts of Scripture, as in the text, " Enter not into the path of the wicked, and go not into the way of evil men. Avoid it, pass not by it, turn from it, and pass away."

THE PRAISE OF MEN.

TO seek the praise of good men is not wrong, any more than to love and to reverence good men; only wrong when it is in excess, when it interferes with exercise of love and reverence towards God. Not wrong while we look on good men singly as instruments and servants of God; or, in the words of Scripture, while "we glorify God in them." But to seek the praise of bad men, is in itself as wrong as to love the company of bad men, or to admire them. It is not, I say, merely the love of praise that is a sin, but love of the corrupt world's praise. This is the case with all our natural feelings and affections; they are all in themselves good, and implanted by God; they are sinful, because we have in us by nature a something more than them, namely, an evil principle which perverts them to a bad end. Adam, before his fall, felt, we may suppose, love, fear, hope, joy, dislike, as we do now; but then he felt them only when he ought, and as he ought; always harmoniously attempered and rightly adjusted in his soul, which was at unity with itself. But, at the fall, this beautiful order and peace was broken up; the same passions remained, but their use and action were changed; they rushed into extremes, sometimes excessive, sometimes the reverse. Indignation was corrupted into wrath, self-love became selfishness, self-respect became pride, and emulation envy and jealousy. They were at variance with each other; pride struggled with self-interest, fear with desire. Thus his soul became a chaos, and needed a new creation. Moreover, his affections were set upon unsuitable objects. The natural man looks to this world, the world is his god; faith, love, hope, joy, are not excited in his mind by things spiritual and divine, but by things seen and temporal.

Considering, then, that love of praise is not a bad principle in itself, it is plain that a parent may very properly teach his child to love his praise, and fear his blame, when that praise, and blame are given in accordance with God's praise and blame, and made subservient to them. And, in like manner, if the world at large took a correct and religious view of things, then its praise and blame would in its place be valuable too. Did the world admire what God admires; did it account humility, for instance, a great virtue, and pride a great sin; did it condemn that spirit of self-importance and sensitiveness of disgrace, which calls itself a love of honour; did it think little of temporal prosperity, wealth, rank, grandeur, and power; did it condemn arrogant and irreverent disputing, the noisy, turbulent spirit of ambition, the love of war and conquest, and the perverse temper which leads to jealousy and hatred; did it prefer goodness and truth to gifts of the intellect; did it think little of quickness, wit, shrewdness, power of speech and general acquirements, and much of patience, meekness, gentleness, firmness, faith, conscientiousness, purity, forgiveness of injuries,—then there would be no sin in our seeking the world's praise; and though we still ought to love God's praise above all, yet we might love the praise of the world in its degree, for it would be nothing more nor less than the praise of good men. But since, alas! the contrary is the case, since the world (as Scripture tells us) "lieth in wickedness," and the principles and practice which prevail on all sides of us are not those which the all-holy God sanctions, we cannot lawfully seek the world's praise. We cannot serve two masters who are enemies the one to the other. We are forbidden to love the world or anything that is of the world, for it is not of the Father, but passeth away.

TEMPORAL ADVANTAGES.

LET me ask any one who has succeeded in any object of his desire, has he experienced in his success that full, that lasting satisfaction which he anticipated? Did not some feeling of disappointment, of weariness, of satiety, of disquietude, after a short time, steal over his mind? I think it did; and if so, what reason has he to suppose that that greater share of reputation, opulence, and influence, which he has not, and which he desires, would, if granted him, suffice to make him happy? No; the fact is certain, however slow and unwilling we may be to believe it, none of these things bring the pleasure which we beforehand suppose they will bring. Watch narrowly the persons who possess them, and you will at length discover the same uneasiness and occasional restlessness which others have; you will find that there is just a something beyond, which they are striving after, or just some one thing which annoys and distresses them. The good things you admire please for the most part only while they are new; now those who have them are accustomed to them, so they care little for them, and find no alleviation in them of the anxieties and cares which still remain. It is fine, in prospect and imagination, to be looked up to, admired, applauded, courted, feared, to have a name among men, to rule their opinions or their actions by our word, to create a stir by our movements, while men cry, "Bow the knee," before us, but none know so well how vain is the world's praise as he who has it. And why is this? It is in a word, because the soul was made for religious employments and pleasures; and hence, that no temporal blessings, however exalted or refined, can satisfy it. As well might we attempt to sustain the body on chaff, as to feed and nourish the immortal soul with the pleasures and occupations of the world.

Much intercourse with the world, which eminence and station render a duty, has a tendency to draw off the mind from God, and deaden it to the force of religious motives and considerations. There is a want of sympathy between much business and calm devotion, great splendour and a simple faith, which will be to no one more painful than to the Christian to whom God has assigned some part of special responsibility and distinction. To maintain a religious spirit in the midst of engagements and excitements of this world is possible only to a saint; nay, the case is the same though our business be one of a charitable and religious nature, and though our chief intercourse is with those whom we believe to have their minds set upon religion, and whose principles and conduct are not likely to withdraw our feet from the narrow way of life. For here we are likely to be deceived from the very circumstance that our enjoyments are religious; and our end, as being a right one, will engross us, and continually tempt us to be inattentive to the means and to the spirit in which we pursue it. Our Lord alludes to the danger of multiplied occupations in the parable of the sower: "He that received seed among thorns, is he that heareth the word, and the cares of this world and the deceitfulness of riches choke the word, and he becometh unfruitful."

Again, these worldly advantages, as they are called, will seduce us into an excessive love of them. We are too well inclined by nature to live by sight, rather than by faith; and besides the immediate enjoyment, there is something so agreeable to our natural tastes in the honours and emoluments of the world, that it requires an especially strong mind, and a large measure of grace, not to be gradually corrupted by them. We are led to set our hearts upon them, and in the same degree to withdraw them from God. We become unwilling to leave this visible state of things, and to be reduced to a level with those multitudes who are at present inferior to ourselves. Prosperity is sufficient to seduce, although not to satisfy. Hence death and judgment are unwelcome subjects of reflection to the rich and powerful; for death takes them from those comforts which habit has made necessary to them, and throws them adrift on a new order of things, of which they know nothing, save that in it there is no respect of persons.

A SOBER MIND.

A SOBER mind never enjoys God's blessings to the full; it draws back and refuses a portion to show its command over itself. It denies itself in trivial circumstances, even if nothing is gained by denying but an evidence of its own sincerity. It makes trial of its own professions; and if it has been tempted to say anything noble and great, or to blame another for sloth or cowardice, it takes itself at its word, and resolves to make some sacrifice (if possible) in little things as a price for the indulgence of fine speaking, or as a penalty on its censoriousness. Much would be gained if we adopted this rule even in our professions of friendship and service one towards another, and never said a word which we were not willing to do.

There is only one place where the Christian allows himself to profess openly, and that is in church. Here, under the guidance of Apostles and Prophets, he says many things boldly, as speaking after them, and as before Him who searcheth the reins. There can be no harm in professing much directly to God, because, *while* we speak, we know He sees through our professions, and takes them for what they really are—*prayers*. How much, for instance, do we profess when we say the creed? and in the collects we put on the full character of a Christian. We desire and seek the best gifts, and declare our strong purpose to serve God with our whole hearts. By doing this, we remind ourselves of our duty; and withal, we humble ourselves by the taunt (so to call it) of putting upon our dwindled and unhealthy forms those ample and glorious garments which befit the "upright" and full-grown believer.

MORAL EFFECTS OF COMMUNION WITH GOD.

'One thing have I desired of the Lord, which I will require, even that I may dwell in the house of the Lord all the days of my life, to behold the fair beauty of the Lord, and to visit his temple."—PSALM xxvii. 4.

I PROPOSE to make some remarks on communion with God, or prayer in a large sense of the word: not as regards its external consequences, but as it may be considered to affect our own minds and hearts.

What, then, is prayer? It is (if it may be said reverently) *conversing* with God. We converse with our fellow men, and then we use familiar language, because they are our fellows. We converse with God, and then we use the lowliest, awfullest, calmest, concisest language we can, because He is God. Prayer, then, is *divine* converse, differing from human as God differs from man. Thus St. Paul says: "Our conversation is in heaven;" not, indeed, thereby meaning converse of words only, but intercourse and manner of living generally; yet still, in an especial way, converse of words or prayer, because language is the special means of all intercourse. Our intercourse with our fellow men goes on, not by sight, but by sound; not by eyes, but by ears. Hearing is the social sense, and language is the social bond. In like manner, as the Christian's conversation is in heaven, as it is his duty, with Enoch and other saints, to *walk with God*, so his voice is in heaven, his heart "inditing of a good matter" of prayers and praises. Prayers and praises are the mode of his intercourse with the next world, as the converse of business or recreation is the mode in which this world is carried on in all its separate courses. He who does not pray, does not claim his citizenship with heaven, but lives, though an heir of the kingdom, as if he were a child of earth.

Now, it is not surprising if that duty or privilege, which is the characteristic token of our heavenly inheritance, should also have an especial influence upon our fitness for claiming it. He who does not use a gift, loses it; the man who does not use his voice or limbs loses power over them, and becomes disqualified for the state of life to which he is called. In like manner, he who neglects to pray, not only suspends the enjoyment, but he is in the way to lose the possession of his divine citizenship. We are members of another world; we have been severed from the companionship of devils, and brought into that invisible kingdom of Christ which faith alone discerns—that mysterious presence of God which encompasses us, which is in us, and around us; which is in our heart, which enfolds us as though with a robe of light, hiding our scarred and discoloured souls from the sight of Divine Purity, and making them shining as the angels; and which flows in upon us too by means of all forms of beauty and grace which this visible world contains, in a starry host, or, if I may so say, a Milky Way of divine companions, the inhabitants of Mount Zion, where we dwell. Faith, I say, alone apprehends all this; and yet there is something which is not left to faith—our own tastes, likings, motives, and habits. Of these we are conscious in one degree, and we can make ourselves more and more conscious; and as consciousness tells us what they are, reason tells us whether they are such as become, as correspond with, that heavenly world into which we have been translated.

I say, then, it is plain to common sense that the man who has not accustomed himself to the language of heaven will be no fit inhabitant of it when, on the Last Day, it is perceptibly revealed. The case is like that of a language, or style of speaking, in this world; we know well a foreigner from a native. Again, we know those who have been used to king's courts or educated society from others. By their voice, accent, and language, and not only so, by their gestures and gait, by their usages, by their mode of conducting themselves, and their principles of conduct, we know well what a vast difference there is between those who have lived in good society and those who have not. What, indeed, is called "good society," is often very worthless society. I am not speaking of it to praise it. I only mean, that as what men call refined or courtly manners are gained only by intercourse with courts and polished circles, and as the influence of the words there used (that is, of the ideas which those words, striking again and again on the ear, convey to the mind) extends in a most subtle way over all that men do—over the tone of their sentences, and the tone of their questions and replies, and their general bearing, and the spontaneous flow of their thoughts, and their mode of viewing things, and the general maxims or heads to which they refer them, and the motives which determine them and their likings and dislikings, hopes and fears, and their relative estimate of persons, and the intensity of their perceptions towards particular objects; so a habit of prayer, the practice of turning to God and the unseen world in every season, in every place, in every emergency (let alone its supernatural effect of prevailing with God)—prayer, I say, has what may be called a *natural* effect in spiritualizing and elevating the soul.

A man is no longer what he was before. Gradually—imperceptibly to himself—he has imbibed a new set of ideas, and become imbued with fresh principles. He is as one coming from kings' courts, with a grace, a delicacy, a dignity, a propriety, a justness of thought and taste, a clearness and firmness of principle, all his own. Such is the power of God's secret grace acting through those ordinances which he has enjoined us; such the evident fitness of those ordinances to produce the results which they set before us. As speech is the organ of human society, and the means of human civilization, so is prayer the instrument of divine fellowship and divine training.

THE MIND OF LITTLE CHILDREN.

"Except ye be converted, and become as little children, ye shall not enter into the kingdom of heaven."—MATT. xviii. 3.

THE longer we live in the world, and the further removed we are from the feelings and remembrances of childhood (and especially if removed from the sight of children), the more reason have we to recollect our Lord's impressive action and words when He called a little child unto Him, and set him in the midst of His disciples, and said, "Verily, I say unto you, Except ye be converted, and become as little children, ye shall not enter into the kingdom of heaven." And in order to remind us of this our Saviour's judgment, the Church, like a careful teacher, calls us back, year by year, upon this day, from the bustle and fever of the world. She takes advantage of the Massacre of the Innocents, recorded in St. Matthew's Gospel, to bring before us a truth which else we might think little of; to sober our wishes and hopes of this world, our high ambitious thoughts, or our anxious fears, jealousies, and cares, by the picture of the purity, peace, and contentment which are the characteristics of little children.

And independently of the benefit thus accruing to us, it is surely right and meet thus to celebrate the death of the Holy Innocents; for it was a blessed one. To be brought near to Christ, and to suffer for Christ, is surely an unspeakable privilege; to suffer anyhow, even unconsciously. The little children whom He took up in His arms were not conscious of His loving condescension, but was it no privilege when He blessed them? Surely this massacre had in it the nature of a sacrament; it was a pledge of the love of the Son of God towards those who were encompassed by it. All who came near Him more or less suffered by approaching Him—just as if earthly pain and trouble went out of Him as some precious virtue for the good of their souls—and these infants in the number. Surely His very presence was a sacrament; every motion, look, and word of His conveying grace to those who would receive it; and much more was fellowship with Him. And hence in ancient times such barbarous murders and martyrdoms were considered as a kind of baptism, a baptism of blood with a sacramental charm in it which stood in the place of the appointed laver of regeneration. Let us, then, take these little children as in some sense martyrs, and see what instruction we may gain from the pattern of their innocence.

There is very great danger of our becoming cold-hearted as life goes on : afflictions which happen to us, cares, disappointments, all tend to blunt our affections and make our feelings callous. That necessary self-discipline, too, which St. Paul enjoins Timothy to practise, tends the same way. And, again, the pursuit of wealth especially ; and much more if men so far openly transgress the word of Almighty God, as to yield to the temptations of sensuality. The glutton and the drunkard brutalize their minds, as is evident. And then, further, we are often smit with the notion of our having become greater and more considerable persons than we were. If we are prosperous, for instance, in worldly matters ; if we rise in the scale of (what is called) society; if we gain a name ; if we change our state by marriage, or in any other way, so as to create a secret envy in the minds of our companions ; in all these cases we shall be exposed to the temptation of *pride*. The deference paid to wealth or talent commonly makes the possessor artificial and difficult to reach, glossing over his mind with a spurious refinement, which deadens feeling and heartiness. Now, after all, there is in most men's minds a secret instinct of reverence and affection for the days of their childhood. They cannot help sighing with regret and tenderness when they think of it; and it is graciously done by our Lord and Saviour to avail Himself (so to say) of this principle of our nature, and, as He employs all that belongs to it, so to turn this also to the real health of the soul. And it is dutifully done on the part of the Church to follow the intimation given her by her Redeemer, and to hallow one day every year, as if for the contemplation of His word and deed.

If we wish to affect a person, and (if so be) humble him, what can we do better than appeal to the memory of times past, and, above all, to his childhood? Then it was that he came out of the hands of God, with all lessons and thoughts of heaven freshly marked upon him. Who can tell how God makes the soul, or how He new makes it? We know not. We know that, besides His part in the work, it comes into the world with the taint of sin upon it; and that even regeneration, which removes the curse, does not extirpate the root of evil. Whether it is created in heaven or hell, how Adam's sin is breathed into it together with the breath of life, and how the Spirit dwells in it, who shall inform us? But this we know full well—we know it from our own recollection of ourselves, and our experience of children—that there is in the infant soul, in the first years of its regenerate state, a discernment of the unseen world in the things that are seen, a realization of what is sovereign and adorable, and an incredulity and ignorance about what is transient and changeable, which mark it as the fit emblem of the matured Christian when weaned from things temporal, and living in the intimate conviction of the Divine Presence. I do not mean, of course, that a child has any formed principle in his heart, any habits of obedience, any true discrimination between the visible and the unseen, such as God promises to reward, for Christ's sake, in those who come to years of discretion. Never must we forget that, in spite of his new birth, evil is within him, though in its seed only; but he has this one great gift, that he seems to have lately come from God's presence, and not to understand the language of this visible scene, or how it is a temptation, how it is a veil interposing itself between the soul and God. The simplicity of a child's ways and notions, his ready belief of everything he is told, his artless love, his frank confidence, his confession of helplessness, his ignorance of evil, his inability to conceal his thoughts, his admiring without coveting, and, above all, his reverential spirit, looking at all things about him as wonderful, as tokens and types of the One Invisible, are all evidence of his being lately (as it were) a visitant in a higher state of things. I would only have a person reflect on the earnestness and awe with which a child listens to any description or tale; or, again, his freedom from that spirit of proud independence which discovers itself in the soul as time goes on. And though, doubtless, children are generally of a weak and irritable nature, and all are not equally amiable, yet their passions go and are over like a shower, not interfering with the lesson we may gain to our own profit from their ready faith and guilelessness.

The distinctness with which the conscience of a child tells him the difference between right and wrong should also be mentioned. As persons advance in life, and yield to the temptations which come upon them, they lose this original endowment, and are obliged to grope about by the mere reason. If they debate whether they should act in this way or that, and there are many considerations of duty and interest involved in the decision, they feel altogether perplexed. Really and truly, not from self-deception, but really, they do not know how they ought to act; and they are obliged to draw out arguments and take a great deal of pains to come to a conclusion. And all this, in many cases at least, because they have lost through sinning a guide which they originally had from God. Hence it is that St. John, in the Epistle for the day, speaks of Christ's undefiled servants as "following the Lamb whithersoever He goeth." They have the minds of children, and are able by the light within them to decide questions of duty at once, undisturbed by the perplexity of discordant arguments. . . . .

In conclusion, I shall but remind you of the difference

on the other hand between the state of a child and that of a matured Christian, though this difference is almost too obvious to be noticed. St. John says, "He that *doeth* righteousness, is righteous, even as He is righteous;" and again, "Every one that doeth righteousness is born of Him." Now it is plain a child's innocence has no share in this higher blessedness. He is but a type of what at length is to be fulfilled in him. The chief beauty of his mind is on its mere surface; and when, as time goes on, he attempts to act (as is his duty to do), instantly it disappears. It is only while he is still that he is like a tranquil water reflecting heaven. Therefore we must not lament that our youthful days are gone, or sigh over the remembrance of pure pleasures and contemplations which we cannot recall. Rather, what we were when children is a blessed intimation, given for our comfort, of what God will make us if we surrender our hearts to the guidance of His Holy Spirit—a prophecy of good to come—a foretaste of what will be fulfilled in heaven. And thus it is that a child is a pledge of immortality, for he bears upon him in figure those high and eternal excellences in which the joy of heaven consists, and which would not be thus shadowed forth by the all-gracious Creator, were they not one day to be realized.

DOCTRINAL.

THE WORD OF GOD.

"THE Voice of the Lord" is mighty in *operation*, the Voice of the Lord is a glorious Voice. It is not like some idle sound, or a vague rumour coming at random, and tending nowhither, but it is "the word which goeth out of His mouth;" it has a sacramental power, being the instrument as well as the sign of His will. It never can "return unto Him void," "but it accomplishes that which He pleases, and prospers in the thing whereto He sends it." Imputed righteousness is the coming in of actual righteousness. They whom God's sovereign voice pronounces just, forthwith become just. He declares a fact, and makes it a fact by declaring it. He imputes, not a name, but a substantial word, which being "ingrafted" in our own hearts, "is able to save our souls."

God's word, I say, effects what it announces. This is its characteristic all through Scripture. Thus in the beginning He *said*, "Let there be light, and there *was* light." Word and deed went together in creation; and so again "in the regeneration," "*The Lord gave the Word*, great was the company of the preachers." So again in His miracles: He *called* Lazarus from the grave, and the dead arose; He *said*, "Be thou cleansed," and the leprosy departed; He *rebuked* the winds and waves, and they were still; He *commanded* the evil spirits, and they fled away; He said to St. Peter and St. Andrew, St. John, St. James, and St. Matthew, "Follow me," and they arose, for "His word was with power;" and so again in the Sacraments His word is the consecrating principle. As He "blessed" the loaves and fishes, and they multiplied, so He "blessed and brake" and the bread became His body. Further, His voice is the instrument of destruction as well as of creation. As He "upholds all things by the word of His power," so "at the voice of the archangel and the trump of God," the visible world will dissolve; and as His "voice" formerly "shook the earth," so once more "the Lord shall roar out of Zion, and utter His voice from Jerusalem, and the heaven and the earth shall shake."

It would seem, then, in all cases, that God's word is the instrument of His deed. When, then, He solemnly utters the command, "Let the soul be just," it becomes just. By what medium or in what manner, is a further question not now to be discussed. Here it will be more in place to mention another analogy in God's dealings with us, which is instanced in the process of justification; I mean the mode in which prophecy is introduced in Scripture, and the purposes it is made answer in sacred history. It has been noticed before now, as a characteristic of Scripture prophecy, that it precedes and introduces into the world the great providences of God's mercy. When He would set apart a family or people for some extraordinary end, He reveals His purposes in the case of the first father of the line. He puts His word upon it in its origin, and seals up for it its destinies in that word, which, like some potent charm, works secretly towards the proposed end. Thus when the chosen people were to be formed, Almighty God not only chose Abraham, but spoke over him the promises which in due time were to be accomplished. The twelve tribes had each its own character and history stamped on it from the first. When the royal line of the Messiah was to be begun in Judah and renewed in David, on each patriarch in turn did Providence inscribe a prediction of what was to be. Such as this is justification as regards an individual. It is a sort of prophecy, recognising God's hidden election, announcing His purposes before the event, and mysteriously working towards their fulfilment; even "the oath which He sware" to us, " more abundantly to show unto the heirs of promise the immutability of His counsel," "that we might have a strong consolation who have fled for refuge to lay hold upon the hope set before us." And in thus openly setting forth what is secretly in course of operation, it is an appointment especially characteristic of that supernatural system which we called revealed religion. As God conducts His Scripture dispensations by prophecy, and anticipates nature by miracle, so does He in a parallel way operate upon our hearts through justification.

THE THOUGHT OF GOD THE STAY OF THE SOUL.

"Ye have not received the spirit of bondage again to fear; but ye have received the Spirit of adoption, whereby we cry, Abba, Father."—ROM. viii. 15.

WHEN Adam fell, his soul lost its true strength; he forfeited the inward light of God's presence, and became the wayward, fretful, excitable, and miserable being which his history has shown him to be ever since; with alternate strength and feebleness, nobleness and meanness, energy in the beginning and failure in the end. Such was the state of his soul in itself, not to speak of the Divine wrath upon it which followed, or was involved in the Divine withdrawal. It lost its spiritual life and health which was necessary to complete its nature, and to enable it to fulfil the ends for which it was created—which was necessary both for its moral integrity and its happiness; and as if faint, hungry, or sick, it could no longer stand upright, but sank on the ground! Such is the state in which every one of us lies as born into the world; and Christ has come to reverse this state, and restore us the great gift which Adam lost in the beginning. Adam fell from his Creator's favour to be a bond-servant; and Christ has come to set us free again, to impart to us the Spirit of adoption, whereby we become God's children, and again approach Him as our Father.

I say, by birth we are in a state of defect and want; we have not all that is necessary for the perfection of our nature. As the body is not complete in itself, but requires the soul to give it a meaning, so again the soul, till God is present with it and manifested in it, has faculties and affections without a ruling principle, object, or purpose. Such it is by birth, and this, Scripture signifies to us by many figures; sometimes calling human nature blind, sometimes hungry, sometimes unclothed; and calling the gift of the Spirit light, health, food, warmth, and raiment; all by way of teaching us what our real state is, and what our gratitude should be to Him who has brought us into a new state. For instance: "Because thou sayest, I am rich and increased in goods, and have need of nothing; and knowest not that thou art wretched, and miserable, and poor, and blind, and naked; I counsel thee to buy of Me gold tried in the fire, that thou mayest be rich; and white raiment, that thou mayest be clothed, . . . and anoint thine eyes with eye-salve, that thou mayest see." Again: "God who commanded the light to shine out of darkness hath shined in our hearts, to give the light of the knowledge of the glory of God, in the face of Jesus Christ." Again: "Awake thou that sleepest, and arise from the dead, and Christ shall give thee light." . . . .

Now the doctrine which these passages contain is often truly expressed thus: that the soul of man is made for the contemplation of its Maker, and that nothing short of that high contemplation is its happiness; that whatever it may possess besides, it is dissatisfied till it is vouchsafed God's presence, and lives in the light of it. I say, then, that the happiness of the soul consists in the exercise of the affections; not in sensual pleasures; not in activity; not in excitement; not in self-esteem; not in the consciousness of power; not in knowledge. In none of these things lies our happiness, but in our affections being elicited, employed, supplied. As hunger and thirst, as taste, sound, and smell are the channels through which this bodily frame receives pleasure, so the affections are the instruments by which the soul has pleasure. When they are exercised duly, they are happy; when they are undeveloped, restrained, or thwarted, it is not happy. This is our real and true bliss—not to know, or to affect, or to pursue; but to love, to hope, to joy, to admire, to revere, to adore. Our real and true bliss lies in the possession of those objects on which our hearts may rest and be satisfied.

Now, if this be so, here is at once a reason for saying that the thought of God, and nothing short of it, is the happiness of man; for though there is much besides to serve as subject of excitement, yet the affections require a something more vast and more enduring than anything created. What is novel and sudden, exalts, but does not influence. What is pleasurable or useful raises no awe; self moves no reverence, and mere knowledge kindles no love. He alone is sufficient for the heart who made it. I do not say, of course, that nothing short of the Almighty Creator can awaken and answer to our love, reverence, and trust; man can do this for man. Man doubtless is an object to rouse his brother's love, and repays it in his measure. Nay, it is a great duty, one of the two chief duties of religion, thus to be minded towards our neighbour. But I am not speaking here of what we can do, or ought to do, but what it is our happiness to do; and surely it may be said that though the love of the brethren, the love of all men, be one half of our obedience, yet exercised by itself, were that possible, which it is not, it were no part of our reward. And for this reason, if for no other, that our hearts require something more permanent and uniform than man can be. We gain much for a time from fellowship with each other. It is a relief to us, as fresh air to the fainting, or meat and drink to the hungry, or a flood of tears to the heavy in mind. It is a soothing comfort to have those whom we may make our confidants; a comfort to have those to whom we may confess our faults; a comfort to have those to whom we may look for sympathy. Love of home and family in these and other ways is sufficient to make this life tolerable to the multitude of men, which otherwise it would not be; but still, after all, our affections exceed such exercise of them, and demand what is more stable. Do not all men die? Are they not taken from us? Are they not as uncertain as the grass of the field? We do not give our hearts to things inanimate, because these have no permanence in them. We do not place our affections in sun, moon, and stars, or this rich and fair earth, because all things material come to nought, and vanish like day and night. Man, too, though he has an intelligence within him, yet in his best estate is altogether vanity. If our happiness consists in our affections being employed and recompensed, "man that is born of a woman" cannot be our happiness; for how can he stay another who continueth not in one stay himself?

But there is another reason why God alone is the happiness of our souls, to which I wish rather to direct attention. The contemplation of Him, and nothing but it, is able fully to open and relieve the mind, to unlock, occupy, and fix our affections. We may indeed love things created with great intenseness; but such affection, when disjoined from the love of the Creator, is like a stream running in a narrow channel, impetuous, vehement, turbid. The heart runs out, as it were, only at one door; it is not an expanding of the whole man. Created natures cannot open us, or elicit the ten thousand mental senses which belong to us, and through which we really live. None but the presence of our Maker can enter us; for to none besides can the whole heart in all its thoughts and feelings be unlocked and subjected. "Behold," He says, "I stand at the door and knock; if any man hear My voice and open the door, I will come in to him and sup with him, and he with Me." "My Father will love him, and We will come unto him, and make Our abode with him." "God hath sent forth the Spirit of His Son into your hearts." "God is greater than our heart, and knoweth all things." It is this feeling of simple and absolute confidence and communion which soothes and satisfies those to whom it is vouchsafed. We know that even our nearest friends enter into us but partially, and hold intercourse with us only at times: whereas the consciousness of a perfect and enduring Presence, and it alone, keeps the heart open. Withdraw the object on which it rests, and it will relapse again into its state of confinement and constraint; and in proportion as it is limited either to certain seasons or to certain affections the heart is straitened and distressed. If it be not over bold to say it, He who is infinite can alone be its measure; He alone can answer to the mysterious assemblage of feelings and thoughts which it has within it. " There is no creature which is not manifest in His sight, but all things are naked and opened unto the eyes of Him with whom we have to do." . . . .

I have been saying that our happiness consists in the contemplation of God;—only such a contemplation is capable of accompanying the mind always and everywhere, for God alone can be always and everywhere present; and that what is commonly said about the happiness of a good conscience confirms this. For what is it to have a good conscience, when we examine the force of our words, but to be ever reminded of God by our own hearts, to have our hearts in such a state as to be led thereby to look up to Him, and to desire His eye to be upon us through the day? It is the feeling attendant in the case of holy men on the contemplation of Almighty God.

But, again, this sense of God's presence is not only the ground of the peace of a good conscience, but of the peace of repentance also. At first sight it may seem strange how repentance can have in it anything of comfort and peace. The Gospel, indeed, promises to turn all sorrow into joy.

It makes us take pleasure in desolateness, weakness, and contempt. "We glory in tribulations also," says the Apostle, "because the love of God is shed abroad in our hearts by the Holy Ghost which is given unto us." It destroys anxiety: "Take no thought for the morrow, for the morrow shall take thought for the things of itself." It bids us take comfort under bereavement: "I would not have you ignorant, brethren, concerning them which are asleep, that ye sorrow not, even as others which have no hope." But if there be one sorrow which might seem to be unmixed misery, if there be one misery left under the Gospel, the awakened sense of having abused the Gospel might have been considered that one. And, again, if there be a time when the presence of the Most High would at first sight seem to be intolerable, it would be then, when the consciousness vividly bursts upon us, that we had ungratefully rebelled against Him. Yet so it is that true repentance cannot be without the thought of God. It has the thought of God, for it seeks Him; and it seeks Him because it is quickened with love, and even sorrow must have a sweetness if love be in it. For what is it to repent, but to surrender ourselves to God for pardon or punishment; as loving His presence for its own sake, and accounting chastisement from Him better than rest and peace from the world? While the prodigal son remained among the swine he had sorrow enough, but no repentance, remorse only; but repentance led him to rise and go to his father, and to confess his sins. Thus he relieved his heart of its misery, which before was like some hard and fretful tumour weighing upon it. . . .

On the other hand, remorse, or what the apostle calls "the sorrow of the world," worketh death. Instead of coming to the Fount of Life, to the God of all consolation, remorseful men feed on their own thoughts, without any confidant of their sorrow. They disburthen themselves to no one; to God they will not, to the world they cannot confess; the world will not attend to their confession; it is a good associate, but it cannot be an intimate. It cannot approach us or stand by us in trouble; it is no paraclete; it leaves all our feelings buried within us, either tumultuous, or at best dead; it leaves us gloomy or obdurate. Such is our state while we live in the world, whether we be in sorrow or in joy. We are pent up within ourselves, and are therefore miserable. Perhaps we may not be able to analyze our misery, or even to realise it, as persons oftentimes who are in bodily sicknesses. We do not know, perhaps, what or where our pain is; we are so used to it that we do not call it pain. Still it is so; we need a relief to our hearts, that they may be dark and sullen no longer, or that they may not go on feeding upon themselves. We need to escape from ourselves to something beyond; and much as we may wish it otherwise, and may try to make idols to ourselves, nothing short of God's presence is our true refuge; everything else is either a mockery, or but an expedient useful for its season or in its measure.

How miserable then is he who does not practically know this great truth! Year after year he will be a more unhappy man, or at least he will emerge into a maturity of misery at once when he passes out of this world of shadows into that kingdom where all is real. He is at present attempting to satisfy his soul with that which is not bread, or he thinks the soul can thrive without nourishment. He fancies he can live without an object. He fancies that he is sufficient for himself; or he supposes that knowledge is sufficient for his happiness; or that exertion, or that the good opinion of others, or what is called fame, or that the comforts and luxuries of wealth are sufficient for him. What a truly wretched state is that coldness and dryness of soul in which so many live and die, high and low, learned and unlearned! Many a great man, many a peasant, many a busy man lives and dies with closed heart, with affections undeveloped, unexercised. You see the poor man passing day after day, Sunday after Sunday, year after year, without a thought in his mind, to appearance almost like a stone. You see the educated man, full of thought, full of intelligence, full of action, but still with a stone heart as cold and dead as regards his affections as if he were the poor ignorant countryman. You see others, with warm affections, perhaps, for their families, with benevolent feelings towards their fellow-men, yet stopping there, centering their heart on what is sure to fail them, as being perishable. Life passes, riches fly away, popularity is fickle, the senses decay, the world changes, friends die. One alone is constant; One alone is true to us; One alone can be true; One alone can be all things to us; One alone can supply our needs; One alone can train us up to our full perfection; One alone can give a meaning to our complex and intricate nature; One alone can give us tune and harmony; One alone can form and possess us. Are we allowed to put ourselves under His guidance? This surely is the only question. Has He really made us His children, and taken possession of us by His Holy Spirit? Are we still in His kingdom of grace, in spite of our sins? The question is not whether we should go, but whether He will receive. And we trust that, in spite of our sins, He will receive us still, every one of us, if we seek His face in love unfeigned and holy fear. Let us then do our part, as He has done His, and much more. Let us say with the Psalmist, "Whom have I in heaven but Thee? and there is none upon earth I desire in comparison of Thee. My flesh and my heart faileth, but God is the strength of my heart, and my portion for ever."

BODILY SUFFERING.

"I fill up that which is behind of the afflictions of Christ in my flesh, for His body's sake, which is the Church."—COL. i. 24.

THE gospel which has shed light in so many ways upon the state of the world has aided especially our view of the *sufferings* to which human nature is subjected ; turning a punishment into a privilege, in the case of all pain, and especially of bodily pain, which is the most mysterious of all. Sorrow, anxiety, and disappointment are more or less connected with sin and sinners ; but bodily pain is involuntary for the most part, stretching over the world by some external irresistible law, reaching to children who have never actually sinned, and to the brute animals, who are strangers to Adam's nature ; while in its manifestations it is far more piteous and distressing than any other suffering. It is the lot of all of us sooner or later ; and that perhaps in a measure which it would be appalling and wrong to anticipate, whether from disease or from the casualties of life. And all of us at length must die; and death is generally ushered in by disease, and ends in that separation of soul and body which itself may, in some cases, involve peculiar pain.

Worldly men put such thoughts aside as gloomy: they can neither deny nor avert the prospect before them: and they are wise, on their own principles, not to embitter the present by anticipating it. But Christians may bear to look at it without undue apprehension; for this very infliction, which most touches the heart and imagination, has (as I have said) been invested by Almighty God with a new and comfortable light, as being the medium of His choicest mercies towards us. Pain is no longer a curse, a necessary evil to be undergone with a dry submission or a passive endurance. It may be considered even as a blessing of the Gospel, and being a blessing, admits of being met either well or ill. In the way of nature, indeed, it seems to shut out the notion of duty, as if so masterful a discipline from without superseded the necessity or opportunity of self-mastery. But now that "Christ hath suffered in the flesh," we are bound "to arm ourselves with the same mind," and to obey, as He did, amid suffering.

Now, as to the effect of pain upon the mind, let it be well understood that it has no sanctifying influence in itself. Bad men are made worse by it. This should be borne in mind, lest we deceive ourselves; for sometimes we speak (at least the poor often so speak) as though present hardship or suffering were in some sense a ground of confidence in ourselves as to our future prospects, whether as expiating our sins or bringing our hearts nearer to God. Nay, even the more religious among us may be misled to think that pain makes them better than it really does; for the effect of it at length, on any but very proud or ungovernable tempers, is to cause a languor and composure of mind, which looks like resignation, while it necessarily throws our reason upon the especial thought of God, our only stay in such times of trial. Doubtless it does really benefit the Christian, and in no scanty measure; and he may thank God who thus blesses it. Only let him be cautious of measuring his spiritual state by the particular exercise of faith and love in his heart at the time, especially if that exercise be limited to the affections themselves, and have no opportunity of showing itself in work. St. Paul speaks of chastisement "yielding *afterwards* the peaceable fruit of righteousness," formed indeed, and ripened at the moment, but manifested in due season. This may be the real fruit of the suffering of a death-bed, even though it may not have time to show itself to others before the Christian departs hence. Surely we may humbly hope that it perfects habits hitherto but partially formed, and blends the several graces of the spirit more entirely. Such is the issue of it in *established* Christians; but it *may* probably effect nothing so blessed. Nay, in the case of those who have followed Christ with but a half heart, it may be a trial too strong for their feebleness, and may overpower them. This is a dreadful reflection for those who put off the day of repentance. Well does our Church pray for us: "Suffer us not, at our last hour, for any pains of death to fall from Thee!" As for unbelievers, we know how it affects them, from such serious passages of Scripture as the following: "They gnawed their tongues for pain, and blasphemed the God of heaven because of their pains and their sores, and repented not of their deeds" (Rev. xvi. 10, 11).

Nay, I would go so far as to say, not only that pain does not commonly improve us, but that without care it has a strong tendency to do our souls harm; viz., by making us selfish, an effect produced even when it does us good in other ways. Weak health, for instance, instead of opening the heart, often makes a man supremely careful of his bodily ease and well-being. Men find an excuse in their infirmities for some extraordinary attention to their comforts; they consider they may fairly consult, on all occasions, their own convenience rather than that of another; they indulge their wayward wishes, allow themselves in indolence when they really might exert themselves, and think they may be fretful because they are weak; they become querulous, self-willed, fastidious, and egotistical. Bystanders, indeed, should be very cautious of thinking any particular sufferer to be thus minded, because, after all, sick people have a multitude of feelings which they cannot explain to any one else, and are often in the right in those matters in which they appear to others most fanciful or unreasonable. Yet this does not interfere with the correctness of my remark on the whole. . . . .

The natural effect then, of pain and fear, is to individualize us in our own minds, to fix our thoughts on ourselves, to make us selfish. It is through pain, chiefly, that we realize to ourselves even our bodily organs; a frame entirely without painful sensations is (as it were) one whole without parts, and prefigures that future spiritual body which shall be the portion of the saints. And to this we most approximate in our youth, when we are not sensible that we are compacted of gross terrestrial matter, as advancing years convince us. The young reflect little upon themselves, they gaze around them, and live out of doors, and say they have souls, little understanding their words. "They rejoice in their youth." This, then, is the effect of suffering, that it arrests us; that it, as it were, puts a finger upon us to ascertain for us our own individuality. But it does no more than this. If such a warning does not lead us, through the stirrings of our conscience, heavenwards, it does but imprison us in ourselves and make us selfish.

Here then it is that the gospel finds us. Heirs to a visitation which, sooner or later, comes upon us, turning our thoughts from outward objects, and so tempting us to idolize self, to the dishonour of that God whom we ought to worship, and the neglect of man, whom we should love as ourselves. Thus it finds us, and it obviates this danger, not by removing pain, but by giving it new associations. Pain, which by nature leads us only to ourselves, carries on the Christian mind from the thought of self to the contemplation of Christ, His passion, His merits, and His pattern; and thence, further to that united company of sufferers who follow Him, and "are what He is in this world." He is the great object of our faith; and while we gaze upon Him we learn to forget ourselves.

No one chooses evil for its own sake, but for the greater good wrought out through it. Jesus underwent it for ends greater than the immediate removal of it. "Not grudgingly or of necessity," but cheerfully doing God's will, as the Gospel history sets before us. When His time was come, we are told, " He steadfastly set His face to go to Jerusalem." His disciples said, " Master, the Jews of late sought to stone Thee, and goest Thou thither again ?" but He persisted. Again, He said to

Judas, "What thou doest, do quickly." He proceeded to the garden beyond Cedron, though Judas knew the place; and when the band of officers came to seize Him, "He went forth and said unto them, I am He." And with what calmness and majesty did He bear His sufferings when they came upon Him, though by His agony in the garden He showed He fully felt their keenness! The Psalmist, in his prediction of them, says, "I am poured out like water, and all my bones are out of joint. My heart is like wax, it is melted;" describing, as it would seem, that sinking of spirit and enfeebling of nerve which severe pain causes. Yet, in the midst of distress which seemed to preclude the opportunity of obedience, He asked questions of the doctors in the Temple; not thinking to be merely passive under the trial, but accounting it as if a great occasion for a noble and severe surrender of Himself to His Father's will. Thus He "learned obedience by the things that He suffered." Consider the deep and serene compassion which led Him to pray for those who crucified Him; His solicitous care of His mother; and His pardoning words addressed to the robber who suffered with Him. And so, when He said, "It is finished," He showed that He was still contemplating with a clear intellect "the travail of His soul, and was satisfied;" and in the solemn surrender of Himself into His Father's hand He showed where His mind rested in the midst of its darkness. Even when He seemed to be thinking of Himself, and said, "I thirst," He really was regarding the words of prophecy, and was bent on vindicating, to the very letter, the divine announcements concerning Him. Thus, upon the cross itself, we discern in Him the mercy of a divine Messenger from heaven, the love and grace of a Saviour, the dutifulness of a son, the faith of a created nature, and the zeal of a servant of God. His mind was stayed upon His Father's sovereign will and infinite perfections, yet could pass, without effort, to the claim of filial duty or the need of an individual sinner. Six out of His seven last words were words of faith and love. For one instant a horrible dread overwhelmed Him, when He seemed to ask why God had forsaken Him. Doubtless "that voice was for our sakes," as when He made mention of His thirst; and, like the other, was taken from inspired prophecy. Perhaps it was intended to set before us an example of a special trial to which human nature is subject, whatever was the real and inscrutable manner of it in Him, who was all along supported by an inherent divinity; I mean the trial of sharp agony hurrying the mind on to vague terrors, and strange, inexplicable thoughts, and is, therefore, graciously recorded for our benefit in the history of His death, "Who was tempted in all points, like as we are, yet without sin."

Such, then, were our Lord's sufferings, voluntarily undergone, and ennobled by an active obedience; themselves the centre of our hopes and worship, yet borne, without thought of self, towards God and for man. And who among us habitually dwells upon them but is led, without deliberate purpose, by the very warmth of gratitude and of adoring love, to attempt bearing his own inferior trials in the same heavenly mind? Who does not see, that to bear pain well is to meet it courageously; not to shrink or waver, but to pray for God's help, then to look at it steadfastly, to summon what nerve we have of mind or body to receive its attack, and to bear up against it (while strength is given us) as against some visible enemy in close combat? Who will not acknowledge that when sent to us we must make its presence (as it were) our own voluntary act, by the cheerful and ready concurrence of our own will with the will of God? Nay, who is there but must own, with Christ's sufferings before us, pain and tribulation are after all not only the most blessed, but even the most congruous attendants upon those who are called to inherit the benefit of them? Most congruous, I say; not as though necessary, but as most natural and befitting, harmonizing most fully with the main object in the group of sacred wonders on which the Church is called to gaze. Who, on the other hand, does not at least perceive that all the glare and gaudiness of this world, its excitements, its keenly-pursued goods, its successes and its transports, its pomp and its luxuries, are not in character with that pale and solemn scene which faith must ever have in its eye? What Christian will not own that to "reign as kings," and to be "full," is not his calling; so as to derive comfort in the hour of sickness, or bereavement, or other affliction, from the thought that he is now in his own place, if he be Christ's, in his true home, the sepulchre in which his Lord was laid. So deeply have His saints felt this, that, when times were peaceful and the Church was in safety, they could not rest in the lap of ease, and have secured to themselves hardnesses, lest the world should corrupt them. They could not bear to see the much-enduring Paul adding to his necessary tribulations a self-inflicted chastisement of the flesh, and yet allow themselves to live delicately and fare sumptuously every day. They saw the image of Christ reflected in tears and blood in the glorious company of the apostles, the goodly fellowship of the prophets, and the noble army of martyrs. They read in prophecy of the doom of the Church, as "a woman fed by God in the wilderness," and her witnesses as "clothed in sackcloth;" and they could not believe they were meant for nothing more but to enjoy the pleasures of this life, however innocent and moderate might be their use of them Without deciding about their neighbours, they felt themselves called to higher things; their own sense of the duty became the sanction and witness of it. They considered that God at least would afflict them in His love, if they spared themselves ever so much. The thorn in the flesh, the buffetings of Satan, the bereavement of their eyes, these were their portion; and in common prudence, were there no higher thought, they could not live out of time and measure with these expected visitations. With no superstitious alarms, or cowardly imagination, or senseless hurrying into difficulty or trial, but calmly, and in faith, they surrendered themselves into His hands who had told them in His inspired Word that affliction was to be their familiar food; till at length they gained that distaste for the luxuries of life as to be impatient of them from their very fulness of grace. It was the temper too of such of the apostles as were removed more than their brethren from the world's buffetings, as if the prospect of suffering afterwards were no dispensation for a present self-inflicted discipline, or rather demanded it. St. James the Less was Bishop of Jerusalem, and was highly venerated for his uprightness by the unbelieving Jews, among whom he lived unmolested. We are told that he drank no wine nor strong drink, nor did he eat any animal food, nor indulge in the luxury of the bath. "So often was he in the Temple on his knees, that they were thin and hard by his continual supplication." Thus he kept his "loins girded about, and his lamp burning," for the blessed martyrdom which was to end his course. Could it be otherwise? How could the great apostle, sitting at home by his Lord's decree, "nourish his heart," as he calls it, "as for the slaughter." How could he eat and drink and live as other men, when "the Ark, and Israel, and Judah, were in tents," encamped in the open fields, and one by one God's chosen warriors were falling before the brief triumph of Satan! How could he be "delicate on the earth, and wanton," when Paul and Barnabas, Peter too, and John, were in stripes and prisons, in labours and perils, in hunger and thirst, in cold and nakedness! Stephen had led the army of martyrs in Jerusalem itself, which was his own post of service. James, the brother of John, had followed him in the same city; he first of the apostles tasting our Lord's cup who had unwittingly asked to drink it. And if this was the feeling of the apostles when in temporary safety, why is it not ours, who altogether live at ease, except that we have not faith enough to realize what is past? Could we see the cross upon Calvary, and the list of sufferers who resisted unto blood in the times that followed it, is it possible that we should feel surprised when pain overtook us, or impatience at its continuance? Is it strange though we are smitten by ever so new a plague? Is it grievous that the cross presses on one nerve or limb ever so many years, till hope of relief is gone? Is it indeed not possible, with the apostle, to rejoice in "bearing in our body the marks of the Lord Jesus?" And much more can we, for very shame's sake, suffer ourselves to be troubled at what is but ordinary pain, to be irritated or saddened, made gloomy or anxious, by inconveniences which never could surprise or unsettle those who had studied and understood their place as servants of a crucified Lord?

Let us then determine with cheerful hearts to sacrifice unto the Lord our God our comforts, and pleasures, however innocent, when He calls for them, whether for the purpose of His Church, or in His own inscrutable Providence. Let us lend to Him a few short hours of present ease, and we shall receive our own with abundant usury in the day of His coming. There is a treasury in heaven stored with such offerings as the natural man abhors; with sighs and tears, wounds and blood, torture and death. The martyrs first began the contribution, and we all may follow them—all of us; for every suffering, great or little, may, like the widow's mite, be sacrificed in faith to Him who sent it. Christ gave us the words of consecration, when He for an ensample said, "Thy will be done." Henceforth, as the apostle speaks, we may "glory in tribulation," as the seed of future glory.

Meanwhile, let us never forget in all we suffer, that, properly speaking, our own sin is the cause of it, and it is only by Christ's mercy that we are allowed to range ourselves at His side. We who are children of wrath, are made through Him children of grace ; and our pains, which are in themselves but foretastes of hell, are changed by the sprinkling of His blood into a preparation for heaven.

THE MINISTRY OF ANGELS.

"Who maketh His angels spirits, His ministers a flaming fire."—
PSALM civ. 4.

THERE have been ages of the world in which men have thought too much of angels, and paid them excessive honour; honoured them so perversely as to forget the supreme worship due to Almighty God. This is the sin of a dark age. But the sin of what is called an educated age, such as our own, is just the reverse: to account slightly of them, or not at all; to ascribe all we see around us, not to their agency, but to certain assumed laws of nature. This, I say, is likely to be our sin in proportion as we are initiated into the learning of this world; and this is the danger of many (so called) philosophical pursuits, now in fashion, and recommended zealously to the notice of large portions of the community hitherto strangers to them—chemistry, geology, and the like; the danger, that is, of resting in things seen and forgetting unseen things, and an ignorance about them.

I will attempt to say what I mean more at length. The text informs us that Almighty God makes His angels spirits or winds, and His ministers a flame of fire. Let us consider what is implied in this.

What a number of beautiful and wonderful objects does nature present on every side of us, and how little we know concerning them! In some, indeed we see symptoms of intelligence, and we get to form some idea of what they are. For instance, the brute animals we know little, but still we see they have sense, and we understand that their bodily form which meets the eye is but the index—the outside token of something we do not see. Much more in the case of men. We see them move, speak, and act, and we know that all we see takes place in consequence of their will, because they have a spirit within them, though we do not see it. But why do rivers flow? Why does rain fall? Why does the sun warm us? And the wind, why does it blow? Here our natural reason is at fault. We know, I say, that it is the *spirit* in man and in beast that makes man and beast move; but reason tells us of no spirit abiding in what is commonly called the natural world, to make it perform its ordinary duties. Of course it is *God's* will which *sustains* it all; so does God's will enable *us* to move also. Yet this does not hinder that, in one sense, we may be truly said to move ourselves. But how do the wind and water, earth and fire, move? Now here Scripture interposes, and seems to tell us that all this wonderful harmony is the work of angels. Those events which we ascribe to chance, as the weather, or to Nature, as the seasons, are duties done to that God who maketh His angels to be winds and His ministers a flame of fire. For example, it was an angel which gave to the pool at Bethesda its medicinal quality; and there is no reason why we should doubt that other health-springs in this and other countries are made such by a like unseen ministry. The fires on Mount Sinai, the thunders and lightnings, were the work of angels; and in the Apocalypse we read of the angels restraining the four winds. Works of vengeance are likewise attributed to them. The fiery lava of the volcanoes, which (as it appears) was the cause of Sodom and Gomorrah's ruin, was caused by the two angels who rescued Lot. The hosts of Sennacherib were destroyed by an angel, by means (it is supposed) of a suffocating wind. The pestilence in Israel, when David numbered the people, was the work of an angel. The earthquake at the resurrection was the work of an angel. And in the Apocalypse the earth is smitten in various ways by angels of vengeance.

Thus, as far as the Scripture communications go, we learn that the course of Nature, which is so wonderful, so beautiful, and so fearful, is effected by the ministry of these unseen beings. Nature is not inanimate; its daily toil is intelligent; its works are *duties*. Accordingly, the Psalmist says, "The heavens declare the glory of God, and the firmament showeth His handywork." "O Lord, Thy word endureth for ever in heaven. Thy truth also remaineth from one generation to another. Thou hast laid the foundation of the earth, and it abideth. They continue this day according to Thine ordinance, for *all things serve Thee.*"

I do not pretend to say that we are told in Scripture what Matter is; but I affirm, that as our souls move our bodies, be our bodies what they may, so there are spiritual intelligences which move those wonderful and vast portions of the natural world which seem to be inanimate; and as the gestures, speech, and expressive countenance of our friends around us enable us to hold intercourse with them, so in the motions of universal Nature, in the interchange of day and night, summer and winter, wind and storm, fulfilling His word, we are reminded of the blessed and dutiful angels. Well, then, may we on this, the Feast of St. Michael and All Angels, sing the hymn of those three holy children whom Nebuchadnezzar cast into the fiery furnace. The angels were bid to change the nature of the flame, and make it harmless unto them; and they in turn called on all creatures of God, on the angels especially, to glorify Him.

Though many hundreds of years have passed since that time, and the world now vainly thinks it knows more than it did, and that it has found the real causes of the things it sees, still may we say, with grateful and simple hearts, " O all ye works of the Lord, O ye angels of the Lord, O ye sun and moon, stars of heaven, showers and dew, winds of God, light and darkness, mountains and hills, green things upon the earth, bless ye the Lord, praise Him, and magnify Him for ever." Thus, whenever we look abroad, we are reminded of those most gracious and holy beings, the servants of the Holiest, who deign to minister to the heirs of salvation. Every breath of air and ray of light and heat, every beautiful prospect is, as it were, the skirts of their garments, the waving of the robes of those whose faces see God in heaven. And I put it to any one, whether it is not as philosophical, and as full of intellectual enjoyment, to refer the movements of the natural world to them, as to attempt to explain them by certain theories of science, useful as these theories certainly are for particular purposes, and capable (in subordination to that higher view) of a religious application. . . . .

Suppose an inquirer into Nature, when examining a flower, or a herb, or a pebble, or a ray of light, which he treats as something so beneath him in the scale of existence, suddenly discovered that he was in the presence of some powerful being who was hidden behind the visible things he was inspecting, who, though concealing his wise hand, was giving them their beauty, grace, and perfection, as being God's instrument for the purpose; nay, whose robe and ornaments those wondrous objects were which he was so eager to analyse; what would be his thoughts? Should we but accidentally show a rudeness of manner towards our fellow man, tread on the hem of his garment, or brush roughly against him, are we not vexed, not as if we had hurt him, but from the fear we may have been disrespectful? David had watched the awful pestilence three days, not with curious eyes, but doubtless with indescribable terror and remorse; but when at length he lifted up his eyes and saw the angel of the Lord (who caused the pestilence) stand between the earth and the heaven, having a drawn sword in his hand stretched out over Jerusalem, then David and the elders, who were clothed in sackcloth, fell upon their faces. The mysterious irresistible pestilence became still more fearful when its cause was known; and what is true of the painful, is true on the other hand of the pleasant and attractive operations of Nature. When, then, when we walk abroad, and "meditate in the field at eventide," how much has every herb and flower in it to surprise and overwhelm us! For even, did we know as much about them as the wisest of men, yet there are those around us, though unseen, to whom our greatest knowledge is as ignorance ; and when we converse on subjects of Nature scientifically, repeating the names of plants and earths, and describing their properties, we should do so religiously, as in the hearing of the great servants of God, with the sort of diffidence which we always feel when speaking before the learned and wise of our own mortal race, as poor beginners in intellectual knowledge as well as in moral attainments.

Now I can conceive persons saying that all this is fanciful. But if it appears so, it is only because we are not accustomed to such thoughts. Surely we are not told in Scripture about the angels for nothing, but for practical purposes. Nor can I conceive a use of our knowledge more practical than to make it connect the sight of this world with the thought of another; nor one more consolatory, for surely it is a great comfort to reflect that wherever we go, we have those about us who are ministering to all the heirs of salvation, though we see them not. In the Communion Service our Church teaches us to join our praises with that of "angels and archangels, and all the company of heaven," and the early Christians even hoped that they waited on the Church's seasons of worship, and glorified God with her. Nor are these thoughts without their direct influence on our faith in God and in His Son ; for the more we can enlarge our view of the next world the better. When we survey Almighty God surrounded by His Holy Angels, His thousand thousands of ministering spirits, and ten thousand times ten thousand standing before Him, the idea of His awful majesty rises before us more powerfully and impressively. We begin to see how little we are, how altogether mean and worthless in ourselves, and how high He is, and fearful. The very lowest of His angels is indefinitely above us in this our present state; how high then must be the Lord of angels! The very Seraphim hide their faces before His glory, while they praise Him; how shamefaced, then, should sinners be, when they come into His presence!

Lastly, it is a motive to our exertions in doing the will of God, to think that, if we attain to heaven, we shall become the fellows of the blessed angels. Indeed, what do we know of the courts of heaven, but as peopled by them? And therefore doubtless they are revealed to us that we may have something to fix our thoughts on when we look heavenwards. Heaven indeed is the palace of Almighty God, and of Him doubtless we must think in the first place; and again of His Son, our Saviour, who died for us, and who is manifested in the Gospels, in order that we may have something definite to look forward to. For the same cause also surely the angels are revealed to us, that heaven may be as little as possible an unknown place in our imaginations.

Let us then entertain such thoughts as these of the angels of God; and while we try to think of them worthily, let us beware lest we make the contemplation of them a mere feeling, a sort of luxury of the imagination. This world is to be a world of practice and labour; God reveals to us glimpses of the third heaven for our comfort; but if we indulge in these as the end of our present being, not trying day by day to purify ourselves for the future enjoyment of the realities, they become but a snare of the enemy. The services of religion day by day; obedience to God in our calling and in ordinary matters; endeavours to imitate our Saviour Christ in word ánd deed; constant prayer to Him and dependence on Him—these are the due preparations for receiving and profiting by His revelations.

WARFARE THE CONDITION OF VICTORY.

" And they worshipped Him, and returned to Jerusalem with great joy : and were continually in the Temple, praising and blessing God."—LUKE xxiv. 52.

FOR forty days after His resurrection did our Saviour Christ continue to remain below, at a distance from that glory which He had purchased. The glory was now His—He might have entered into it. Had he not had enough of earth? What should detain him here, instead of returning to His Father, and taking possession of His throne? He delayed in order to comfort and instruct those who had forsaken Him in the hour of trial. A time had just passed when their faith had all but failed, even while they had His pattern before their eyes; and a time, or rather a long period, was in prospect, when far heavier trials were to come upon them. Yet He was to be withdrawn. They hitherto understood not that suffering is the path to glory, and that none sit down upon Christ's throne who do not first overcome as He overcame. He stayed to impress upon them this lesson, lest they should still misunderstand the Gospel and fail a second time. "Ought not Christ," He said, "to suffer these things, and to enter into His glory?" And having taught them fully, after forty days, at length He rose above the troubles of this world. He rose above the atmosphere of sin, sorrow, and remorse, which broods over it. He entered into the region of peace and joy, into the pure light, the dwelling-place of angels, the courts of the Most High, through which resound continually the chants of blessed spirits and the praises of the Seraphim. There He entered, leaving His brethren in due season to come after Him, by the light of His example and the grace of His Spirit.

Yet, though the forty days was a long season for Him to stay, it was but a short time for the apostles to have Him among them. What feelings must have been theirs when He parted from them? So late found, so early lost again; hardly recognized, and then snatched away. The history of the two disciples at Emmaus was a figure or picture of the condition of the eleven. Their eyes were holden that they should not know Him while He talked with them for three years; then suddenly they were opened, and he forthwith vanished away. So had it been, I say, with all of them. "Have I been so long time with you, and yet hast thou not known Me, Philip?" had already been His expostulation with one of them. They had not known Him all through His ministry. Peter, indeed, had confessed Him to be the Christ, the Son of the living God; but even he showed inconsistency and change of mind in his comprehension of this great truth. They did not understand at that time who and what He was. But after His resurrection it was otherwise. Thomas touched His hands and His side, and said, "My Lord and my God!" In like manner they all began to know Him. At length they recognized Him as the Living Bread which came down from heaven, and was the life of the world. But hardly had they recognized Him, when He withdrew Himself once for all from their sight, never to see them again or to be seen by them on earth; never to visit earth again, till He comes at the last day to receive all saints unto Himself, and to take them to their rest. "So then, after the Lord had spoken unto them, He was received up into heaven, and sat on the right hand of God."

Late found, early lost. This perhaps was the Apostles' first feeling on His parting from them. And the like often happens here below. We understand our blessings just when about to forfeit them; prospects are most hopeful just when they are most hopelessly clouded. Years upon years we have had great privileges, the light of truth, the presence of holy men, opportunities of religious improvement, kind and tender parents. Yet we knew not, or thought not of our happiness; we valued not our gift; and then it is taken away just when we have begun to value it.

What a time must that forty days have been, during which, while He taught them, all His past teaching must have risen in their minds, and their thoughts then must have recurred in overpowering contrast to their thoughts now: His manner of life, His ministry, His discourses, His parables, His miracles, His meekness, gravity, incomprehensible majesty, the mystery of His thoughts and feelings; the agony, the scourge, the cross, the crown of thorns, the spear, the tomb; their despair, their unbelief, their perplexity, their amazement, their sudden joy, their triumph. All this was in their minds, and surely not the least at that awful hour when He led His breathless followers out to Bethany on the fortieth day. "He led them out as far as to Bethany, and He lifted up His hands and blessed them. And it came to pass while He blessed them, He was parted from them and carried up into heaven." Surely all His history, all His dealings with them, came before them, gathered up in that moment. Then, as they gazed upon that divine countenance and that dreadful form, every thought and feeling which they ever had had about Him, came upon them at once. He had gone through His work; theirs was to come—their work and their sufferings. He was leaving them just at the most critical time. When Elijah went up, Elisha said, "My father, my father, the chariot of Israel and the horsemen thereof!" With a like feeling might the apostles now gaze up into heaven, as if with the hope of arresting His ascent. Their Lord and their God, the light of their eyes, the stay of their hearts, the guide of their feet, was taken away. "My beloved had withdrawn Himself and was gone: my soul failed when He spake. I sought Him, but I could not find Him: I called Him, but He gave me no answer." Well might they use the Church's words, as now: "We beseech Thee, leave us not comfortless." O Thou who wast so gentle and familiar with us, who didst converse with us by the way, and sit at meat with us, and didst enter the vessel with us, and teach us on the Mount, and hear the malice of the Pharisees, and feast with Martha, and raise Lazarus, art Thou gone, and shall we see Thee no more? Yet so it was determined. Privileges they were to have, but not the same; and their thoughts henceforth were to be of another kind than heretofore. It was in vain wishing back what was past and over. They were but told, as they gazed, "This same Jesus, which is taken up from you into heaven, shall so come in like manner as ye have seen Him go into heaven."

Such are some of the feelings which the apostles may

have experienced on our Lord's ascension; but these are after all but human and ordinary, and of a kind which all of us can enter into. But other than these were sovereign with them at that solemn time; for upon the glorious ascension of their Lord, "they worshipped Him," says the text, "and returned to Jerusalem with *great joy*, and were continually in the Temple, praising and blessing God." Now, how was it, that when Nature would have wept, the apostles rejoiced? There was no sorrow in the apostles in spite of their loss, in spite of the prospect before them, but " great joy," and " continued praise and blessing." May we venture to surmise that this rejoicing was the high temper of the brave and noble-minded, who have faced danger in idea, and are prepared for it? Christ in forty days trains His apostles to be bold and patient, instead of cowards. "They mourned and wept" at the beginning of the season, but at the end they are full of courage for the good fight; their spirits mount high with their Lord, and when He is received out of their sight, and their own trial begins, "they return to Jerusalem with great joy, and are continually in the Temple, praising and blessing God."

For Christ surely had taught them what it was to have their treasure in heaven; and they rejoiced not that their Lord was gone, but that their hearts had gone with Him. Their hearts were no longer on earth, they were risen aloft. Before He was seized they had said to Him, "Lord, whither goest Thou? Lord, we know not whither Thou goest." They could but follow Him to the grave, and there mourn, for they knew no better; but now they saw Him ascend on high, and in spirit they ascended with Him. Mary wept at the grave because she thought enemies had taken Him away, and she knew not where they had laid Him. "Where your treasure is, there will your heart be also." Strengthened, then, with this knowledge, they were able to face those trials which Christ had first undergone Himself, and had foretold as their portion. "Whither I go," He had said to St. Peter, "thou canst not follow Me now, but thou shalt follow Me afterwards." And He told them, "They shall put you out of the synagogues. Yea, the time cometh that whosoever killeth you will think that he doeth God service." That time was now coming, and they were able to rejoice in what so troubled them forty days before. For they understood the promise, "To him that overcometh, will I grant to sit with Me in My throne, even as I also overcame, and am sat down with My Father in His throne."

It will be well if we take this lesson to ourselves, and learn that great truth which the apostles shrank from at first, but at length rejoiced in. Christ suffered, and entered into joy: so did they, in their measure, after Him: and in our measure, so do we. It is written, that

S

"through much tribulation we must enter into the Kingdom of God." God has all things in His own hands. He can spare, He can inflict: He often spares (may He spare us still!), but He often tries us—in one way or another He tries every one. At some time or other of the life of every one there is pain, and sorrow, and trouble. So it is, and the sooner, perhaps, we can look upon it as a law of our Christian condition, the better. One generation comes, and then another. They issue forth and succeed like leaves in spring; and in all, this law is observable. They are tried, and then they triumph; they are humbled, and then are exalted; they overcome the world, and then they sit down on Christ's throne. . . . . Let us try to accustom ourselves to this view of the subject. The whole church, all elect souls, each in its turn is called to this necessary work. Once it was the turn of others, and now it is our turn. Once it was the apostles' turn. It was St. Paul's turn once. He had all cares on him at once—covered from head to foot with cares, as Job was with sores. And, as if all this were not enough, he had a thorn in his flesh added—some personal discomfort ever with him. Yet he did his part well: he was as a strong and bold wrestler in his day, and at the close of it was able to say, " I have fought a good fight, I have finished my course, I have kept the faith." And after him, the excellent of the earth, the white-robed army of martyrs and the cheerful company of confessors, each in his turn, each in his day, likewise played the man. And so down to this very time, when faith has well-nigh failed, first one and then another have been called out to exhibit before the Great King. It is as though all of us were allowed to stand around His throne at once, and He called on first this man, and then that, to take up the chant by himself, each in his turn having to repeat the melody which his brethren have before gone through; or as if He held a solemn dance to His honour in the courts of heaven, and each had by himself to perform some one and the same solemn and graceful movement at a signal given; or as if it were some trial of strength, or of agility, and, while the ring of bystanders beheld and applauded, we in succession, one by one, were actors in the pageant. Such is our state. Angels are looking on. Christ has gone before. Christ has given us an example, that we may follow His steps. He went through far more, infinitely more, than we can be called to suffer. Our brethren have gone through much more, and they seem to encourage us by their success, and to sympathise in our essay. Now it is our turn, and all ministering spirits keep silence and look on. Oh, let not your foot slip, or your eye be false, or your ear dull, or your attention flagging! Be not dispirited; be not afraid; keep a good heart; be bold; draw not back; you will be carried through. Whatever troubles come on you, of mind, body, or estate; from within or from without; from chance or from intent; from friends or foes; whatever your trouble be; though you be lonely, O children of a heavenly Father, be not afraid! Quit you like men in your day; and when it is over Christ will receive you to Himself, and your heart shall rejoice, and your joy no man taketh from you. Christ is already in that place of peace which is all in all. He is on the right hand of God—He is hidden in the brightness of the radiance which issues from the everlasting throne—He is in the very abyss of peace, where there is no voice of tumult or distress, but a deep stillness—stillness, that greatest and most awful of all goods which we can fancy— that most perfect of joys, the utter, profound ineffable tranquillity of the divine essence. He has entered into His rest. Oh, how great a good will it be, if, when this troublesome life is over, we in our turn also enter into that same rest; if the time shall one day come when we shall enter into His tabernacle above, and hide ourselves under the shadow of His wings! Here we are tossing upon the sea, and the wind is contrary. All through the day we are tried and tempted in various ways. We cannot speak, think, or act, but infirmity and sin are at hand. But in the unseen world, where Christ has entered, all is peace. "There is no more death, neither sorrow nor crying, neither any more pain; for the former things are passed away." Nor any more sin; nor any more guilt; no more remorse; no more punishment; no more penitence; no more trial; no infirmity to depress us; no affection to mislead us; no passion to transport us; no prejudice to blind us; no sloth, no pride, no envy, no strife; but the light of God's countenance, and a pure river of water of life, clear as crystal, proceeding out of the throne. That is our home. Here we are but on pilgrimage, and Christ is calling us home. He calls us to His many mansions, which He has prepared. And the Spirit and the Bride call us too, and all things will be ready for us by the time of our coming. "Seeing, then, that we have a great High Priest, that is passed into the heavens, Jesus the Son of God, let us hold fast our profession;" seeing we have "so great a cloud of witnesses, let us lay aside every weight;" "let us labour to enter into our rest;" "let us come boldly unto the Throne of Grace, that we may obtain mercy, and find grace to help in time of need."

SECRECY AND SUDDENNESS OF DIVINE VISITATIONS.

"The kingdom of God cometh not with observation."—
LUKE xvii. 20.

THE event in our Saviour's infancy which we this day celebrate, is His presentation in the Temple, when His Virgin Mother was ceremonially purified. It was made memorable at the time by the hymns and praises of Simeon and Anna, to whom He was then revealed. And there were others besides these, who had been "looking for redemption in Jerusalem," who were also vouchsafed a sight of the Infant Saviour. But the chief importance of this event consists in its being a fulfilment of prophecy. Malachi had announced the Lord's visitation of His Temple in these words: "The Lord, whom ye seek, shall suddenly come to His Temple;" words which, though variously fulfilled during His ministry, had their first accomplishment in the humble ceremony commemorated on this day. And when we consider the grandeur of the prediction, and how unostentatious this accomplishment was, we are led to muse upon God's ways, and to draw useful lessons for ourselves.

I say, we are to-day reminded of the noiseless course of God's providence; His tranquil accomplishment in the course of nature of great events, long designed; and again, the suddenness and stillness of His visitations. Consider what the occurrence in question consists in. A little child is brought to the Temple, as all first-born children were brought. There is nothing here uncommon or striking, so far. His parents are with Him, poor people, bringing the offering of pigeons or doves, for the purification of the mother. They are met in the Temple by an old man, who takes the child in his arms, offers a thanksgiving to God, and blesses the parents; and next are joined by a woman of a great age, a widow of eighty-four years, who had exceeded the time of useful service, and seemed to be but a fit prey for death. She gives thanks also, and speaks concerning the child to other persons who are present. Then all retire.

Now there is evidently nothing great or impressive in this; nothing to excite the feelings or interest the imagination. We know what the world thinks of such a group as I have described. The weak and helpless, whether from age or infancy, it looks upon negligently and passes by. Yet all this that happened was really the solemn fulfilment of an ancient and emphatic prophecy.

The infant in arms was the Saviour of the world, the rightful heir come in the guise of a stranger to visit His own house. The Scripture had said: "The Lord, whom ye seek, shall suddenly come to His Temple; but who may abide the day of His coming? and who may stand when He appeareth?" He had now taken possession. And further, the old man who took the child in his arms had upon him gifts of the Holy Ghost; had been promised the blessed sight of his Lord before his death; came into the Temple by heavenly guidance, and now had within him thoughts unutterable, of joy, thankfulness, and hope, strangely mixed with awe, fear, painful wonder, and "bitterness of spirit." Anna too, the woman of four score and four years, was a prophetess; and the bystanders to whom she spoke were the true Israel, who were looking out in faith for the predicted redemption of mankind, those who (in the words of the prophecy) "sought," and in prospect "delighted" in the "messenger" of God's covenant of mercy. "The glory of this latter house shall be greater than of the former," was the announcement of another prophecy. Behold the glory! A little child and his parents, two aged persons, and a congregation without name or memorial. "The kingdom of God cometh not with observation."

Such has ever been the manner of His visitations, in the destruction of His enemies as well as in the deliverance of His own people; silent, sudden, unforeseen, as regards the world, though predicted in the face of all men, and in their measure comprehended and waited for by His true Church. Such a visitation was the flood. Noah, a preacher of righteousness, but the multitude of sinners judicially blinded. "They did eat, they drank, they married wives, they were given in marriage, until the day that Noah entered into the ark, and the flood came and destroyed them all." Such was the overthrow of Sodom and Gomorrah. "Likewise as it was in the days of Lot, they did eat, they drank, they bought, they sold, they planted, they builded; but the same day that Lot went out of Sodom, it rained fire and brimstone from heaven, and destroyed them all." Again: "The horse of Pharaoh went in with his chariots and with his horsemen into the sea; and the Lord brought again the waters of the sea upon them." The overthrow of Sennacherib was also silent and sudden, when his vast army least expected it. "The angel of the Lord went forth and smote in the camp of the Assyrians a hundred four score and five thousand." Belshazzar and Babylon were surprised in the midst of the king's great feast to his thousand lords. While Nebuchadnezzar boasted, his reason was suddenly taken from him. While the multitude shouted with impious flattery at Herod's speech, then "the angel of the Lord smote him, because he gave not God the glory." Whether we take the first or the final judgment upon Jerusalem, both visitations were foretold as sudden. Of the former, Isaiah had declared it should come " suddenly — at an instant." Of the latter, Malachi : " The Lord, whom ye seek, shall suddenly come to His Temple." And such too will be His final visitation of the whole earth. Men will be at their work, in the city and in the field, and it will overtake them like a thunder-cloud. " Two women shall be grinding together; the one shall be taken, and the other left. Two men shall be in the field; the one shall be taken, and the other left."

And it is impossible that it should be otherwise, in spite of warnings ever so clear, considering how the world goes on in every age. Men who are plunged in the pursuits of active life are no judges of its course and tendency on the whole. They confuse great events with little, and measure the importance of objects as in perspective, by the mere standard of nearness or remoteness. It is only at a distance that one can take in the outlines and features of a whole country. It is but holy Daniel, solitary among princes, or Elijah, the recluse of Mount Carmel, who can withstand Baal, or forecast the time of God's providences among the nations. To the multitude all things continue to the end as they were from the beginning of the creation. The business of state affairs, the movements of society, the course of nature, proceed as ever, till the moment of Christ's coming. "The sun was risen upon the earth," bright as usual, on that very day of wrath on which Sodom was destroyed. Men cannot believe their own time is an especially wicked time; for with Scripture unstudied, and hearts untrained in holiness, they have no standard to compare it with. They take warning from no troubles or perplexities, which rather carry them away to search out the earthly causes of them, and the possible remedies. When the power of Assyria became great (we might suppose), the Jews had a plain call to repentance. Far from it; they were led to set power against power, they took refuge against Assyria in Egypt, their old enemy. Probably they reasoned themselves into what they considered a temperate, enlightened, cheerful view of national affairs; perhaps they might consider the growth of Assyria an advantage rather than otherwise, as balancing the power of Egypt, and so tending to their own security. Certain it is, we find them connecting themselves first with one kingdom and then with the other, as men who could read (as they thought) "the signs of the times," and made some pretence to political wisdom. Thus the world proceeds till wrath comes upon it, and there is no escape. "To-morrow," they say, "shall be as this day, and much more abundant."

And in the midst of this their revel, whether of sensual pleasure, or of ambition, or of covetousness, or of pride and self-esteem, the decree goes forth to destroy. The decree goes forth in secret; angels hear it, and the favoured few on earth; but no public event takes place to give the world warning. The earth was doomed to the flood one hundred and twenty years before "the decree brought forth," or men heard of it (Zeph. ii. 2). The waters of Babylon had been turned, and the conqueror was marching into the city when Belshazzar made his great feast. Pride infatuates man, and self-indulgence and luxury work their way unseen—like some smouldering fire, which for a while leaves the outward forms of things unaltered. At length the decayed mass cannot hold together, and breaks by its own weight, or on some slight and accidental external violence. . . . .

Thoughts such as the foregoing are profitable at all times; for in every age the world is profane and blind, and God hides His Providence, yet carries it forward. Let us then turn this festival to account by taking it as the memorial-day of His visitations. Let us, from the events it celebrates, lay up deep in our hearts the recollection how mysteriously little things are in this world connected with great; how single moments, improved or wasted, are the salvation or ruin of all-important interests. Let us bear the thought upon us when we come to worship in God's house, that any such season of service may, for what we know, be wonderfully connected with some ancient purpose of His, announced before we were born, and have its determinate bearing on our eternal welfare. Let us fear to miss the Saviour, while Simeon and Anna find Him. Let us remember that He was not manifested again in the Temple, except once, for thirty years, while a whole generation who were alive at His first visitation died off in the interval. Let us carry this thought into our daily conduct, considering that, for what we know, our hope of salvation may in the event materially depend on our avoiding this or that momentary sin. And further, from the occurrences of this day, let us take comfort when we despond about the state of the Church. Perhaps we see not God's tokens; we see neither prophet nor teacher remaining to His people; darkness falls over the earth, and no protesting voice is heard. Yet, granting things to be at the very worst, yet, when Christ was presented in the Temple, the age knew as little of it as it knows of His Providence now. Rather, the worse our condition is, the nearer to us is the Advent of our Deliverer. Even though He is silent, doubt not that His army is on the march towards us. He is coming through the sky, and has even now His camp upon the outskirts of our own world.

Nay, though He still for a while keep His seat at His

Father's right hand, yet surely He sees all that is going on, and waits, and will not fail His hour of vengeance. Shall He not hear His own elect, when they cry day and night to Him? His services of prayer and praise continue, and are scorned by the multitude. Day by day, festival by festival, fast after fast, season by season, they continue according to His ordinance, and are scorned. But the greater His delay, the heavier will be His vengeance, and the more complete the deliverance of His people.

THE VISIBLE TEMPLE.

"Whether is the greater, the gold, or the Temple that sanctifieth the gold?"—MATT. xxiii. 17.

A TEMPLE there has been upon earth, a Spiritual Temple, made up of living stones; a Temple, as I may say, composed of souls; a Temple with God for its Light, and Christ for the High Priest; with wings of angels for its arches, with saints and teachers for its pillars, and with worshippers for its pavement. Such a Temple has been on earth ever since the Gospel was first preached. This unseen, secret, mysterious, Spiritual Temple exists everywhere throughout the Kingdom of Christ, in all places, as perfect in one place as if it were not in another. Wherever there is faith and love, this Temple is; faith and love, with the name of Christ, are as heavenly charms and spells to make present to us this Divine Temple in every part of Christ's kingdom. This Temple is invisible, but it is perfect and real because it is invisible, and gains nothing in perfection by possessing visible tokens. There needs no outward building to meet the eye in order to make it more of a Temple than it is in itself. God, and Christ, and angels, and souls—are not these a heavenly court, all perfect, to which this world can add nothing? Though faithful Christians worship without splendour, without show, in a homely and rude way, still their worship is as acceptable to God, as excellent, as holy, as though they worshipped in the public view of men, and with all the glory and riches of the world.

Such was the Church in its beginning, "built upon the foundation of apostles and prophets, Jesus Christ Himself being the chief corner stone;" "builded together for an habitation of God through the Spirit." In the apostles' lifetime it was poor and persecuted, and the Holy Temple was all but invisible. There were no edifying rites, no various ceremonies, no rich music, no high Cathedrals, no mystic vestments, no solemn altars, no stone, or marble, or metals, or jewels, or woods of cost, or fine linen, to signify outwardly, and to honour duly the Heavenly Temple in which we stand and serve. The place where our Lord and Saviour first celebrated the Holy Sacrament of the Eucharist was the upper room of a house, hired too, or used for the occasion. That in which the apostles and the holy women waited for the promised coming of the Comforter was also "an upper room; and that also in which St. Paul preached at Troas was an upper chamber, "where they were gathered together." What other places of worship do we hear of? The water-side, out in the open air; as at Philippi, where, we are told, "on the Sabbath," St. Paul and his companions "went out of the city by a river-side, where prayer was wont to be made." And the sea-shore: "They all brought us on our way, with wives and children, till we were out of the city; and we kneeled down on the shore, and prayed." And St. Peter was in prayer on the house-top.; and St. Paul and St. Silas sang their hymns and praises in prison, with their feet in the stocks; and St. Philip baptized the Ethiopian eunuch in the desert. Yet, wherever they were, whether in prison, or on the house-top, or in the wilderness, or by the river-side, or on the sea-shore, or in a private room, God and Christ were with them. The Spirit of Grace was there, the Temple of God was around them. They were come into the mystical Sion, and to the Heavenly Jerusalem, and to an innumerable company of angels, and to the spirits of the just. There needed not gold, nor jewels, nor costly array for those who had what, according to the text, was greater—who had the Temple. It might be right and fitting, if possible, to have these precious things also, but it was not necessary; for which was the greater? Such things did not make the Temple

T

more holy, but became themselves holy by being used for the Temple. The gold did not sanctify the Temple, for the Temple was greater, and sanctified the gold. Gold is a thing of nought without Christ's presence; and with His presence, as in the days of His earthly ministry, it might be dispensed with.

The case is the same as regards the immediate successors of the apostles, who were in still more forlorn circumstances, as regards worship, than the apostles themselves. The Christians who came after them were obliged to worship in caves and tombs, to save their lives from their persecutors. In the eastern and southern parts, where the apostles and the first converts lived, before the glad sound of the Gospel had reached these northern and distant countries, they were accustomed to bury in caves dug out of the rock. Long galleries there are still remaining, in some places for miles underground, on each side of which the dead were placed. There the poor persecuted Christians met for worship, and that by night. Or the great people of the time built for themselves high and stately tombs above ground, as large as houses for the living. Here too, in the darkness and solitude of the night, did the saints worship; or in the depth of some wood, perhaps, where no one was likely to discover them. Such were the places in which the Invisible Temple was revealed in times of heathenism, and who shall say that it wanted aught of outward show to make it perfect?

This is true, and ever to be borne in mind; and yet no one can deny, on the other hand, that a great object of Christ's coming was to subdue this world, to claim it as His own, to assert His rights as its Master, to destroy the usurped dominion of the enemy, to show Himself to all men, and to take possession. He is that mustard-tree which was destined silently to spread and to shadow all lands; He is that leaven which was secretly to make its way through the mass of human opinions and institutions till the whole was leavened. Heaven and earth had hitherto been separate. His gracious purpose was to make them one, and that by making earth like heaven. He was in the world from the beginning, and man worshipped other gods; He came into the world in the flesh, and the world knew Him not; He came unto His own, and His own received Him not. But He came in order to *make* them receive Him, know Him, worship Him. He came to absorb this world into Himself; that, as He was light, so it might be light also. When He came He had not a place to lay His head; but He came to make Himself a place, to make Himself a home, to make Himself houses, to fashion for Himself a glorious dwelling out of this whole world, which the powers of evil had taken captive. He came in the dark, in the dark night was He born, in a cave underground; in a cave where cattle were stabled, there was He housed; in a rude manger was He laid. There first He laid His head; but He meant not, blessed be His name! He meant not there to remain for ever. He did not resign Himself to that obscurity; He came into that cave to leave it. The King of the Jews was born to claim the kingdom—yea, rather, the Hope of all nations and the King of the whole earth, the King of kings, and the Lord of lords; and He gave not "sleep to His eyes, or slumber to His eyelids," till He had changed His manger for a royal throne, and His grot for high palaces. Lift up your eyes, my brethren, and look round, for it is fulfilled at this day; yea, long ago, for many ages and in many countries. "Wisdom hath builded her house, she hath hewn out her seven pillars." Where is the grot? Where the stall for cattle? Where the manger? Where the grass and straw? Where the unseemly furniture of that despised place? Is it possible that the Eternal Son should have been born in a hole of the earth? Was the great miracle there wrought, whereby a pure and spotless virgin brought forth God? Strange condescension undergone to secure a strange triumph! He purposed to change the earth, and He began "in the lowest pit, in a place of darkness, and in the deep." All was to be by Him renewed, and He availed Himself of nothing that was, that out of nothing

He might make all things. He was not born in the Temple of Jerusalem; He abhorred the palace of David. He laid Himself on the damp earth in the cold night, a light shining in a dark place; till by the virtue that went out of Him He should create a Temple worthy of His name.

And lo! in omen of the future, even in His cradle, the rich and wise of the earth seek Him with gold, and frankincense, and myrrh, as an offering. And He puts aside the swaddling clothes, and takes instead "a coat without seam, woven from the top throughout." And He changes water into wine; and Levi feasts Him; and Zaccheus receives Him; and Mary anoints His head. Pass a few generations, and the whole face of things is changed; the earth is covered with His Temples; as it has been for ages. Go where you will you will find the eternal mountains hewn and fashioned into shrines where He may dwell, who was an outcast in the days of His flesh. Rivers and mines pay tribute of their richest jewels; forests are searched for their choicest woods; the skill of man is put to task to use what Nature furnishes. Go through the countries where His name is known, and you will find all that is rarest and most wonderful in nature or art has been consecrated to Him. King's palaces are poor, whether in architecture or in decoration, compared with the shrines which have been reared to Him.

The invisible Temple has become visible. As on a misty day the gloom gradually melts and the sun brightens, so have the glories of the spiritual world lit up this world below. The dull and cold earth is penetrated by the rays. All around we see glimpses of reflections of those heavenly things which the elect of God shall one day see face to face. The kingdoms of this world are become the kingdoms of our Lord and of His Christ. "The Temple has sanctified the gold," and the prophecies made to the Church have been fulfilled to the letter. "The glory of Lebanon" has been "given unto it, the excellency of Carmel and Sharon." "The glory of Lebanon, the fir-tree, the pine-tree, and the box together, to beautify the place of His sanctuary, and to make the place of His feet glorious. The multitude of camels have covered it, the dromedaries of Midian and Ephah: all they from Sheba have come; they have brought gold and incense, and shown forth the praise of the Lord." "The labour of Egypt, and merchandize of Ethiopia, and of the Sabeans, men of stature, have come over to it, in chains have they come over; they have fallen down, they have made supplication."

And He has made Him a Temple, not only out of inanimate things, but of men also as parts of it. Not gold and silver, jewels and fine linen, and skill of man to use them, make the House of God; but worshippers, the souls and bodies of men whom He has redeemed. Not souls alone, He takes possession of the whole man, body as well as soul; for St. Paul says, "I beseech you therefore, brethren, by the mercies of God, that ye present your *bodies* a living sacrifice, holy, acceptable unto God, which is your reasonable service." And He claims us as His own, not one by one, but altogether, as one great company. Our tongues must preach Him, and our voices sing of Him, and our countenances beam of Him, and our gait herald him. And hence arise joint worship, forms of prayer, ceremonies of devotion, the course of services, orders of ministers, holy vestments, solemn music, and other things of a like nature; all which are, as it were, the incoming into this world of the invisible kingdom of Christ, the fruit of its influence, the sample of its power, the earnest of its victories, the means of its manifestations.

Things temporal have their visible establishment. Kings' courts and palaces, councils and armies, have dazzled the multitude, and blinded them, till they worshipped them as idols. Such is our nature, we must have something to look up to. We cannot help admiring *something;* and if there is nothing good to admire we admire what is bad. When then men see proud Babel set up on high, with all her show and pomp, when they see or hear of great cities with their stately mansions, the streets swarming with chariots and horses innumerable, and the shops filled with splendid wares, and great men and women richly dressed, with many attendants, and men crying, "Bow the knee," and soldiers in bright array, with the sound of the trumpets and other military music, and other things which one could mention were it reverent to be particular, simple men are tempted to look up to all this as the summit of perfection and blessedness; nay, as I have said, to worship what seems to them, though they do not express it, the presence of the Unseen. Hence come in servility, coveting, jealousy, ambition; men wish to be great in this world, and try to be great; they aim at riches, or they lie in wait for promotion. Christ, then, in order to counteract this evil, has mercifully set up His own court and His own polity, that men might have something to fix their eyes upon of a more divine and holy character than the world can supply; that poverty, at least, might divide men's admiration with riches; that meekness might be set up on high as well as pride, and sanctity become our ambition as well as luxury. Saintly bishops with their clergy, officials of all kinds, religious bodies, austere Nazarites, prayer and praise without ceasing—all this hath Christ mercifully set up, to outshine the fascinations of the world. So ran the promise, "I have set watchmen upon thy walls, O Jerusalem! which shall never hold their peace day nor night." "Sing unto the Lord a new song, and His praise from the end of the earth; ye that go down to the sea and all that is therein. . . . Let the wilderness and the cities thereof lift up their voice, the villages that Kedar doth inhabit; let the inhabitants of the rock sing, let them shout from the top of the mountains. Let them give glory unto the Lord, and declare His praise in the islands." And these words began to have their fulfilment even from the time that Christ came; for, as I said when I began, St. Paul and St. Silas *sang* in the prison; and when he and his party left Tyre, the men, women, and children, who accompanied them out, kneeled down on the shore with them, and prayed. Such were the forms of worship in the beginning; till, as time went on, the Church, like some fair tree, put out her branches and foliage, and stood complete in all manner of holy symbols and spiritual ordinances, an outward sign of that unseen Temple in which Christ had dwelt from the first.

In conclusion, let me observe, that such a view as has been taken of the connection of the ritual of religion with its spiritual and invisible powers, will enable us to form a right estimate of things external, and keep us both from a curious and superstitious use and an arrogant neglect of them. The Temple is greater than the gold; therefore, care not though the gold be away: it sanctifies it;

therefore cherish the gold while it is present. Christ is with us, though there be no outward show. Suppose all the comely appendages of our worship stripped off; yet, where two or three are gathered together in His Name, He is in the midst of them. Be it a cottage or the open fields, or even a prison or a dungeon, Christ can be there, and will be there if His servants are there. Stone walls do not make a church. Though they were in the vastest, noblest, richest building on earth, still Christ would not be with those who preach another gospel than that which He delivered once for all. This is the very point I am insisting on. It is the Temple which sanctifieth the gold; it is nothing but the invisible and heavenly Presence which sanctifieth any place or anything. Magnificent or mean, costly or common, it alone sanctifies either worshippers or building. As it avails not to have sumptuous churches without the Spirit of Christ, so it is but a mockery to have large congregations, eloquent preachers, and much excitement, if that gracious Spirit is away. But where He really places His *Name*, there, be the spot a palace or a cottage, it is sacred and glorious. He who once lay in a manger will still condescend to manifest Himself anywhere, as He did in primitive times. No indignities can be done to Him who inhabiteth eternity. "Heaven is His throne, and earth His footstool." The very heaven of heavens cannot contain Him; much less any house which we can build. High and low is alike to Him. . . . .

They who profane His presence, who treat its resting-place as a common house, and make free with it, these men do not hurt Christ, but they hurt themselves. The Temple is greater than the gold.

And while He is displeased with the profane, He accepts our offerings made in faith, whether they be greater or less. He accepts our gold and our silver, not to honour Himself thereby, but in mercy to us. When Mary poured the ointment on His head, it was her advantage, not His. He praised her, and said, "She hath done what she could."

Every one must do his best; he must attend his best. If we did all, it would be little—not worthy of Him. If we do little, it may suffice to show our faith, and He in His mercy will accept whatever we can offer. He will accept what we prefer giving to Him instead of giving to ourselves. When, instead of spending money on our own homes, we spend it on His house; when we prefer that He should have the gold and silver to our having it, we do not make our worship more spiritual, but we bring Christ nearer to us; we show that we are in earnest—we evidence our faith. It requires very little of true faith and love to feel an unwillingness to spend money on one's self. Fine dresses, fine houses, fine furniture, fine establishments, are painful to a true Christian; they create misgivings in his mind whether his portion is with the saints or with the world. Rather he will feel it suitable to lay out his money in God's service—to feed the hungry, to clothe the naked, to educate the young, to spread the knowledge of the truth, and, among other pious objects, to build and to decorate the visible house of God.

"Remember me, O my God, concerning this, and wipe not out my good deeds that I have done for the house of my God, and for the offices thereof." Such was Nehemiah's prayer when he had been stirred up to cleanse the sanctuary. May God in His mercy grant that our outward show does not outstrip our inward progress; that whatever gift, rare or beautiful, we introduce here, may be but a figure of inward beauty and unseen sanctity ornamenting our hearts. Hearts are the true shrine wherein Christ must dwell. "The King's daughter is all glorious within;" and when we are repenting of past sin, and cleansing ourselves from all defilements of flesh and spirit, and perfecting holiness in the fear of the Lord, then, and then only, may we safely employ ourselves in brightening, embellishing, and making glorious the dwelling-place of His invisible presence, doing it with that severity, gravity, and awe, which a chastened heart and sober thoughts will teach us.

THE RESURRECTION OF THE BODY.

'Now that the dead are raised, even Moses showed at the bush, when he calleth the Lord the God of Abraham, and the God of Isaac, and the God of Jacob. For He is not a God of the dead, but of the living; for all live unto Him."—LUKE xx. 37, 38.

THESE words of our Saviour show us how much more there is in Scripture than at first sight appears. God spoke to Moses in the burning bush, and called Himself "the God of Abraham;" and Christ tells us that in this simple announcement was contained the promise that Abraham should rise again from the dead. In truth, if we may say it with reverence, the All-wise, All-knowing God, cannot speak without meaning many things at once. He sees the end from the beginning; He understands the numberless connexions and relations of all things one with another. Every word of His is full of instruction, looking many ways; and though it is not often given to us to know these various senses, and we are not at liberty to attempt lightly to imagine them, yet, as far as they are told us, and as far as we may reasonably infer them, we must thankfully accept them. Look at Christ's words, and this same character of them strikes us: whatever He says is fruitful in meaning, and refers to many things. It is well to keep this in mind when we read Scripture, for it may hinder us from self-conceit, from studying it in an arrogant, critical temper, and from giving over reading it, as if we had got from it all that can be learned.

When God called Himself the God of Abraham, Isaac, and Jacob, He implied that those holy patriarchs were still alive, though they were no more seen on earth. This may seem evident at first sight; but it may be asked how the text proves that their *bodies* would live; for, if their souls were still living, that would be enough to account for their being still called, in the Book of Exodus, servants of God. This is the point to be considered. Our blessed Lord seems to tell us that in some sense or other Abraham's body might be considered still alive as a pledge of his resurrection, though it was dead in the common sense in which we apply the word. His announcement is, Abraham shall rise from the dead, because in truth he is still alive. He cannot in the end be held under the power of the grave, more than a sleeping man can be kept from waking. Abraham is still alive in the dust, though not risen thence. He is alive, because all God's saints live to Him, though they seem to perish.

It may seem a paradox to say that our bodies even when dead are still alive; but since our Lord seems to countenance us in saying so, I will say it, though a strange saying, because it has an instructive meaning. We are apt to talk about our bodies as if we knew how or what they really were, whereas we only know what our eyes tell us. They seem to grow, to come to maturity, to decay; but after all we know no more about them than meets our senses, and there is doubtless much which God sees in our material frames which we cannot see. We have no direct cognizance of what may be called the substantive existence of the body, only of its accidents. Again, we are apt to speak of soul and body as if we could distinguish between them, and knew much about them; but for the most part we use words without meaning. It is useful indeed to make the distinction, and Scripture makes it; but after all, the Gospel speaks of our nature, in a religious sense, as one. Soul and body make up one man, which is born once and never dies. Philosophers of old time thought the soul indeed might live for ever, but that the body perished at death; but Christ tells us otherwise. He tells us the body will live for ever. In the text He seems to intimate that it never really dies; that we lose sight indeed of what we are accustomed to see; but that God still sees the elements of it which are not exposed to our senses.

God graciously called Himself the God of Abraham. He did not say the God of Abraham's soul, but simply of Abraham. He blest Abraham, and He gave him eternal life; not to his soul only without his body, but to Abraham as one man. And so He is *our* God, and it is not given us to distinguish between what He does for our different natures, spiritual and material. These are mere words. Each of us may feel himself to be one, and that one being, in all its substantial parts and attributes, will never die. . . . . . .

Among the wise men of the heathen, as I have said, it was usual to speak slightingly and contemptuously of the mortal body; they knew no better. They thought it scarcely a part of their real selves, and fancied they should be in a better condition without it. Nay, they considered it to be the cause of their sinning; that the soul of man was pure, and the material body was gross, and defiled the soul. We have been taught the truth, viz., that sin is a disease of *our minds*, of ourselves; and that all of us, not body alone, but soul and body, is naturally corrupt, and that Christ has redeemed and cleansed whatever we are, sinful soul and body. Accordingly their chief hope in death was the notion they should be rid of their body. Feeling they were sinful, and not knowing how, they laid the charge on their body; and knowing they were badly circumstanced here, they thought death perchance might be a change for the better. Not that they rested on the hope of returning to a God and Father; but they thought to be unshackled from the earth, and able to do what they would. It was consistent with this slighting of their earthly tabernacle that they burned the dead bodies of their friends; not burying them, as we do, but consuming them, as a mere worthless case of what had been precious, and was then an encumbrance to the ground. Far different is the temper which the glorious light of the Gospel teaches us. Our bodies shall rise again and live for ever; they may not be irreverently handled. How they will rise we know not; but surely, if the word of Scripture be true, the body from which the soul departed shall come to life. . . . . We cannot determine in what exact sense our bodies will be on the resurrection the same as they are at present, but we cannot harm ourselves by taking God's declaration simply, and acting upon it. And it is as believing this comfortable truth that the Christian Church put aside that old irreverence of the funeral pile, and consecrated the ground for the reception of the saints that sleep. We deposit our departed friends calmly and thoughtfully in faith, not ceasing to love or remember that which once lived among us, but marking the place where it lies, as believing that God has set His seal upon it, and His angels guard it. His angels surely guard the bodies of His servants; Michael the archangel thinking it no unworthy task to preserve them from the powers of evil. . . . .

And in this view what a venerable and fearful place is a church, in and around which the dead are deposited! Truly it is chiefly sacred as being the spot where God has for ages manifested Himself to His servants; but add to this the thought that it is the actual resting-place of those very servants, through successive times, who still live unto Him! The dust around us will one day become animate. We may ourselves be dead long before, and not see it. We ourselves may elsewhere be buried, and should it be our exceeding blessedness to rise to life eternal, we may rise in other places, far in the east or west. But as God's work is sure, what is sown is raised. The earth to earth, ashes to ashes, dust to dust, shall become glory to glory, and life to the living God, and a true incorruptible image of the spirit made perfect. Here the saints sleep, here they shall rise. A great sight will a Christian country then be, if earth remains what it is, when holy places pour out the worshippers who have for generations kept vigil therein, waiting through the long night for the bright coming of Christ. And, if this be so, what pious, composed thoughts should be ours when we enter churches! God indeed is everywhere, and His angels go to and fro; yet can they be more worthily employed in their condescending care of man, than where good men sleep? In the service of the Communion we magnify God together with angels and archangels, and all the company of heaven. Surely there is more meaning in this than we know of. What a "dreadful" place would this appear if our eyes were opened as those of Elisha's servant: "This is none other than the house of God, and this is the gate of heaven!"

SCRIPTURE A RECORD OF HUMAN SORROW.

"There is at Jerusalem by the sheep-market a pool, which is called in the Hebrew tongue Bethesda, having five porches. In these lay a great multitude of impotent folk, of blind, halt, withered, waiting for the moving of the water."—JOHN v. 2, 3.

WHAT a scene of misery this pool of Bethesda must have presented! of pain and sickness triumphing unto death; the "blind, halt, withered, and impotent," persuaded by the hope of cure to disclose their sufferings in the eye of day in one large company! This pool was endued at certain times with a wonderful virtue by the descent of an angel into it, so that its waters effected the cure of the first who stepped into it, whatever was his disease. However, I shall not speak of this wonderful pool, nor of our Saviour's miracle wrought there upon the man who had no one to put him in before the rest, when the water was troubled, and had been for thirty-eight years afflicted with his infirmity. Without entering into these subjects, let us take the text as it stands, and deduce a lesson from it.

There lay about the pool "a great multitude of impotent folk, of blind, halt, and withered." This is a painful picture, such as we do not like to dwell upon, —a picture of a chief kind of human suffering, bodily disease; one which suggests to us and typifies all other suffering—the most obvious fulfilment of that curse which Adam's fall brought upon his descendants. Now it must strike every one, who thinks at all about it, that the Bible is full of such descriptions of human misery. We know it also abounds in accounts of human sin; but not to speak of these, it abounds in accounts of human distress and sufferings, of our miserable condition, of the vanity, unprofitableness, and trials of life. The Bible begins with the history of the curse pronounced on the earth and man; it ends with the book of Revelation, a portion of Scripture fearful for its threats, and its prediction of judgments. Spite of the peculiar promises made to the Church in Christ our Saviour, yet as regards the world, the volume of inspiration is still a dreary record, "written within and without with lamentations, and mourning, and woe." And further, you will observe that it seems to drop what might be said in favour of this life, and enlarges on the unpleasant side of it. The history passes quickly from the garden of Eden, to dwell on the sufferings which followed when our first parents were expelled thence; and though, in matter of fact, there are traces of

Paradise still left among us, yet it is evident Scripture says little of them in comparison of its accounts of human misery. Little does it say concerning the innocent pleasures of life; of those temporal blessings which rest upon our worldly occupations, and make them easy; of the blessings which we derive from the sun, and moon, and the "everlasting hills;" from the succession of the seasons and the produce of the earth; little about our recreations, and our daily domestic comforts; little about the ordinary occasions of festivity and mirth which occur in life; and nothing at all about those various other enjoyments which it would be going too much into detail to mention. Human tales and poems are full of pleasant sights and prospects; they make things better than they are, and portray a sort of imaginary perfection; but Scripture (I repeat) seems to abstain even from what might be said in praise of human life as it is. "Vanity of vanities, all is vanity;" "Man is born to trouble;" these are its customary lessons. The text is but a specimen of the descriptions repeated again and again throughout Scripture of human infirmity and misery. . . . .

In truth, this view is the ultimate *true* view of human life. But this is not all; it is a view which it concerns us much to know. It concerns us (I say) much to be told that this world is, after all, in spite of first appearances and partial exceptions, a dark world; else we shall be obliged to learn it (and sooner or later we must learn it) by sad *experience;* whereas, if we are forewarned, we shall unlearn false notions of its excellence, and be saved the disappointment which follows them. And therefore it is that Scripture omits even what might be said in praise of this world's pleasures; not denying their value, such as it is, or forbidding us to use them religiously, but knowing that we are sure to find them out for ourselves without being told of them, and that our danger is on the side, not of undervaluing, but of overvaluing them; whereas, by being told of the world's vanity *at first*, we shall learn (what else we should only attain *at last*), not indeed to be gloomy and discontented, but to bear a sober and calm heart under a smiling cheerful countenance. This is one chief reason of the solemn character of the Scripture history; and if we keep it in view, so far from being offended and frightened away by its notes of sorrow, because they grate on the ear at first, we shall steadfastly listen to them and get them by heart, as a gracious gift from God, sent to us as a remedy for all dangerous overflowing joy in present blessings, in order to save us far greater pain (if we use the lesson well), the pain of actual disappointment, such as the overthrow of vainly-cherished hopes of lasting good upon earth will certainly occasion.

Do but consider what is the consequence of ignorance

or distrust of God's warning voice, and you will see clearly how merciful He is, and how wise it is to listen to Him. I will not suppose a case of gross sin, or of open contempt for religion; but let a man have a general becoming reverence for the law and Church of God, and an unhesitating faith in his Saviour Christ, yet suppose him to be so taken with the goods of this world, as (without his being aware of it) to give his heart to them. Let him have many good feelings and dispositions, but let him love his earthly pursuits, amusements, friends, too well—by which I mean so well as to forget that he is bound to live in the spirit of Abraham's faith, who gave up home, kindred, possessions, all his eye ever loved, at God's word; in the spirit of St. Paul's faith, who "counted all things but loss for the excellency of the knowledge of Christ Jesus his Lord," to win whose favour "he suffered the loss of all things." How will the world go with a man thus forgetful of his real interests? For a while all will be enjoyment: if at any time weariness comes, he will be able to change his pleasure, and the variety will relieve him. His health is good, and his spirits high, and easily master and bear down all the accidental troubles of life. So far all is well; but as years roll on, by little and little he will discover that, after all, he is not, as he imagined, possessed of any real substantial good. He will begin to find, and be startled at finding, that the things which once pleased, please less and less, or not at all. He will be unable to recall those lively emotions in which he once indulged; and he will wonder why thus, by degrees, the delightful visions which surrounded him will fade away, and in their stead melancholy forms will haunt him, such as crowded round the pool of Bethesda. Then will be fulfilled the words of the wise man. The days will have come "when thou shalt say, I have no pleasure in them; the sun, and the light, and the moon, and the stars shall be darkened, and the clouds return after the rain; then they who look out of the window shall be darkened, the doors shall be shut in the streets, all the daughters of music shall be brought low, fears shall be in the way, and desire shall fail." Then a man will begin to be restless and discontented, for he does not know how to amuse himself. Before, he was cheerful only from the natural flow of his spirits, and when such cheerfulness is lost with increasing years he becomes evil-natured. He has made no effort to change his heart, to raise, strengthen, and purify his faith, to subdue his bad passions and tempers. Now their day is come; they have sprung up, and begin to domineer. When he was in health he thought about his farm or his merchandise, and lived to himself; he laid out his strength on the world, and the world is nothing to him, as a worthless bargain (so to say), seeing it is nothing worth to one who cannot take pleasure in it. He had no habitual thought of God in the former time, however he might have a general reverence for His name; and now he dreads Him, or (if the truth must be said) even begins to hate the thought of Him. Where shall he look for succour? Perhaps, moreover, he is a burthen to those around him; they care not for him, he is in their way. And so he will lie year after year by the pool of Bethesda, by the waters of health, with no one helping him; unable to advance himself towards a cure, in consequence of his long habits of sin, and others passing him by, perhaps unable to help one who obstinately refuses to be comforted. Thus he has at length full, personal, painful experience that this world is really vanity, or worse, and all this because he would not believe it from Scripture.

Now should the above description appear overcharged; should it be said that it supposes a man to be possessed of more of the pleasures of life than most men have, and of keener feelings; should it be said that most men have little to enjoy, and that most of those who have much go on in an ordinary tranquil way, and take and lose things without much thought, not pleased much in their vigorous days, and not caring much about the change when the world deserts them; then I must proceed to a more solemn consideration still, on which

I do not like to dwell, but would rather leave it for your own private reflection upon it. There is a story in the Gospel of a man who was taken out of this life before he had turned his thoughts heavenward, and in another world he lifted up his eyes, being in torments. Be quite sure that every one of us, even the poorest and the most dull and insensible, is far more attached to this world than he can possibly imagine. We get used to the things about us, and forget they are necessary for our comfort. Every one, when taken out of this world, would miss a great deal that he is used to depend on, and would in consequence be in great discomfort and sorrow in his new abode, as a stranger in an unknown place; every one, that is, who had not, while on earth, made God his Father and Protector—that great God who alone will there be found. We do not then mend the matter at all in supposing a man not to find out the world's vanity here; for even should the world remain his faithful friend, and please him with its goods to his dying day, still that world will be burnt up at the day of his resurrection; and even had he little of its comforts here, that little he will then miss. Then all men, small and great, will know it to be vanity, and feel their infinite loss if they have trusted it, when all the dead stand before God.

Let this suffice on the use we must make of the solemn view which the Scripture takes of this life. Those disclosures are intended to save us pain, by preventing us enjoying the world unreservedly; that we may use it as not abusing it.

Nor let it seem as if this view of life must make a man melancholy and gloomy. The great rule of our conduct is to take things as they come. He who goes out of his way as shrinking from the varieties of human life which meet him, has weak faith or a strangely-perverted conscience—he wants elevation of mind. The true Christian rejoices in those earthly things which give joy, but in such a way as not to care for them when they go. For no blessings does he care much, except those which are immortal, knowing that he shall receive all such again in the world to come. But the least and the most fleeting, he is too religious to contemn, considering them God's gift; and the least and most fleeting, thus received, yield a purer and deeper, though a less tumultuous joy. And if he at times refrains, it is lest he should encroach upon God's bounty, or lest by a constant use of it he should forget how to do without it.

Our Saviour gives us a pattern which we are bound to follow. He was a far greater than John the Baptist, yet He came, not with St. John's outward austerity, condemning the *display* of strictness or gloominess, that we, His followers, might fast the more in private, and be the more austere in our secret hearts. True it is that such self-command, composure, and inward faith, are not learned in a day; but if they were, why should this life be given us? It is given us as a very preparation time for obtaining them. Only look upon the world in this light. Its sights of sorrows are to calm you, and its pleasant sights to try you. There is a bravery in thus going straight forward, shrinking from no duty little or great, passing from high to low, from pleasure to pain, and making your principles strong without their becoming formal. Learn to be as the angel, who could descend among the miseries of Bethesda without losing his heavenly purity or his perfect happiness. Gain healing from troubled waters. Make up your mind to the prospect of sustaining a certain measure of pain and trouble in your passage through life. By the blessing of God this will prepare you for it; it will make you thoughtful and resigned without interfering with your cheerfulness. It will connect you in your own thoughts with the saints of Scripture, whose lot it was to be patterns of patient endurance; and this association brings to the mind a peculiar consolation. View yourself and all Christians as humbly following the steps of Jacob, whose days were few and evil; and David, who in his best estate was as a shadow that declineth, and was withered like grass; and Elijah, who despised soft raiment and sumptuous fare; and forlorn Daniel, who led an angel's life; and be lighthearted and contented, *because* you are thus called to be a member of Christ's pilgrim Church. Realize the paradox of making merry and rejoicing in the world because it is not yours. And if you are hard to be affected (as many men are), and think too little of the changes of life, going on in a dull way without hope or fear, feeling neither your need nor the excellence of religion; then, again, meditate on the mournful histories recorded in Scripture, in order that your hearts may be opened thereby and roused. Read the Gospels in particular; you there find accounts of sick and afflicted persons in every page as mementoes. Above all, you there read of Christ's sufferings, which I am not now called upon to speak of; but the thought of which is far more than enough to make the world, bright as it may be, look dark and miserable in itself to all true believers, even if the record of *them* were the only sorrowful part of the whole Bible.

HOLINESS NECESSARY FOR FUTURE BLESSEDNESS.

"Holiness, without which no man shall see the Lord."—
HEB. xii. 14.

IN this text it has seemed good to the Holy Spirit to convey a chief truth of religion in a few words. It is this circumstance which makes it especially impressive; for the truth itself is declared in one form or other in every part of Scripture. It is told us again and again, that to make sinful creatures holy was the great end which our Lord had in view in taking upon Him our nature, and that none but the holy will be accepted for His sake at the last day. . . . .

To be holy, is in our Church's words, to have "the true circumcision of the Spirit;" that is, to be separate from sin, to hate the works of the world, the flesh, and the devil; to take pleasure in keeping God's commandments; to do things as He would have us do them; to live habitually as in the sight of the world to come, as if we had broken the ties of this life, and were dead already.

Why cannot we be saved without possessing such a frame and temper of mind?

I answer as follows: that, even supposing a man of unholy life were suffered to enter heaven, *he would not be happy there;* so that it would be no mercy to permit him to enter.

We are apt to deceive ourselves, and to consider heaven a place like this earth; I mean, a place where every man may choose and take his *own* pleasure. We see that in this world active men have their own enjoyments, and domestic men have theirs; men of literature, of science, of political talent, have their respective pursuits and pleasures. Hence we are led to act as if it will be the same in another world. The only difference we put between this world and the next, is that *here* (as we know well) men are *not always sure*, but *there*, we suppose they *will be always sure*, of obtaining what they seek after. And accordingly we conclude that *any man*, whatever his habits, tastes, or manner of life, if once admitted into heaven, would be happy there. Not that we altogether deny that some preparation is necessary for the next world; but we do not estimate its real extent and importance. We think we can reconcile ourselves to God when we will; as if nothing were required in the case of men in general but some temporary attention, more than ordinary, to our religious duties; some strictness, during our last sickness, to the services of the Church, as men of business arrange their letters and papers on taking a journey or balancing an account. But an opinion like this, though commonly acted upon, is refuted as soon as put into words. For heaven, it is plain from Scripture, is not a place where many different and discordant pursuits can be carried on at once, as is the case in this world. Here every one can do his own pleasure, but there he must do God's pleasure. It would be presumption to attempt to determine the employments of that eternal life which good men are to pass in God's presence, or to deny that that state which eye hath not seen, nor ear heard, nor mind conceived, may comprise an infinite variety of pursuits and occupations. Still, so far we are distinctly told, that that future life will be spent in God's *presence*, in a sense which does not apply to our present life; so that it may be best described as an endless and uninterrupted worship of the Eternal Father, Son, and Spirit. "They serve Him day and night in His temple, and He that sitteth on the throne shall dwell among them. . . . The Lamb which is in the midst of the throne shall feed them, and shall lead them unto living fountains of waters." Again: "The city had no need of the sun, neither of the moon to shine in it, for the glory of God did lighten it, and the Lamb is the light thereof. And the nations of them which are saved shall walk in the light of it, and the kings of the earth do bring their glory and honour into it." These passages of St. John are sufficient to remind us of many others.

Heaven, then, is not like this world. I will say what it is much more like—*a church*. For in a place of public worship no language of this world is heard; there are no schemes brought forward for temporal objects, great or small; no information how to strengthen our worldly interests, extend our influence, or establish our credit. These things indeed may be right in their way, so that we do not set our hearts upon them; still (I repeat), it is certain that we hear nothing of them in a church. Here we hear solely and entirely of *God*. We praise Him, worship Him, sing to Him, thank Him, confess to Him, give ourselves up to Him, and ask His blessing. And, *therefore*, a church is like heaven, viz., because both in the one and the other there is one single sovereign subject—religion—brought before us.

Supposing, then, instead of its being said that no irreligious man could serve and love God in heaven (or see Him, as the text expresses it), we were told that no irreligious man could worship, of spiritually see Him in church; should we not at once perceive the meaning of the doctrine? namely, that were a man to come hither, who had suffered his mind to grow up its own way, as nature or chance determined, without any deliberate habitual effort after truth and purity, he would find no real pleasure here, but would soon get weary of the place; because in this house of God he would hear only of that one subject which he cared little or nothing about, and nothing at all of those things which excited his hopes and fears, his sympathies and energies. If, then, a man without religion (supposing it possible) were admitted into heaven, doubtless he would sustain a great disappointment. Before, indeed, he fancied that he could be happy there; but when he arrived there he would find no discourse but that which he had shunned on earth; no pursuits but those he had disliked or despised; nothing which bound him to aught else in the universe, and made him feel at home; nothing which he could enter into and rest upon. He would perceive himself to be an isolated being, cut away by Supreme Power from those objects which were still entwined about his heart. Nay, he would be in the presence of that Supreme Power whom he never on earth could bring himself steadily to think upon, and whom now he regarded only as the destroyer of all that was precious and dear to Him. Ah! he could not *bear* the face of the Living God; the Holy God would be no object of joy to him. "Let us alone! what have we to do with Thee?" is the sole thought and desire of unclean souls, even while they acknowledge His majesty. None but the holy can look upon the Holy One: without holiness no man can endure to see the Lord.

When, then, we think to take part in the joys of heaven without holiness, we are as inconsiderate as if we supposed we could take an interest in the worship of Christians here below without possessing it in our measure. A careless, a sensual, an unbelieving mind; a mind destitute of the love and fear of God; with narrow views and earthly aims, a low standard of duty, and a benighted conscience; a mind contented with itself, and unresigned to God's will, would not feel pleasure at the last day at the words, "Enter into the joy of thy Lord," more than it does now at the words, "Let us pray." Nay, much less; because while we are in a church we may turn our thoughts to other subjects, and contrive to forget that God is working on us; but that will not be possible in heaven.

We see, then, that holiness, or inward separation from the world, is necessary to our admission into heaven; because heaven is *not* heaven, is not a place of happiness, *except* to the holy. There are bodily indispositions which affect the taste, so that the sweetest flavours become ungrateful to the palate; and indispositions which impair the sight, tinging the fair face of nature with some sickly hue. In like manner there is a moral malady which disorders the inward sight and taste; and no man labouring under it is in a condition to enjoy what Scripture calls "the fulness of joy in God's presence, and pleasures at His right hand for evermore."

Nay, I will venture to say more than this—it is fearful, but it is right to say it—that if we wished to imagine a punishment for an unholy, reprobate soul, we perhaps could not fancy a greater than to summon it to heaven. Heaven would be hell to an irreligious man. We know how unhappy we are apt to feel at present, when alone in the midst of strangers, or of men of different tastes and habits to ourselves. How miserable, for example, would it be to have to live in a foreign land, among a people whose faces we never saw before, and whose language we could not learn. And this is but a faint illustration of the loneliness of a man of earthly dispositions and tastes thrown into the society of saints and angels. How forlorn would he wander through the courts of heaven! He would find no one like himself; he would see in every direction the marks of God's holiness, and these would make him shudder. He would feel himself always in His presence. He could no longer turn his thoughts another way, as he does now, when conscience reproaches him. He would know that the eternal eye was ever upon him; and that eye of holiness, which is joy and life to holy creatures, would seem to him an eye of wrath and punishment. God cannot change His nature. Holy He must ever be. But while He is holy no unholy soul can be happy in heaven. Fire does not inflame iron, but it inflames straw. It would cease to be fire if it did not. And so heaven itself would be fire to those who would fain escape across the great gulf from the torments of hell. The finger of Lazarus would but increase their thirst. The very "heaven that is over their heads" will be "brass" to them.

I will now mention two important truths which seem to follow from what has been said.

First, if a certain character of mind, a certain state of the heart and affections, be necessary for entering heaven, our actions will avail for our salvation chiefly as they tend to produce or evidence this frame of mind. Good works (as they are called) are required, not as if they had anything of merit in them, not as if they could of themselves turn away God's anger for our sins, or purchase heaven for us, but because they are the means, under God's grace, of strengthening and showing forth that holy principle which God implants in the heart, and without which (as the text tells us) we cannot see Him. The more numerous are our acts of charity, self-denial, and forbearance, of course the more will our minds be schooled into a charitable, self-denying, and forbearing temper. The more frequent are our prayers, the more humble, patient, and religious are our daily deeds, this communion with God, these holy works, will be the means of making our hearts holy, and of preparing us for the future presence of God. Outward acts, done on principle, create inward habits. I repeat, the separate acts of obedience to the will of God, good works as they are called, are of service to us, as gradually severing us from this world of sense, and impressing our hearts with a heavenly character. . . . The mere outward acts of coming to church and saying prayers, which are of course duties imperative upon all of us, are really serviceable to those only who do them in a heavenly spirit, because such men only use these good deeds to the improvement of the heart; whereas even the most exact outward devotion avails not a man if it does not improve it.

Secondly, if holiness be not merely the doing a certain number of actions, but is an inward character which follows, under God's grace, from doing them, how far distant from that holiness are the multitude of men. . . . . Most men who are living in neglect of God, silence their consciences when troublesome with the promise of repenting some future day. How often are they thus led on till death surprises them! But we will suppose they do begin to repent when that future day comes. Nay, we will even suppose that Almighty God were to forgive them, and to admit them into His holy heaven. Well, but is nothing more requisite? Are they in a fit state to do Him service in heaven? Is not this the very point I have been so insisting upon, that they are not in a fit state? has it not been shown, that even if admitted there without a change of heart, they would find no pleasure in heaven? and is a change of heart wrought in a day? Which of our tastes or likings can we change at our will in a moment? Not the most superficial. Can we then at a word change the whole character and frame of our minds? Is not holiness the result of many patient, repeated efforts after obedience gradually working on us, and first modifying and then changing our hearts? We dare not, of course, set bounds to God's mercy and power in cases of repentance late in life, even where He has revealed to us the general rule of His moral governance; yet surely it is our duty ever to keep steadily before us and act upon those general truths which His holy word has declared. His holy word in various ways warns us that, as no one will find happiness in heaven who is not holy, so no one can learn to be so in a short time, and when he will. It implies it in the text, which names a qualification, which we know in matter of fact does ordinarily take time to gain. It propounds it clearly, though in figure, in the parable of the wedding garment, in which inward sanctification is made a condition distinct from our acceptance of the proffer of mercy, and not negligently to be passed over in our thoughts as if a necessary consequence of it. And it solemnly assures us in St. Paul's epistles that it is possible so to presume on Divine grace as to let slip the accepted time, and be sealed even before the end of life to a reprobate mind (Heb. vi. 4-6; x. 26-29). . . . . . .

To obtain the gift of holiness is the work of *a life*. No man will ever be perfect here, so sinful is our nature. Thus, in putting off the day of repentance, these men are reserving for a few chance years, when strength and vigour are gone, that work for which a whole life would not be enough. That work is great and arduous beyond expression. There is much of sin remaining even in the best of men, and if the righteous scarcely be saved, where shall the ungodly and the sinner appear (1 Peter iv. 18)? Their doom may be fixed any moment; and though this thought should not make a man despair to-day, yet it should ever make him tremble for to-morrow. . . . .

Be you content with nothing short of perfection; exert yourselves day by day to grow in knowledge and grace; that, if so be, you may at length attain to the presence of Almighty God.

Lastly, while we thus labour to mould our hearts after the pattern of the holiness of our heavenly Father, it is one comfort to know, what I have already implied, that we are not left to ourselves, but that the Holy Ghost is graciously present with us, and enables us to triumph over and to change our own minds. It is a comfort and encouragement, while it is an anxious and an awful thing, to know that God works in and through us. We are the instruments, but we are only the instruments, of our own salvation. Let no one say that I discourage him, and propose to him a task beyond his strength. All of us have the gifts of grace pledged to us from our youth up. We know this well, but we do not use our privilege. We form mean ideas of the difficulty of our duties, and in consequence never enter into the greatness of the gifts given us to meet it. Then afterwards, if perchance we gain a deeper insight into the work we have to do, we think God a hard master, who commands much from a sinful race. Narrow indeed is the way of life, but infinite is His love and power who is with the Church, in Christ's place, to guide us along it.

WATCHING.

"Take ye heed, watch and pray; for ye know not when the time is."—MARK xiii. 33.

OUR Saviour gave this warning when He was leaving this world—leaving it, that is, as far as His visible presence is concerned. He looked forward to the many hundred years which were to pass before He came again. He knew His own purpose and His Father's purpose, gradually to leave the world to itself, gradually to withdraw from it the tokens of His gracious presence. He contemplated, as contemplating all things, the neglect of Him which would spread even among His professed followers; the daring disobedience, and the loud words which would be ventured against Him and His Father by many whom He had regenerated; and the coldness, cowardice, and tolerance of error which would be displayed by others who did not go so far as to speak or to act against him. He foresaw the state of the world and the Church, as we see it this day, when His prolonged absence has made it practically thought that He never will come back in visible presence : and in the text He mercifully whispers into our ears not to trust in what we see, not to share in that general unbelief, not to be carried away by the world; but to "take heed, pray, watch," and look out for His coming.

Surely this gracious warning should be ever in our thoughts, being so precise, so solemn, so earnest. He foretold His first coming, yet He took His Church by surprise when He came. Much more will He come suddenly the second time, and overtake men, now that He has not measured out the interval before it, as then He did, but left our watchfulness to the keeping of faith and love. . . . .

Now I consider this word *watching*, first used by our Lord, then by the favoured disciple, then by the two great apostles, Peter and Paul, is a remarkable word; remarkable because the idea is not so obvious as might appear at first sight, and next because they all inculcate it. We are not simply to believe, but to watch; not simply to love, but to watch; not simply to obey, but to watch. To watch for what? for that great event, Christ's coming! Whether then we consider what is the obvious meaning of the word, or the object towards which it directs us, such as does not naturally come into our minds, most of us have a general idea what is meant by believing, fearing, loving, and obeying; but perhaps we do not contemplate or apprehend what is meant by watching. I conceive it may be explained as follows. Do you know the feeling in matters of this life, of expecting a friend, expecting him to come, and he delays? Do you know what it is to be in unpleasant company, and wish for the time to pass away, and the hour strike when you may be at liberty? Do you know what it is to be in anxiety lest something should happen, which may happen or may not; or to be in suspense about some important event, which makes your heart beat when you are reminded of it, and of which you think the first thing in the morning? Do you know what it is to have a friend in a distant country, to expect news of him, and to wonder from day to day what he is now doing, and whether he is well? Do you know what it is so to live upon a person who is present with you, that your eyes follow his, that you read his soul, that you see all its changes in his countenance, that you anticipate his wishes, that you smile in his smile, and are sad in his sadness, and are downcast when he is vexed, and rejoice in his successes? To watch for Christ is a feeling such as all these, as far as feelings of this world are fit to shadow out those of another.

He watches *for* Christ who has a sensitive, eager, apprehensive mind; who is awake, alive, quick-sighted, zealous in seeking and honouring Him; who looks out for Him in all that happens, and who would not be surprised, who would not be over-agitated or overwhelmed, if he found that He was coming at once.

And he watches *with* Christ, who, while he looks on to the future, looks back on the past, and does not so contemplate what his Saviour has purchased for him as to forget what He has suffered for him. He watches with Christ who ever commemorates and renews in his own person Christ's cross and agony, and gladly takes up that mantle of affliction which Christ bore here, and left behind Him when He ascended. . . . .

This then is to watch; to be detached from what is present, and to live in what is unseen; to live in the thought of Christ as He came once, and as He will come again; to desire His second coming, from our affectionate and grateful remembrance of His first. "I will stand upon my watch, and set me upon the tower, and will watch to see what He will say unto me, and what I shall answer when I am reproved." When we reflect how rarely this temper of mind is found among professing Christians, we shall see why our Lord is so urgent in enforcing it; as if He said, "I am not warning you, my followers, against open apostacy—that will not be ; but I foresee that very few will keep awake and watch while I am away. Blessed are the servants who do so; few will open to Me immediately when I knock. They will have something to do first; they will have to get ready. They will have to recover from the surprise and confusion which overtake them on the first news of my coming, and will need time to collect themselves, and summon about them their better thoughts and affections. They feel themselves very well off as they are, and wish to serve God as they are. They are satisfied to remain on earth; they do not wish to move; they do not wish to change."

Without denying, then, to these persons the praise of many religious habits and practices, I would say that they want the tender and sensitive heart which hangs on the thought of Christ, and lives in His love. The breath of the world has a peculiar power in what may be called rusting the soul. The mirror within them, instead of reflecting back the Son of God, their Saviour, has become dim and discoloured; and hence, though (to use a common expression) they have a good deal of good in them, it is not through them, around them, and upon them. An evil crust is on them; they think with the world; they are full of the world's notions and modes of speaking; they appeal to the world, and have a sort of reverence for what the world will say. There is a want of naturalness, simplicity, and childlike teachableness in them. It is difficult to touch them, or (what may be called) get at them, and to persuade them to a straightforward course in religion. They start off when you least expect it; they have reservations, make distinctions, take exceptions, indulge in refinements, in questions where there are really but two sides, a right and a wrong. Their religious feelings do not flow forth easily; at times when they ought to flow, either they are diffident and can say nothing, or else they are affected and strained in their mode of conversing. And as a rust preys upon metal and eats into it, so does this worldly spirit penetrate more and more deeply into the soul which once admits it. And this is one great end, as it would appear, of afflictions, viz., to rub away and clear off these outward defilements, and to keep the soul in a measure of its baptismal purity and brightness.

Now it cannot surely be doubted that multitudes in the Church are such as I have been describing, and that they would not, could not, at once welcome our Lord on His coming. We cannot indeed apply what has been said to this or that individual; but on the whole, viewing the multitude, one cannot be mistaken. There may be exceptions; but after all conceivable deductions, a large body must remain thus double-minded, thus attempting to unite things impossible. This we might be sure of, though Christ had said nothing on the subject; but it is a most affecting and solemn thought that He has actually called our attention to this very danger, the danger of a worldly religiousness, for so it may be called, though it *is* religiousness, this mixture of religion and unbelief which serves God indeed, but loves the fashions, the distinctions, the pleasures, the comforts of this life—which feels a satisfaction in being prosperous in circumstances, likes pomps and vanities, is particular about food, raiment, house, furniture, and domestic matters, courts great people, and aims at having a position in society. He warns His disciples of the danger of having their minds drawn off from the thought of Him, by whatever cause. He warns them against all excitements, all allurements of this world. He solemnly warns them that the world will not be prepared for His coming, and tenderly entreats of them not to take their portion with the world. He warns them by the instance of the rich man whose soul was required, of the servant who ate and drank, and of the foolish virgins. When He comes, they will one and all want time; their heads will be confused, their eyes will swim, their tongues falter, their limbs totter, as men who are suddenly awakened. They will not all at once collect their senses and faculties. O fearful thought! the bridal train is sweeping by—angels are there—the just made perfect are there—little children, and holy teachers, and white-robed saints, and martyrs washed in blood; the marriage of the Lamb is come, and His wife hath made herself ready. She has already attired herself while we have been sleeping. She has been robing; she has been adding jewel to jewel, and

Y

grace to grace; she has been gathering in her chosen ones one by one, and has been exercising them in holiness, and purifying them for her Lord; and now her marriage hour is come. The holy Jerusalem is ascending, and a loud voice proclaims: "Behold the Bridegroom cometh, go ye out to meet Him!" But we, alas! are but dazzled with the blaze of light, and neither welcome the sound, nor obey it—and all for what? What shall we have gained then? What will this world have then done for us? Wretched, deceiving world, which will then be burnt up, unable not only to profit us, but to save itself. Miserable hour, indeed, will that be, when the full consciousness breaks on us of what we will not believe now, that we are at present serving the world. We trifle with our conscience now; we deceive our better judgment; we repel the hints of those who tell us that we are giving ourselves to this perishing world. We will taste a little of its pleasures, and follow its ways, and think it no harm so that we do not altogether neglect religion.

Year passes after year silently; Christ's coming is ever nearer than it was. O that, as He comes nearer earth, we may approach nearer heaven! Oh, my brethren, pray Him to give you the heart to seek Him in sincerity! Pray Him to make you in earnest. You have one work only, to bear your cross after Him. Resolve, in His strength, to do so; resolve to be no longer beguiled by "shadows of religion," by words, or by disputings, or by notions, or by high professions, or by excuses, or by the world's promises or threats. Pray Him to give you what Scripture calls "an honest and good heart," or "a perfect heart;" and, without waiting, begin at once to obey Him with the best heart you have. Any obedience is better than none—any profession which is disjoined from obedience is a mere pretence and deceit. Any religion which does not bring you nearer God is of the world. You have to seek his face; obedience is the only way of seeing Him. All your duties are obediences. If you are to believe the truths He has revealed, to regulate yourselves by His precepts, to be frequent in His ordinances, to adhere to His church and people, why is it, except because *He* has bid you? and to do what He bids is to obey Him, and to obey Him is to approach Him. Every act of obedience is an approach—an approach to Him who is not far off, though He seems so, but close behind this visible screen of things which hides Him from us. He is behind this material framework; earth and sky are but a veil going between Him and us; the day will come when He will rend that veil, and show Himself to us. And then, according as we have waited for Him, will He recompense us. If we have forgotten Him, He will not know us; but "blessed are those servants whom the Lord, when He cometh, shall find watching. . . . . . He shall gird Himself, and make them sit down to meat, and will come forth and serve them. And if He shall come in the second watch, or come in the third watch, and find them so, blessed are those servants." May this be the portion of every one of us! It is hard to attain it, but it is woful to fail. Life is short; death is certain; and the world to come is everlasting.

WAITING FOR CHRIST.

"He who testifieth these things saith, Surely I come quickly. Amen. Even so, come, Lord Jesus."—REV. xxii. 20.

WHEN our Lord was going away, He said He would quickly come again; yet, knowing that by "quickly" He did not mean what would be at first sight understood by the word, He added, "suddenly," or "as a thief." "Behold I come as a thief; blessed is he that watcheth, and keepeth his garments" (Rev. xvi. 15). Had His coming been soon, in our sense of the word, it could not well have been sudden. Servants who are bid to wait for their master's return from an entertainment, could not, one should think, be overtaken by that return. It was because to us His coming would not *seem* soon, that it *was* sudden. What you expect to come, you wait for; what fails to come, you give up. While, then, Christ said that His coming would be soon, yet by saying it would be sudden, He said that to us it would seem long.

Is it not something significant that, in the last book of

Scripture, which more than any other implies a long continuance to the Christian Church, that there we should read such express and repeated assurances that Christ's coming would be speedy? Even in the last chapter we are told it three times. "Behold, I come quickly; blessed is he that keepeth the sayings of the prophecy of this book." "Behold, I come quickly, and My reward is with Me." And again, in the text, "He that testifieth these things saith, Surely I come quickly." Such is the announcement; and in consequence we are commanded to be ever looking out for the great day, to "wait for His Son from heaven;" to "look and haste unto the coming of the day of God."

It is true, indeed, that in one place St. Paul cautions his brethren against expecting the immediate coming of Christ, but he does not say more than that Christ will send a sign immediately before His coming—a certain dreadful enemy of the truth—which is to be followed by Himself at once, and therefore does not stand in our way, or prevent eager eyes from looking out for Him. And, in truth, St. Paul seems rather to be warning his brethren against being disappointed if Christ did not come, than hindering them from expecting Him.

Now it may be objected that this is a kind of paradox. How is it possible, it may be asked, ever to be expecting what has so long been delayed? What has been so long coming, may be longer still. It was possible, indeed, for the early Christians, who had no experience of the long period which the Church was to remain on earth, to look out for Christ, but we cannot help using *our* reason. There are no more grounds to expect Christ now than at those many former times when, as the events showed, He did not come. Christians have ever been expecting the last day, and have ever been disappointed. They have seen what they thought symptoms of His coming, and peculiarities in their own times, which a little more knowledge of the world, a more enlarged experience, would have shown them to be common to all times. They have been ever frightened without good reason, fretting in their narrow minds, and building on their superstitious fancies. What age of the world has there been in which people did not think the Day of Judgment coming? Such expectation has but evidenced and fostered indolence and superstition: it is to be considered as a mere weakness.

Now I shall attempt to say something in answer to this objection.

First, considered as an objection to a habit of continual waiting, it proves too much, as it is called. If it is consistently followed up, no age ought ever to expect the day of Christ; the age in which He shall come (whatever it is) ought not to expect him—which is the very thing He has warned us against. He nowhere warns us against what is contemptuously called superstition; but He expressly warns us against highminded security. If it be true that Christians have expected Him when He did not come, it is quite as true that when He does come the world will not expect Him. If it be true that Christians have fancied signs of His coming when there were none, it is equally true that the world will not see the signs of His coming when they are present. His signs are not so plain but you have to search for them; not so plain but you may be mistaken in your search; and your choice lies between the risk of thinking you see what is not, and of not seeing what is. True it is, that many times, many ages, have Christians been mistaken in thinking they discerned Christ's coming; but better a thousand times think Him coming when he is not, than once think Him not coming when He is. Such is the difference between Scripture and the world: judging by Scripture, you would ever be expecting Christ; judging by the world, you would never expect Him. Now He must come one day, sooner or later. Worldly men have their scoff at our failure of discernment now; but whose will be the want of discernment, whose the triumph then? And what does Christ think of their present scoff? He expressly warns us, by His apostle, of scoffers, who shall say, "Where is the promise of His coming? for since the fathers fell asleep, all things continue as they were from the beginning of the creation . . . . But, beloved," continues St. Peter, " be not ignorant of this one thing, that one day is with the Lord as a thousand years, and a thousand years as one day."

It should be recollected, too, that the enemies of Christ have ever been expecting the downfall of His religion age after age; and I do not see why the one expectation is more unreasonable than the other; indeed, they illustrate each other. So it is, undeterred by the failure of former anticipations, unbelievers are ever expecting that the Church and the religion of the Church are coming to an end. They thought so in the last century; they think so now. They ever think the light of truth is going out, and that their hour of victory is come. . . .

Now, when Christians and unbelievers thus unite in expecting substantially the same thing, though they view it differently, according to their respective modes of thought, there cannot be anything very extravagant in the expectation itself. The Christian has said: "All looks so full of tumult, that the world is coming to an end." The unbeliever has said: "All is so full of tumult, that the Church is coming to an end ;" and there is nothing surely more superstitious in the one opinion than in the other. Ever since Christianity came into the world, it has been, in one sense, going out of it. It is so uncongenial to the human mind; it is so spiritual, and man is so earthly; it is apparently so defenceless, and has so many strong enemies, so many false friends, that every age, as it comes, may be called "the last time." It has made great conquests and done great works; but still it has done all, as the apostle says of himself, "in weakness and in fear, and in much trembling." *How* it is that it is always failing, yet always continuing, God only knows who wills it—but so it is; and it is no paradox to say, on the one hand, that it has lasted eighteen hundred years, that it may last many years more, and yet that it draws to an end, nay, is likely to end any day. And God would have us give our minds and hearts to the latter side of the alternative, to open them to impressions *from* this side, viz., that the end is coming—it being a wholesome thing to live as if *that* will come in our day which may come any day.

It was different during the ages before Christ came. *He* was to come. He was to bring perfection, and religion was to grow *towards* that perfection. There was a system of successive revelations going on, first one and then another; each prophet in his turn adding to the store of divine truth, and gradually tending towards the full Gospel. Time was measured out for believing minds before Christ came, by the word of prophecy; so that He never could be expected in any age before the "fulness of time" in which He came. The chosen people were not bidden to expect Him at once; but after a sojourning in Canaan, and a captivity in Egypt, and a wandering in the wilderness, and judges, and kings, and prophets, at length seventy long weeks were determined to introduce Him into the world. Thus His delay was, as I may say, *recognized* then; and *during* His delay, other doctrines, other rules, were given to fill the interval. But when once the Christ had come, as the Son over His own house, and with His perfect Gospel, nothing remained but to gather in His saints. No higher priest could come—no truer doctrine. The Light and Life of men had appeared, and had suffered, and had risen again; and nothing more was left to do. Earth had had its most solemn event, and seen its most august sight; and therefore it was the last time. And hence, though time intervene between Christ's first and second coming, it is not *recognized* (as I may say) in the Gospel scheme, but is, as it were, an accident. For so it was, that up to Christ's coming in the flesh, the course of things ran straight towards it, nearing it by every step; but now, under the Gospel, that course has (if I may so speak) altered its direction as regards His second coming, and runs, not towards it, but along it, and on the brink of it, and is at all times equally near that great event which, did it run towards, it would at once run into. Christ, then, is ever at our doors; as near eighteen hundred years ago as now, and not nearer now than then; and not nearer when He comes than now. When He says that He will come soon, "soon" is not a word of time, but of natural order. This present state of things, "the present distress," as St. Paul calls it, is ever *close upon* the next world, and resolves itself into it. As when a man is given over, he may die any moment, yet lingers; as an implement of war may any moment explode, and must at some time; as we listen for a clock to strike, and at length it surprises us; as a crumbling arch hangs, we know not how, yet is not safe to pass under; so creeps on this feeble, weary world; and one day, before we know where we are, it will end. . . . .

I observe then, that though Christians might be mistaken in what they took to be signs of Christ's coming, yet they were not wrong in their state of mind; they were not mistaken in looking out, and that for Christ. Whether credulous or not, they only acted as one acts towards some person beloved, or revered, or admired on earth. Consider the mode in which loyal persons look up to a good prince. You will find stories current up and down the country in his favour; people delight in believing that they have fallen in with tokens of his beneficence, nobleness, and paternal kindness. Many of these reports are false, yet others are true; and, on the whole, we should not think highly of that man who, instead of being touched at this mutual sympathy between sovereign and people, occupied himself merely in carping at what he called their credulity, and sifting the accuracy of this or that particular story. A great thing, truly, after all, to be able to detect a few misstatements, and to expose a few fictions, and to be without a heart! And, forsooth, on the other hand, a sad deficiency in that people, I suppose, merely to be right on the whole, not in every particular, and to have the heart right! Who would envy such a man's knowledge? Who would not rather have that people's ignorance? And in like manner, I had rather be he who, from love of Christ and want of science, thinks some strange sight in the sky, comet or meteor, to be the sign of His coming, than the man who, from more knowledge and from lack of love, laughs at the mistake. . . . .

And you will observe that, in the case of which I am speaking, persons who are looking out for Christ are not only *in* looking out acting in obedience to Him, but are looking out in the very *way* they look out, through the very signs through which they look out, in obedience to Him. Always since the first, Christians have been looking out for Christ *in* the signs of the natural and moral world. If they have been poor and uneducated, strange sights in the sky, or tremblings in the ground, torms, failure of harvest, or disease, or anything monstrous and unnatural, has made them think that He was at hand. If they were in a way to take a view of the social and political world, then the troubles of states, wars, revolutions, and the like, have been additional circumstances which served to impress them, and kept their hearts awake for Christ. Now all these are nothing else but those very things which He Himself has told us to dwell upon, and has given us as signs of His coming. "There shall be signs," He says, "in the sun, and in the moon, and in the stars; and upon the earth distress of nations, with perplexity, the sea and the waves roaring; men's hearts failing them for fear, and for looking after those things which are coming on the earth; for the powers of heaven shall be shaken. . . . . And when these things begin to come to pass, then look up and lift up your heads, for your redemption draweth nigh." One day the lights of heaven *will* be signs; one day the affairs of nations also *will* be signs. Why, then, is it superstitious to *look* towards them? It is not. We may be wrong in the particulars we rest upon, and may show our ignorance in doing so; but there is nothing ridiculous or contemptible in our ignorance, and there is much that is religious in our watching. It is better to be wrong in our watching, than not to watch at all. . . . .

Surely there can be no great harm, and nothing very ridiculous, where men are religious, in thus thinking the events of their day more than ordinary; in fancying that the world's matters are winding up, and that events are thickening for a final visitation; for, let it be observed, Scripture sanctions us in interpreting all that we see in the world in a religious sense, and as if all things were tokens and revelations of Christ, His providence and will. I mean, that if this lower world, which seems to go on in its own way, independently of Him, governed by fixed laws or swayed by lawless hearts, will nevertheless, in an awful way, herald His coming to judge it, surely it is not impossible that the same world, both in its physical order and its temporal course, speaks of Him also in other manners. At first, indeed, one might argue that this world did but speak a language contrary to him; that in Scripture it is described as opposed to God, to truth, to faith, to heaven; that it is said to be a deceitful veil, misrepresenting things, and keeping the soul from God. How then, it may be asked, can this world have upon it tokens of His presence, or bring us near to Him? Yet certainly so it is, that in spite of the world's evil, after all, He is in it, and speaks through it, though not loudly. When He came in the flesh, "He was in the world, and the world was made by Him, and the world knew Him not." Nor did He strive nor cry, nor lift up His voice in the streets. So it is now. He still is here; He still whispers to us; He still makes signs to us. But His voice is so low, and the world's din is so loud, and His signs are so covert, and the world is so restless, that it is difficult to determine when He addresses us and what He says. Religious men cannot but feel in various ways that His providence is guiding them and blessing them personally on the whole; yet when they attempt to put their finger upon the times and places, the traces of His presence disappear. Who is there, for instance, but has been favoured with answers to prayer, such that, at the time, he has felt he never could again be unbelieving? Who has not had strange coincidences in his course of life which brought before him in an overpowering way the hand of God? Who has not had thoughts come upon him with a sort of mysterious force, for his warning or his direction? And some persons, perhaps, experience stranger things still. Wonderful providences have before now been brought about by means of dreams; or in other still more unusual ways Almighty God has at times interposed. And then, again, things which come before our eyes, in such wise take the form of types and omens of things moral or future, that the spirit within us cannot but reach forward and presage what it is not told from what it sees. And sometimes these presages are remarkably fulfilled in the event. And then, again, the fortunes of men are so singularly various, as if a law of success and prosperity embraced a certain number, and a contrary law others. All this being so, and the vastness and mystery of the world being borne in upon us, we begin to think that there is nothing here below but, for what we know, may have a connexion with everything else. The most distant events may yet be united, and meanest and highest may be parts of one; and God may be teaching us and offering us knowledge of His ways, if we will but open our eyes, in all the ordinary matters of the day This is what thoughtful persons come to believe; and they begin to show a sort of faith in the divine meaning of the accidents (as they are called) of life, and a readiness to take impressions from them, which may easily become excessive, and which, whether excessive or not, is sure to be ridiculed by the world at large as superstitious. Yet, considering Scripture tells us that the very hairs of our head are all numbered by God, that all things work together for our good, it does certainly encourage us in thus looking out for His presence in everything that happens, however trivial, and in trusting that to religious ears even the bad world prophesies of Him.

PRESENT BLESSINGS.

"I have all, and abound; I am full."—PHIL. iv. 18.

SUCH is St. Paul's confession concerning his temporal condition, even in the midst of his trials. Those trials brought with them spiritual benefits, but even as regarded this world he felt he had cause for joy and thankfulness, in spite of sorrows, pains, labours, and self-denials. He did not look on this life with bitterness, complain of it morosely, or refuse to enjoy it; he was not soured as the children of men often are by his trials; but he felt that if he had troubles in this world, he had blessings also; and he did not reject these, but made much of them. "I have all, and abound; I am full," he says. And elsewhere he tells us, that "every creature of God is good;" and that "godliness is profitable unto all things, having the promise of the life that now is, and of that which is to come."

Gloom is no Christian temper; that repentance is not real which has not love in it; that self-chastisement is not acceptable which is not sweetened by faith and cheerfulness. We must live in sunshine, even when we sorrow; we must live in God's presence; we must not shut ourselves up in our own hearts, even when we are reckoning up our past sins. . . . .

We ought to bless and praise God that we have the gift of life. By this I mean not merely that we live, but for those blessings which are included in the notion of our living. He has made life in its very nature to imply the existence of certain blessings which are themselves a happiness, and which bring it to pass, that in spite of all evils, life in itself, except in rare cases, cannot be otherwise than desirable. We cannot live without the means of life; without the means of life we should die; and the means of life are means of pleasure. It might have been so ordered that life could not have been sustained without the use of such means as were indifferent, neither pleasurable nor painful, or of means which were even painful; as in the case of illness or disease, when we actually find that we cannot preserve it without painful remedies. Now, supposing the ordinary ways of preserving it had been what are now but extraordinary; supposing food were medicine; supposing wounds or blows imparted health and strength. But it is not so. On the contrary, life consists in things pleasant; it is sustained by blessings. And moreover, the Gospel, by a solemn grant, guarantees these things to us. After the flood, God Almighty condescended to promise that there never should be such a flood again; that seed-time and harvest should not fail. He ratified the stability of nature by His own word, and by that word it is upheld. And in like manner He has, in a special way, guaranteed to us in the Gospel that law of nature whereby good and pleasant gifts are included in our idea of life, and life becomes a blessing. He might, did He so will, sustain us Christians not by bread only, but by every word that proceedeth out of His mouth. But He has not done so. He has pledged to us those ordinary means of sustenance which we naturally like. " Bread shall be given us, our water shall be sure." " All these things shall be added unto us." He has not indeed promised us what the world calls its great prizes; He has not promised us those goods, so called, of which the goodness depends on the imagination; He has not promised us large estates, magnificent domains, houses like palaces, sumptuous furniture, retainers and servants, chariots and horses, rank, name, credit, popularity, power, the deference of others, the indulgence of our wills, luxury, sensual enjoyments. These, on the contrary, He denies us; and withal He declares, that, specious and inviting as they are, really they are evil. But still He has promised that this shall be His rule; that thus shall it be fulfilled to us as His ordinary providence; that life shall not be a burthen to us, but a blessing, and shall contain more to comfort than to afflict. And giving us as much as this, He bids us be satisfied with it. He bids us confess that we "have all" when we have so much; that we "abound" when we have enough. He promises us food, raiment, and lodging; and He bids us, "having food and raiment, therewith to be content." He bids us be content with those gifts, and withal unsolicitous about them; tranquil, secure, and confident, because He has promised them. He bids us be sure that we shall have so much, and not be disappointed that it is no more. Such is His merciful consideration of us. He does not separate us from this world, though He calls us out of it; He does not reject our old nature when He gives us a new one; He does but redeem it from the curse, and purify it from the infection which came through Adam, and is none of His. He especially blesses the creation to our use, though we be regenerate. "Every creature of God," says the Apostle, "is good, and nothing to be refused, if it be received with thanksgiving, for it is sanctified by the word of God and prayer." He does not bid us renounce the creation, but associates us with the most beautiful portions of it. He likens us to the flowers with which He has ornamented the earth, and to the birds that live solitary under heaven, and makes them the type of a Christian. He denies us Solomon's regal magnificence, to unite us to the lilies of the field and the fowls of the air. "Take no thought for your life, what ye shall eat or what ye shall drink; nor yet for your body, what ye shall put on. Is not the life more than meat, and the body than raiment? Behold the fowls of the air, for they sow not, neither do they reap, nor gather into barns; yet your heavenly Father feedeth them. Are ye not much better than they? . . . . And why take ye thought for raiment? Consider the lilies of the field, how they grow; they toil not, neither do they spin; and yet I say unto you, that even Solomon in all his glory was not arrayed like one of these." Here, then, surely, is a matter for joy and thankfulness at all seasons. . . . .

Again, what a great blessing is the gift of sleep! Almighty God does not suffer us to be miserable for a long time together, even when He afflicts us, but He breaks our trials into portions; takes us out of this world ever and anon, and gives us a holiday-time, like children at school, in an unknown and mysterious country.

All this, then, must be borne in mind in reflecting on those solemn and sobering truths concerning the Christian's calling which it is necessary often to insist upon. It is often said, and truly, that the Christian is born to trouble, that sorrow is the rule with him, and pleasure the exception. But when this is said, the question is one of seasons, circumstances, events, such things as are adventitious and additional to the gift of life itself. The Christian's lot is one of sorrow; but, as the regenerate life within him is happiness, so is the gift of natural life also. We live, therefore we are happy; *upon* this life of ours come joys and sorrows; and in proportion as we are favourites of God, it is sorrow that comes, not joy. Still, after all, considered in ourselves, that we live; that God breathes in us; that we exist in Him; that we think and act; that we have the means of life; that we have food, and sleep, and raiment, and lodging; and that we are not lonely, but in God's Church, and are sure of brethren by the very token of our having a Father which is in heaven;—so far, rejoicing is the very condition of our being, and all pain is little more than external, not reaching to our inmost heart. So far, all men almost are on a level, seasons of sickness excepted. Even delicate health and feebleness of life does not preclude these pleasures. And as to seasons of sickness, or even long and habitual pain or disease, the good Lord can compensate for them in His own way by extraordinary supplies of grace; as in early times He made even the torments of Christians in persecution literally pleasant to them. He who so ordered it that even the red-hot iron did feel pleasant to the martyrs after a while, cannot fail of means to support His servants when life becomes a burthen. But, generally speaking, it is a happiness, and that to all ranks. High and low, rich and poor, have the same refreshment in their pilgrimage. Hunger is as pleasantly appeased by the low as by the high, on coarse fare as on delicate. Sleep is equally the comfort and recruiting of rich and poor. We eat, drink, and sleep, whether we are in sorrow or in joy, in anxiety or in hope. Our natural life is the type of our spiritual life, and thus, in a literal as well as higher sense, we may bless Him "who saveth our life from destruction, and crowneth us with mercy and loving-kindness; who satisfieth our mouth with good things, making us young and lusty as an eagle."

Again, consider the blessings which we have in Christian brotherhood. In the beginning, woman was made, that man might not be alone, but might have a helpmate for him; and our Lord promised that all who gave up this world and this world's kindred for Him should "receive manifold more in this present time, houses, and brethren, and sisters, and mothers, and children, and lands, with persecutions." You see He mentions the troubles of Christians, which were their lot *as* Christians; but still these did not interfere with the prior law of their very nature, that they should not be friendless. As food and raiment are necessary conditions of life, society is an inseparable adjunct of it. God does not take away food and raiment when He gives us grace, nor does He take away brotherhood. He removes from the world to put into the Church. Religion without a Church is as unnatural as life without food and raiment. He began our life anew, but He built it up upon the same foundations; and as He did not strip us of our body when He made us Christians, neither did He of social ties. Christ finds us in the double tabernacle of a house of flesh and a house of brethren, and He sanctifies both, not pulls them down. Our first life is in ourselves; our second in our friends. They whom God forces to part with their near of kin for His sake, find brethren in the spirit at their side. They who remain solitary for His sake, have children in the spirit raised up to them. How should we thank God for this great benefit!

We, through God's mercy, whether we be young or old, whether we have many friends or few, if we be Christ's, shall all along our pilgrimage find those in whom we may live, who will love us, and whom we may love; who will aid us, and help us forward, and comfort us, and close our eyes. For His love is a secret gift, which, unseen by the world, binds together those in whom it lives, and makes them love and sympathize in one another.

THE DANGER OF RICHES.

"Woe unto you that are rich! for ye have received your consolation."—LUKE vi. 24.

UNLESS we were accustomed to read the New Testament from our childhood, I think we should be very much struck with the warnings which it contains, not only against the love of riches, but the very possession of them. We should wonder with a portion of that astonishment which the apostles at first felt, who had been brought up in the notion that they were a chief reward which God bestowed on those He loved. As it is, we have heard these most solemn declarations so continually, that we have ceased to attach any distinct meaning to them; or if our attention is at any time drawn more closely to them, we soon dismiss the subject, on some vague imagination that what is said in Scripture had a reference to the particular times when Christ came, without attempting to settle its exact application to us, or whether it has any such application at all; as if the circumstance that the application requires care and thought were an excuse for giving no thought nor care whatever to the settling of it.

But even if we had ever so little concern in the Scripture denunciations against riches and the love of riches, the very awfulness of them might have seemed enough to save them from neglect; just as the Flood and the judgment upon Sodom and Gomorrah are still dwelt upon by Christians with solemn attention, though we have a promise against the recurrence of the one, and trust we shall never be so deserted by God's grace as to call down upon us the other. And this consideration may lead a man to suspect that the neglect in question does not entirely arise from unconcern, but from a sort of misgiving that the subject of riches is one which cannot be safely or comfortably discussed without placing the claims of God's law and the pride of life into visible and perplexing opposition. Let us then see what the letter of Scripture says on the subject. For instance, consider the text: "Woe unto you that are rich! for ye have received your consolation." The words are sufficiently clear, it will not be denied, as spoken of rich persons in our Saviour's days. Let the full force of the word "consolation" be observed. It is used by way of contrast to the comfort which is promised to the Christian in the list of beatitudes. Comfort, in all the fulness of that word, as including help, guidance, encouragement, and support, is the promise of the Gospel. The promised Spirit who has taken Christ's place was called by Him the "Comforter." There is then something very fearful in the intimation of the text, that those who have riches thereby receive their portion, such as it is, in full, instead of the heavenly gift of the Gospel. The same doctrine is implied in our Lord's words in the parable of Dives and Lazarus. "Son, remember thou in thy lifetime receivedst *thy* good things, and likewise Lazarus evil things; but *now* he is *comforted*, and thou art tormented." At another time He said to His disciples, "How hardly shall they that have riches enter into the kingdom of God! For it is easier for a camel to go through a needle's eye than for a rich man to enter into the kingdom of God."

Now it is usual to dismiss such passages with the remark that they are directed, not against those who have, but against those who trust in riches; as if, forsooth, they implied no connection between the having and the trusting; no warning lest the possession lead to the idolatrous reliance on them; no necessity of fear and anxiety in the possessors, lest they should become castaways. And this irrelevant distinction is supposed to find countenance in our Lord's own language on one of the occasions above referred to, in which he first says, "How hardly shall they that *have* riches;" then, "How hard it is for them that *trust* in riches to enter into the kingdom of God;" whereas surely He only removes His disciples' false impression that the bare circumstance of possessing wealth was inconsistent with a state of salvation, and no more interprets *having* by *trusting* than makes *trusting* essential to *having*. He connects the two without identifying, without explaining away; and the simple question which lies for our determination is this: Whether, considering that they who had riches when Christ came were likely in His judgment idolatrously to trust in them, there is, or is not, reason for thinking that this likelihood varies materially in different ages? and according to the solution of this question must we determine the application of the woe pronounced in the text to these times. And, at all events, let it be observed, it is for those who would make out that these passages do *not* apply now, to give their reasons for their opinion: the burden of proof is with them. Till they draw their clear and reasonable distinction between the first and nineteenth century, the denunciation hangs over the world that is, as much as over the Pharisees and Sadducees at our Lord's coming.

But, in truth, that our Lord meant to speak of riches as being in some sense a calamity to the Christian, is plain, not only from such texts as the foregoing, but from His praises and recommendation on the other hand of poverty. For instance: "Sell that ye have and give alms; provide yourselves bags which wax not old." "If thou wilt be perfect, go and sell that thou hast, and give to the poor, and thou shalt have treasure in heaven." "Blessed be ye poor, for yours is the kingdom of God." "When thou makest a dinner or a supper, call not thy friends, nor thy brethren, neither thy kinsmen, nor thy rich neighbours—but—call the poor, the maimed, the lame, the blind." And in like manner St. James: "Hath He not chosen the poor of this world, rich in faith, and heirs of that kingdom which He hath promised to them that love Him?" Now I cite these texts in the way of doctrine, not of precept. Whatever be the line of conduct they prescribe to this or that individual (with which I have nothing to do at present), so far seems clear, that according to the rule of the Gospel, the absence of wealth is, as such, a more blessed and a more Christian state than the possession of it.

The most obvious danger which worldly possessions present to our spiritual welfare is, that they become practically a substitute in our hearts for that one object to which our supreme devotion is due. They are present; God is unseen. They are means at hand of effecting what we want: whether God will hear our petitions for such things is uncertain; or rather, I may say, certain in the negative. Thus they minister to the corrupt inclinations of our nature. They promise and are able to be gods to us, and such gods, too, as require no service; but, like dumb idols, exalt the worshipper, impressing him with a notion of his own power and security. And in this consists their chief and most subtle mischief. Religious men are able to repress, nay, extirpate sinful desires, the lust of the flesh and of the eyes, gluttony, drunkenness, and the like, love of amusements, and frivolous pleasures and display, indulgences or luxuries of whatever kind; but as to wealth, they cannot easily rid themselves of a secret feeling that it gives them a footing to stand upon, an importance, a superiority; and in consequence they get attached to this world, lose sight of the duty of bearing the cross, become dull and dim-sighted, and lose their delicacy and precision of touch; are numbed (so to say) in their fingers'-ends as regards religious interests and prospects. To risk all upon Christ's word seems somehow unnatural to them, extravagant, and evidences a morbid excitement; and death, instead of being a gracious, however awful release, is not a welcome subject of thought. They are content to remain as they are, and do not contemplate a change. They desire and mean to serve God; they actually do serve Him in their measure; but not with the keen sensibilities, the noble enthusiasm, the grandeur and elevation of soul, the dutifulness and affectionateness towards Christ which becomes a Christian; but as Jews might obey, who had no image of God given them except this created world, "eating their bread with joy, and drinking their wine with a merry heart;" caring that "their garments be always white, and their head lacking no ointment; living joyfully with the wife whom they love all the days of the life of their vanity," and "enjoying the good of their labour" (Eccles. ix. 7-9, v. 18). Not of course that the due use of God's temporal blessings is wrong; but to make them the object of our affections, to allow them to beguile us from the "one husband" to whom we are espoused, is to mistake the Gospel for Judaism.

This then, if we may venture to say so, was some part of our Saviour's meaning, when He connected together the having with the trusting in riches. Our Saviour seems further to warn us in His description of the thorns, in the parable of the Sower, as being the cares of this world, and the "deceitfulness of riches;" and more clearly in the parable of the Great Supper, where the guests excuse themselves, one as having "bought a piece of ground," another, "five yoke of oxen." Still more openly does St. Paul speak in his first Epistle to Timothy: "They that desire to be rich fall into temptation and a snare, and into many foolish and hurtful lusts, which drown men in destruction and perdition.

For the love of money is the root of all evil; which, while some coveted after, they have erred from the faith, and pierced themselves through with many sorrows."

The danger of *possessing* riches is the carnal security to which they lead; that of *desiring* and *pursuing* them is, that an object of this world is thus set before us as the aim and end of life. It seems to be the will of Christ that His followers shall have no aim or end, pursuit or business, merely of this world. Here, again, I speak as before, not in the way of precept, but of doctrine. I am looking at His holy religion as at a distance, and determining what is its general character and spirit, not what may happen to be the duty of this or that individual who has embraced it. It is His will that all we do should be done, not unto men, or to the world, or to self, but to His glory; and the more we are enabled to do this simply, the more favoured we are whenever we act with reference to an object of this world. Even though it be ever so pure, we are exposed to the temptation (not irresistible, God forbid! still to the temptation) of setting our hearts upon obtaining it. And, therefore, we call all such objects *excitements*, as stimulating us incongruously; casting us out of the serenity and stability of heavenly faith; attracting us aside by their proximity from our harmonious round of duties; and making our thoughts converge to something short of that which is infinitely high and eternal. Such excitements are of perpetual occurrence, and the mere undergoing them, so far from involving guilt in the act itself or its results, is the great business of life and the discipline of our hearts. It is often a sin to withdraw from them, as has been the case of some perhaps who have gone into monasteries to serve God more entirely. On the other hand, it is the very duty of the spiritual ruler to labour for the flock committed to him, to suffer and to dare. St. Paul was encompassed with excitements hence arising, and his writings show the agitating effect of them on his mind. He was like David, a man of war and blood, and that for our sakes. Still it holds good that the essential spirit of the Gospel is "quietness and confidence;" that the possession of these is the highest gift, and to gain them perfectly our main aim. Consequently, however much a duty it is to undergo excitements when they are sent upon us, it is plainly unchristian, a manifest foolishness and sin, to seek out any such, whether secular or religious. . . . .

Men of energetic minds and talents for action are called to a life of trouble; they are the compensations and antagonists of the world's evils; still let them never forget their place. They are men of war, and we war that we may obtain peace. They are but men of war, honoured indeed by God's choice, and in spite of all momentary excitements, resting in the depth of their hearts upon the one true vision of Christian faith. Still after all they are but soldiers in the open field, not builders of the Temple, nor inhabitants of those "amiable" and specially blessed "tabernacles," where the worshipper lives in praise and intercession, and is militant amid the unostentatious duties of ordinary life. "Martha, Martha, thou art anxious and troubled about many things : but one thing is needful, and Mary has chosen that good part which shall not be taken away from her." Such is our Lord's judgment, showing that our true happiness consists in being at leisure to serve God without excitements. For this gift we specially pray in one of our collects : " Grant, O Lord, that the course of this world may be so peaceably ordered by Thy governance, that Thy Church may joyfully serve Thee in all godly quietness." Persecution, civil changes, and the like, break in upon the Church's calm. The greatest privilege of a Christian is to have nothing to do with worldly politics—to be governed, and to submit obediently; and, though here again, selfishness may creep in, and lead a man to neglect public concerns in which he is called to take his share, yet, after all, such participation must be regarded as a duty, scarcely as a privilege ; as the fulfilment of trusts committed to him for the good of others, not as the enjoyment of rights (as men talk in these days of delusion), not as if political power were in itself a good.

I say, then, that it is a part of Christian caution to see that our engagements do not become pursuits. Engagements are our portion, but pursuits are for the most part of our own choosing. We may be engaged in worldly business without pursuing worldly objects. "Not slothful in business," yet "serving the Lord." In this then consists the danger of the pursuit of gain, as by trade and the like. It is the most common and widely-spread of all excitements. It is one in which every one almost may indulge, nay, and will be praised by the world for indulging. And it lasts through life; in that differing from the amusements and pleasures of the world, which are short-lived, and succeed one after another. Dissipation of mind, which these amusements create, is itself indeed miserable enough; but far worse than this dissipation is the concentration of mind upon some worldly object which admits of being constantly pursued; and such is the pursuit of gain. Nor is it a slight aggravation of the evil that anxiety is almost sure to attend it. A life of money-getting is a life of care. From the first there is a fretful anticipation of loss in various ways to depress and unsettle the mind, nay, to haunt it, till a man finds he can think about nothing else, and is unable to give his mind to religion from the constant whirl of business in which he is involved. It is well this should be understood. You may hear men talk as if the pursuit of wealth was the business of life. They will argue that, by the law of nature, a man is bound to gain a livelihood for his family, and that he finds a reward in doing so—an innocent and honourable satisfaction—as he adds one sum to another, and counts up his gains. And perhaps they go on to argue that it is the very duty of man, since Adam's fall, "in the sweat of his face," by effort and anxiety, "to eat bread." How strange it is that they do not remember Christ's gracious promise, repealing that original curse, and obviating the necessity of any real pursuit after "the meat that perisheth." In order that we might be delivered from the bondage of corruption, He has expressly told us that the necessaries of life shall never fail His faithful follower any more than the meal and oil the widow woman of Sarepta; that while he is bound to labour for his family, he need not be engrossed by his toil—that while he is busy, his heart may be at leisure for his Lord. "Be not anxious, saying, What shall we eat? or, What shall we drink? or, Wherewithal shall we be clothed? For after all these things do the Gentiles seek; and your heavenly Father knoweth that ye have need of all these things." . . . .

I have now given the main reason why the pursuit of gain, whether in a large or small way, is prejudicial to our spiritual interests—that it fixes the mind upon an object of this world. Yet others remain behind. Money is a sort of creation, and gives the acquirer even more than the possessor an imagination of his own power, and tends to make him idolize self. Again, what we have hardly won, we are unwilling to part with; so that a man who has himself made his wealth will commonly be penurious, or at least will not part with it except in exchange for what will reflect credit on himself, and increase his importance. Even when his conduct is most disinterested and amiable (as in spending for the comfort of those who depend on him), still this indulgence of self, of pride and worldliness, insinuates itself. Very unlikely therefore is it that he should be liberal towards God; for religious offerings are an expenditure without sensible return, and that upon objects for which the very pursuit of wealth has indisposed his mind. Moreover, if it may be added, there is a considerable tendency in occupations connected with gain to make a man unfair in his dealings; that is, in a subtle way. There are so many conventional deceits and prevarications in the details of the world's business, so much intricacy in the management of accounts, so many perplexed questions about justice and equity, so many plausible subterfuges and fictions of law, so much confusion between the distinct yet approximating outlines of honesty and civil enactment, that it requires a very straightforward mind to keep firm hold of strict conscientiousness, honour, and truth, and to look at matters in which he is engaged as he would have looked on them supposing he now came upon them all at once as a stranger.

And if such be the effect of the pursuit of gain on an individual, doubtless it will be the same on a nation. Only let us consider the fact that we *are* a money-making people, with our Saviour's declaration before us against wealth, and trust in wealth, and we shall have abundant matter for serious thought.

Lastly, the pattern of St. Matthew is our consolation, for it suggests that we, Christ's ministers, may use great freedom of speech, and state unreservedly the peril of wealth and gain, without aught of harshness or uncharitableness towards individuals who are exposed to it. They may be brethren of the evangelist, who left all for Christ's sake. Nay, such there have been (blessed be God !) in every age ; and in proportion to the strength of the temptation which surrounds them is their blessedness and their praise, if they are enabled amid the "wares of the seas " and the "great wisdom of their traffick," to hear Christ's voice, to take up their cross, and follow Him.

TEARS OF CHRIST AT THE GRAVE OF LAZARUS.

"Jesus said, Where have ye laid him? They say unto him, Lord, come and see. Jesus wept. Then said the Jews, Behold how He loved him."—JOHN xi. 34—36.

WHAT led our Lord to weep over the dead, who could at a word restore him; nay, had it in purpose to do so?

1. First of all, as the context informs us, He wept from very sympathy with the grief of others. "When Jesus saw Mary weeping, and the Jews also weeping which came with her, He groaned in the spirit and was troubled." It is the very nature of compassion or sympathy, as the word implies, "to rejoice with those who rejoice, and weep with those who weep." We know it is so with men, and God tells us He also is compassionate, and full of tender mercy. Yet we do not well know what this means, for how can God rejoice or grieve? By the very perfection of His nature, Almighty God cannot

show sympathy, at least to the comprehension of beings of such limited minds as ours. He indeed is hid from us; but if we were allowed to see Him, how could we discern in the Eternal and Unchangeable signs of sympathy? Words and works of sympathy He does display to us; but it is the very sight of sympathy in another that affects and comforts the sufferer more even than the fruits of it. Now we cannot see God's sympathy; and the Son of God, though feeling for us as great compassion as His Father, did not show it to us while He remained in His Father's bosom. But when He took flesh and appeared on earth, He showed us the Godhead in a new manifestation. He invested Himself with a new set of attributes, those of our flesh, taking into Him a human soul and body, in order that thoughts, feelings, affection might be His, which could respond to ours, and certify to us His tender mercy. When, then, our Saviour weeps from sympathy at Mary's tears, let us not say it is the love of a man overcome by natural feeling. It is the love of God, the bowels of compassion of the Almighty and Eternal condescending to appear as we are capable of receiving it, in the form of human nature.

Jesus wept, therefore, not merely from the deep thoughts of His understanding, but from spontaneous tenderness, from the gentleness and mercy, the encompassing loving-kindness and exuberant fostering affection of the Son of God for His own work, the race of man. Their tears touched Him at once, as their miseries had brought Him down from heaven. His ear was open to them, and the sound of weeping went at once to His heart.

2. But next we may suppose (if it is allowable to conjecture) that His pity thus spontaneously excited was led forward to dwell on the various circumstances in man's condition which excite pity. It was awakened, and began to look around upon the miseries of the world. What was it He saw? He saw visibly displayed the *victory of death;* a mourning multitude, everything present which might awaken sorrow, except him who was the chief object of it. He was not—a stone marked the place where he lay. Martha and Mary, whom He had known and loved in their brother's company, now solitary, approached Him, first one and then the other, in far other mood and circumstance than heretofore—in deep affliction; in faith and resignation, yet, apparently, with somewhat of a tender complaint: "Lord, if Thou hadst been here, my brother had not died." Such has been the judgment passed, or the doubt raised, concerning Him in the breast of the creature in every age. Men have seen sin and misery around them, and, whether in faith or unbelief, have said, "If Thou hadst been here," if Thou hadst interfered, it might have been otherwise. Here,

then, was the Creator surrounded by the works of His hands, who adored Him indeed, yet seemed to ask why He suffered what He Himself had made so to be marred. Here was the Creator of the world at a scene of death, seeing the issue of His gracious handiwork. Would not He revert in thought to the hour of creation, when He went forth from the bosom of the Father to bring all things into existence? There had been a day when He had looked upon the work of His love, and seen that it was "very good." Whence had the good been turned to evil, the fine gold become dim? "An enemy had done this." Why it was allowed, and how achieved, was a secret with Him, a secret from all who were about Him, as it is a secret to us at this day. Here He had incommunicable thoughts with His Eternal Father. He would not say why it was. He chose another course for taking away their doubts and complaints. "He opened not His mouth," but He wrought wondrously. What He has done for all believers, revealing His atoning death, yet not explaining it, this He did for Martha and Mary also, proceeding to the grave in silence, to raise their brother while they complained that he had been allowed to die.

Here, then, I say, were abundant sources for His grief (if we may be permitted to trace them), in the contrast between Adam, in the day in which he was created, innocent and immortal, and man as the devil had made him, full of the poison of sin and the breath of the grave; and again, in the timid complaint of His sorrowing friends that that change had been permitted. And though He was about to turn back the scene of sorrow into joy again, yet, after all, one day Lazarus must die again— He was but delaying the fulfilment of His own decree. A stone lay upon him now; and though he was raised from the grave, yet, by His own inscrutable law, one day he must lie down again in it. It was a respite, not a resurrection. . . . .

Alas! there were other thoughts still to call forth His tears. This marvellous benefit to the forlorn sisters— how was it to be attained? At His own cost. Joseph knew he could bring joy to his brethren, but at no sacrifice of his own. Christ was bringing life to the dead by His own death. His disciples would have dissuaded Him from going into Judea, lest the Jews should kill Him. Their apprehension was fulfilled. He went to raise Lazarus, and the fame of that miracle was the immediate cause of His seizure and crucifixion. This He knew beforehand. He saw the prospect before Him;— He saw Lazarus raised—the supper in Martha's house— Lazarus sitting at table—joy on all sides of Him—Mary honouring her Lord on this festive occasion by the outpouring of the very costly ointment upon His feet—the

Jews crowding, not only to see Him, but Lazarus also—His triumphant entry into Jerusalem—the multitude shouting Hosanna—the people testifying to the raising of Lazarus—the Greeks, who had come up to worship at the feast, earnest to see Him—the children joining in the general joy; and then the Pharisees plotting against Him—Judas betraying Him—His friends deserting Him, and the cross receiving Him. These things doubtless, among a number of thoughts unspeakable, passed over His mind. He felt that Lazarus was wakening to life at His own sacrifice; that He was descending into the grave which Lazarus had left. He felt that Lazarus was to live and He to die; the appearance of things was to be reversed; the feast was to be kept in Martha's house, but the last passover of sorrow remained for Him. And He knew that this reverse was altogether voluntary with Him. He had come down from His Father's bosom to be an atonement of blood for all sin, and thereby to raise all believers from the grave, as He was then about to raise Lazarus; and to raise them, not for a time, but for eternity. And now the sharp trial lay before Him, through which He was to "open the kingdom of heaven to all believers." Contemplating then the fulness of His purpose while going about a single act of mercy, He said to Martha, "I am the resurrection and the life: he that believeth in Me, though he were dead, yet shall he live; and whosoever liveth and believeth in Me shall never die."

Let us take to ourselves these comfortable thoughts, both in the contemplation of our own death, or upon the death of our friends. Wherever faith in Christ is, there is Christ Himself. He said to Martha, " Believest thou this?" Wherever there is a heart to answer, " Lord, I believe," there Christ is present; there our Lord vouchsafes to stand, though unseen—whether over the bed of death or over the grave—whether we ourselves are sinking or those who are dear to us. Blessed be His name ! nothing can rob us of this consolation; we will be as certain, through His grace, that He is standing over us in love, as though we saw Him. We will not, after our experience of Lazarus' history, doubt an instant that He is thoughtful for us. He knows the beginnings of our illness, though He keeps at a distance. He knows when to remain away, and when to draw near. He notes down the advances of it, and the stages. He tells truly when His friend Lazarus is sick, and when he sleeps. We all have experience of this in the narrative before us, and henceforth, so be it! will never complain of the course of His providence. Only we will beg of Him an increase of faith; a more lively perception of the curse under which the world lies, and of our own personal demerits; a more understanding view of the mystery of His cross;

a more devout and implicit reliance on the virtue of it; and a more confident persuasion that He will never put on us more than we can bear, never afflict His brethren with any woe except for their own highest benefit.

A PARTICULAR PROVIDENCE AS REVEALED IN THE GOSPEL.

"Thou God seest me."—GEN. xvi. 13.

WHEN Hagar fled into the wilderness from the face of her mistress, she was visited by an Angel, who sent her back, but, together with this implied reproof of her impatience, gave her a word of promise to encourage her. In the mixture of humbling and cheerful thoughts thus wrought in her, she recognized the presence of her Maker and Lord, who ever comes to His servants in a twofold aspect; severe, because He is holy; yet soothing, as abounding in mercy. In consequence, she called the name of the Lord that spake unto her, "Thou God seest me."

Such was the condition of man before Christ came, favoured with some occasional notices of God's regard for individuals; but, for the most part, instructed merely in His general Providence as seen in the course of human affairs. In this respect even the Law was deficient, though it abounded in proofs that God was a living, all-seeing, all-recompensing God. It was deficient, in comparison of the Gospel, in evidence of the really existing relation between each soul of man and its Maker, independently of everything else in the world. Of Moses, indeed, it is said, that "the Lord spake unto him *face to face*, as a man speaketh unto his friend." But this was an especial privilege vouchsafed to him only, and to some others, as to Hagar, who records it in the text, not to all the people. But under the New Covenant this distinct regard vouchsafed by Almighty God to every one of us is clearly revealed. It was foretold of the Christian Church: "*All* thy children shall be taught of the Lord; and great shall be the peace of thy children" (Is. liv. 13). When the Eternal Son came on earth in our flesh, men saw their invisible Maker and Judge. He showed Himself no longer through the mere powers of nature, or the maze of human affairs, but in our own likeness. "God, who commanded the light to shine out of darkness, hath shined in our hearts, to kindle the knowledge of His glory in the face of Jesus Christ;" that is, in a sensible form, as a really existing individual being. And, at the same time, He forthwith began to speak to *us* as individuals. He, on the one hand, addressed each of us on the other. Thus it was in some sense a revelation face to face.

A PARTICULAR PROVIDENCE AS REVEALED IN THE GOSPEL.

"Thou God seest me."—GEN. xvi. 13.

WHEN Hagar fled into the wilderness from the face of her mistress, she was visited by an Angel, who sent her back, but, together with this implied reproof of her impatience, gave her a word of promise to encourage her. In the mixture of humbling and cheerful thoughts thus wrought in her, she recognized the presence of her Maker and Lord, who ever comes to His servants in a twofold aspect; severe, because He is holy; yet soothing, as abounding in mercy. In consequence, she called the name of the Lord that spake unto her, "Thou God seest me."

Such was the condition of man before Christ came, favoured with some occasional notices of God's regard for individuals; but, for the most part, instructed merely in His general Providence as seen in the course of human affairs. In this respect even the Law was deficient, though it abounded in proofs that God was a living, all-seeing, all-recompensing God. It was deficient, in comparison of the Gospel, in evidence of the really existing relation between each soul of man and its Maker, independently of everything else in the world. Of Moses, indeed, it is said, that "the Lord spake unto him *face to face*, as a man speaketh unto his friend." But this was an especial privilege vouchsafed to him only, and to some others, as to Hagar, who records it in the text, not to all the people. But under the New Covenant this distinct regard vouchsafed by Almighty God to every one of us is clearly revealed. It was foretold of the Christian Church: "*All* thy children shall be taught of the Lord ; and great shall be the peace of thy children " (Is. liv. 13). When the Eternal Son came on earth in our flesh, men saw their invisible Maker and Judge. He showed Himself no longer through the mere powers of nature, or the maze of human affairs, but in our own likeness. "God, who commanded the light to shine out of darkness, hath shined in our hearts, to kindle the knowledge of His glory in the face of Jesus Christ;" that is, in a sensible form, as a really existing individual being. And, at the same time, He forthwith began to speak to *us* as individuals. He, on the one hand, addressed each of us on the other. Thus it was in some sense a revelation face to face.

This is the subject on which I propose now to make a few remarks. And first, let me observe, it is very difficult, in spite of the revelation made us in the Gospel, to master the idea of this particular providence of God. If we allow ourselves to float down the current of the world, living as other men, gathering up our notions of religion here and there, as it may be, we have little or no true comprehension of a particular Providence. We conceive that Almighty God works on a large plan; but we cannot realize the wonderful truth that He sees and thinks of individuals. We cannot believe that He is really present everywhere; that He is wherever we are, though unseen. For instance, we can understand, or think we understand, that He was present on Mount Sinai—or within the Jewish Temple—or that He clave the ground under Dathan and Abiram; but we do not in any sufficient sense believe that He is in like manner "about *our* path, and about *our* bed, and spieth out all *our* ways." We cannot bring ourselves to get fast hold of the solemn fact that He sees what is going on among ourselves at this moment; that this man falls, and that man is exalted, at His silent, invisible appointment. We use, indeed, the prayers of the Church, and intercede, not only for all conditions of men, but for the king, and the nobility, and the court of parliament, and so on, down to individual sick people in our own parish; yet, in spite of all this, we do not bring home to us the truth of His omniscience. We know He is in heaven, and forget that He is also on earth. This is the reason why the multitude of men are so profane; they use light words; they scoff at religion; they allow themselves to be lukewarm and indifferent; they take the part of wicked men; they push forward wicked measures; they defend injustice, or cruelty, or sacrilege, or infidelity, because they have no grasp of a truth, while, nevertheless, they have no intention to deny that God sees them. There is, indeed, a self-will, a self-deceit, which would sin on even in God's visible presence. This was the sin of Balaam, who took part with the enemies of Israel for reward; and of Zimri, the son of Salu, a prince of the Simeonites, on whom Phineas did judgment; and such the sin of Saul, of Judas, of Ananias and Sapphira. Alas! doubtless such is the sin of many a man now in England, unless human nature is other than it was aforetime. Alas! such a sin is in a measure our own from time to time, as any one may know for certain who is used to self-examination. Yet, over and above this, there is certainly a great deal of profane sinning from our *forgetting*, not comprehending that we are in God's presence; not comprehending, or (in other words) believing, that He sees and hears and notes down everything we do. This, again, is often the state in which persons find themselves on falling into trouble. The world fails them, and they despair, because they do not realize to themselves the loving-kindness and the presence of God. They find no comfort in a truth which to them is not a substance, but an opinion. Therefore it was that Hagar, when visited in the wilderness by the angel, called the name of the Lord that spake unto her, "Thou God seest me!" It came as a new truth to her, that, amid her trouble and her waywardness, the eye of God was upon her. The case is the same now. Men talk in a general way of the goodness of God, His benevolence, compassion, and long-suffering; but they think of it as a flood pouring itself out through all the world—as the light of the sun, not as the continually repeated action of an intelligent and living mind, contemplating whom it visits, and intending what it effects. Accordingly, when they come into trouble, they can but say, " It is all for the best—God is good!" and the like; and it all falls as cold comfort upon them, and does not lessen their sorrow, because they have not accustomed their minds to feel that He is a merciful God, regarding them individually, and not a mere universal Providence acting by general laws. And then, perhaps, all of a sudden the new notion breaks on them, as it did upon Hagar. Some especial Providence, amid their infliction, runs right into their hearts; brings it close home to them, in a way they never experienced before, that God sees them. And then, surprised at this, which is a something quite new to them, they go into the other extreme, in proportion to their former apathy, and are led to think that they are especial objects of God's love more than all other men. . . . .

The most winning property of our Saviour's mercy (if it is right so to speak of it), is its dependence on time and place, person and circumstance; in other words, its tender discrimination. It regards and consults each individual as he comes before it. It is called forth by some as it is not by others; it cannot (if I may so say) manifest itself to every object alike; it has its particular shade and mode of feeling for each; and in some it is so wrapt up as to seem to depend for its own happiness on their well-being. This might be illustrated, as is often done, by our Lord's tender behaviour towards Lazarus and his sisters, or His tears over Jerusalem; or by His conduct towards St. Peter, before and after his denial of Him; or towards St. Thomas when he doubted; or by His love of His mother or of St. John. But I will direct your attention rather to His treatment of the traitor Judas, both because it is not so commonly referred to, and also, if there was a being in the whole world whom one might suppose cast out of His presence as hateful and reprobate, it was he who He foresaw would betray Him. Yet we shall find that even this wretched man was followed and encompassed by His serene though solemn regard till the very hour He betrayed Him.

Judas was in darkness and hated the light, and "went to his own place;" yet he found it, not by the mere force of certain natural principles working out their inevitable results—by some unfeeling fate, which sentences the wicked to hell—but by a Judge who surveys him from head to foot, who searches him through and through, to see if there is any ray of hope, any latent spark of faith; who pleads with him again and again, and, at length abandoning him, mourns over him the while with the wounded affection of a friend rather than the severity of the Judge of the whole earth. For instance, first, a startling warning a year before his trial: "Have I not chosen you twelve, and one of you is a devil?" Then, when the time was come, the lowest act of abasement towards one who was soon to betray Him and to suffer the unquenchable fire: "He riseth from supper, poureth water into a basin, and began to wash the disciples' feet," and Judas in the number. Then a second warning at the same time, or rather a sorrowful lament, spoken as if to Himself: "Ye are not all clean." Then openly: "Verily, verily, I say unto you, that one of you shall betray Me." "The Son of Man goeth, as it is written of

Him; but woe unto that man by whom the Son of Man is betrayed! it had been good for that man if he had not been born. Then Judas, which betrayed Him, answered and said, Master, is it I? He said unto him, Thou hast said it." Lastly, when He was actually betrayed by him: "Friend, wherefore art thou come?" "Judas (He addresses him by name), betrayest thou the Son of Man with a kiss?" I am not attempting to reconcile His Divine foreknowledge with this special and prolonged anxiety, this personal feeling towards Judas; but wish you only to observe the latter, to observe what is given us by the revelation of Almighty God in the Gospels, viz., an acquaintance with His providential regard for *individuals*, making His sun to rise on the evil as well as on the good. And, in like manner doubtless, at the last day, the wicked and impenitent shall be condemned, not in a mass, but one by one— one by one appearing, each in his own turn, before the righteous Judge, standing under the full glory of His countenance, carefully weighed in the balance, and found wanting; dealt with, not, indeed, with a weak and wavering purpose, where God's justice claims satisfaction, yet, at the same time, with all the substantial solicitude and awful care of one who would fain make, if He could, the fruit of His passion more numerous than it is.

This solemn reflection may be further enforced by considering our Lord's behaviour towards strangers who came to Him. Judas was His friend; but we have never seen Him. How will He look, and how does He look upon us? Let His manner in the Gospels towards the multitude of men assure us. All holy and all almighty as He is, and has shown Himself to be, yet in the midst of His divine majesty He could display a tender interest in all who approached Him; as if He could not cast His eyes on any of His creatures without the overflowing affection of a parent for his child, regarding it with a full satisfaction, and simply desiring its happiness and highest good. Thus, when the rich young man came to Him, it is said: "And Jesus beholding him, *loved him*, and said unto him, One thing thou lackest." When the Pharisees asked a sign, "He sighed deeply in His spirit." At another time, "He looked round about on them,"—as if on every one, to see if here and there perchance there might be an exception to the general unbelief, and to condemn, one by one, those who were guilty,—"He looked round about on them with anger, being grieved for the hardness of their hearts." Again, when a leper came to Him, He did not simply heal him, but, "moved with compassion, He put forth His hand."

How gracious is this revelation of God's particular providence to those who seek Him! How gracious to those who have discovered that this world is but vanity, and who are solitary and isolated in themselves, whatever shadows of power and happiness surround them! The multitude, indeed, go on without these thoughts; either from insensibility, as not understanding their own hearts, or changing from one idol to another, as each successively fails. But men of keener hearts would be overpowered by despondency, and would even loathe existence, did they suppose themselves under the mere operation of fixed laws, powerless to excite the pity or the attention of Him who has appointed them. What should they do especially who are cast among persons unable to enter into their feelings, and thus strangers to them, though by long custom ever so much friends? or have perplexities of mind they cannot explain to themselves, much less remove, and no one to help them? or have affections and aspirations pent up within them, because they have not met with objects to which to devote them? or are misunderstood by those around them, and find they have no words to set themselves right with them, or no principles in common by way of appeal? or seem to themselves to be without place or purpose in the world, or to be in the way of others? or have to follow their own sense of duty without advisers or supporters, nay, to resist the wishes and solicitations of superiors or relatives? or have the burden of some painful secret, or of some incommunicable solitary grief?

In all such cases the gospel narrative supplies our very need, not simply presenting to us an unchangeable Creator to rely upon, but a compassionate Guardian, a discriminating Judge and Helper. God beholds thee individually, whoever thou art. "He calls thee by thy name." He sees thee, and understands thee. He knows what is in thee, all thy own peculiar feelings and thoughts, thy dispositions and likings, thy strength and thy weakness. He views thee in thy day of rejoicing and in thy day of sorrow. He sympathises in thy hopes and in thy temptations. He interests Himself in all thy anxieties and thy remembrances, in all the risings and fallings of thy spirit. He has numbered the very hairs of thy head, and the cubits of thy stature. He compasses thee round, and bears thee in His arms; He takes thee up and sets thee down. He notes thy very countenance, whether smiling or in tears, whether healthful or sickly. He looks tenderly upon thy hands and thy feet; He hears thy voice, the beating of thy heart, and thy very breathing. Thou dost not love thyself better than He loves thee. Thou canst not shrink from pain more than He dislikes thy bearing it; and if He puts it on thee, it is as thou wilt put it on thyself, if thou art wise, for a greater good afterwards. Thou art not only His creature (though for the very sparrows He has a care, and pitied the "much cattle" of Nineveh), thou art man redeemed and sanctified, His adopted son, favoured with a portion of that glory and blessedness which flows from Him everlastingly unto the Only-begotten. Thou art chosen to be His, even above thy fellows who dwell in the east and south. Thou wast one of those for whom Christ offered up His last prayer, and sealed it with His precious blood. What a thought is this, a thought almost too great for our faith! Scarce can we refrain from acting Sarah's part, when we bring it before us, so as to "laugh" from amazement and perplexity. What is man, what are we, what am I, that the Son of God should be so mindful of me? What am I, that He should have raised me from almost a devil's nature to that of an angel's? that He should have changed my soul's original constitution, new-made me, who from my youth up have been a transgressor, and should Himself dwell personally in this very heart of mine, making me His temple? What am I, that God the Holy Ghost should enter into me, and draw up my thoughts heavenward "with plaints unutterable?"

These are the meditations which come upon the Christian to console him while he is with Christ upon the holy mount. And when he descends to his daily duties they are still his inward strength, though he is not allowed to tell the vision to those around him. They make his countenance to shine; make him cheerful, collected, serene, and firm in the midst of all temptation, persecution, or bereavement. And with such thoughts before us, how base and miserable does the world appear in all its pursuits and doctrines! How truly miserable does it seem to seek good from the creature; to court station, health, or credit; to choose for ourselves, in fancy, this or that mode of life; to affect the manners and fashions of the great; to spend our time in follies; to be discontented, quarrelsome, jealous or envious, censorious or resentful, full of unprofitable talk, and eager for the news of the day; busy about public matters which concern us not; hot in the cause of this or that interest or party; or set upon gain; or devoted to the increase of barren knowledge! And at the end of our days, when flesh and heart fail, what will be our consolation, though we have made ourselves rich, or have served an office, or been the first man among our equals, or have depressed a rival, or managed things our own way, or have settled splendidly, or have been intimate with the great, or have fared sumptuously, or have gained a name! Say, even if we obtain that which lasts longest, a place in history, yet, after all, what ashes shall we have eaten for bread! And in that awful hour, when death is in sight, will He, whose eye is now so loving towards us, and whose hand falls on us so gently, will He acknowledge us any more? Or if He still speaks, will His voice have any power to stir us? Rather, will it not repel us, as it did Judas, by the very tenderness with which it would invite us to Him?

Let us then endeavour, by His grace, to understand rightly where we stand, and what He is towards us : most tender and pitiful, yet, for all His pity, not passing by the breadth of a single hair the eternal lines of truth, holiness, and justice; He who can condemn to the woe everlasting, though He weeps and laments beforehand, and who, when once the sentence of condemnation has gone forth, will wipe out altogether the remembrance of us, "and know us not." The tares were "bound in bundles" for the burning, indiscriminately, promiscuously, contemptuously. "Let us then fear, lest a promise being left us of entering into His rest, any of us should seem to come short of it."

TIMES OF PRIVATE PRAYER.

"Thou, when thou prayest, enter into thy closet, and when thou hast shut thy door, pray to thy Father which is in secret; and thy Father, which seeth in secret, shall reward thee openly."—MATT. vi. 6.

HERE is our Saviour's own sanction and blessing vouchsafed to private prayer, in simple, clear, and most gracious words. The Pharisees were in the practice, when they prayed by themselves, of praying in *public*, in the corners of the streets; a strange inconsistency, according to our notions, since in our language prayer by one's self is ever called *private* prayer. Public private prayer, this was their self-contradictory practice. Warning, then, His disciples against the particular form of hypocrisy in which the self-conceit of human nature at that day showed itself, our Lord promises in the text His Father's blessing on such humble supplications as were really addressed to Him, and not made to gain the praise of men. Those who seek the unseen God (He seems to say) seek Him in their hearts and hidden thoughts, not in loud words, as if He were far off from them. Such men would retire from the world into places where no human eye saw them, there to meet Him humbly and in faith who is "about their path and about their bed, and spieth out all their ways." And He, the searcher of hearts, would reward them openly. Prayers uttered in secret, according to God's will, are treasured up in God's Book of Life. They seem, perhaps, to have sought an answer here, and to have failed of their object. Their memory perishes even in the mind of the petitioner, and the world never knew of them. But God is ever mindful, and in the last day, when the books are opened, they shall be disclosed and rewarded before the whole world.

Such is Christ's gracious promise in the text, acknowledging and blessing, according to His own condescension, those devotional exercises which were a duty even before Scripture enjoined them; and changing into a privilege that work of faith which, though bidden by conscience, and authorised by reason, yet before He revealed His mercy, is laden, in every man's case who attempts it, with guilt, remorse, and fear. It is the Christian's unspeakable privilege, and his alone, that he has at all times free access to the throne of grace boldly through the mediation of his Saviour.

But in what I shall now say concerning prayer I shall

not consider it as a privilege, but as a duty. For till we have some experience of the duties of religion, we are incapable of entering duly into the privileges; and it is too much the fashion of the day to view prayer chiefly as a mere privilege, such a privilege as it is inconsiderate indeed to neglect—but only inconsiderate, not sinful—and optional to use.

Now we know well enough that we are bound to be, in one sense, in prayer and meditation all the day long. The question then arises, are we to pray in any other way? Is it enough to keep our minds fixed upon God through the day, and to commune with Him in our hearts? or is it necessary, over and above this habitual faith, to set apart particular times for the more systematic and earnest exercise of it? Need we pray at certain times of the day in a set manner? *Public* worship indeed, from its very nature, requires *places, times,* and even set *forms.* But *private* prayer does not necessarily require set *times,* because we have no one to consult but ourselves, and we are always with ourselves. Nor *forms;* for there is no one else whose thoughts are to keep pace with ours. Still, though set forms and times of prayer are not absolutely *necessary* in private prayer, yet they are highly expedient; or, rather, times are actually commanded to us by our Lord in the text: "Thou, when thou prayest, enter into thy closet, and when thou hast shut thy door, pray to thy Father which is in secret; and thy Father, which seeth in secret, shall reward thee openly."

In these words certain *times* for private prayer, over and above the secret thought of God which must ever be alive in us, are clearly enjoined; and the practice of good men in Scripture gives us an example in confirmation of the command. Even our Saviour had His peculiar seasons of communing with God. *His* thoughts indeed were one continued sacred service offered up to His Father. Nevertheless, we read of His going up "into a mountain apart to pray;" and again, of His "continuing all night in prayer to God." Doubtless you will recollect that solitary prayer of His, before His Passion, thrice repeated, "that the cup might pass from Him." St. Peter too, as in the narrative of the conversion of Cornelius, the Roman centurion, went up upon the house-top to pray about the sixth hour: then God visited him. And Nathaniel seems to have been in prayer under the fig-tree at the time our Saviour saw him, and Philip called him. I might multiply instances from Scripture of such Israelites without guile; which are of course applicable to us; because, though they were under a divine government in many respects different from the Christian, yet *personal* religion is the same at all times. "The just," in every dispensation, "shall live by faith;"

and whatever reasons there were then for faith to display and maintain itself by stated prayer remain substantially the same now. Let two passages suffice. The Psalmist says, "*Seven* times a day do I praise Thee, because of Thy righteous judgments." And Daniel's practice is told us on a memorable occasion: "Now when Daniel knew that the writing was signed (the impious decree forbidding prayer to any but King Darius for thirty days), he went into his house, and his windows being open in his chamber towards Jerusalem, he kneeled upon his knees *three times* a day, and prayed, and gave thanks before his God, *as he did aforetime.*"

It is plain, then, besides the devotional temper in which we should pass the day, more solemn and direct acts of worship, nay, regular and periodical, are required of us by the precept of Christ and His own example, and that of His apostles and prophets under both covenants.

Now it is necessary to insist upon this duty of observing private prayer at stated times, because amid the cares and hurry of life men are very apt to neglect it; and it is a much more important duty than it is generally considered, even by those who perform it.

The following are two chief reasons for its importance.

First, it brings religious subjects before the mind in regular course. Prayer through the day is indeed the characteristic of a Christian spirit; but we may be sure that, in most cases, those who do not pray at stated times, in a more solemn and direct manner, will never pray well at other times. We know in the common engagements of life the importance of collecting and arranging our thoughts calmly and accurately before proceeding to any important business, in order to the right performance of it; and so in that one really needful occupation, the care of our eternal interests, if we would have our minds composed, our desires subdued, and our tempers heavenly through the day, we must, before commencing the day's employment, stand still awhile to look into ourselves and commune with our hearts, by way of preparing ourselves for the trials and duties on which we are entering. A like reason may be assigned for evening prayer, viz., as affording us a time of looking back on the day past, and summing up (as it were) that account which, if *we* do not reckon, at least God has reckoned, and written down in that book which will be produced at the judgment. . .

Stated times of private prayer are useful as impulses (so to say) to the continuous devotion of the day. They instruct us and engage us in what is ever our duty. It is commonly said that what is every one's business is practically no one's: this applies here. I repeat it, if we leave religion as a subject of thought for all hours of the day equally, it will be thought of in none. In all things it is by small beginnings and appointed channels that an advance is made to extensive works. Stated times of prayer put us in that posture (as I may call it) in which we ought ever to be; they urge us forward in a heavenly direction, and then the stream carries us on. For the same reason it is expedient, if possible, to be solemn in the forms of our private worship, in order to impress our minds. Our Saviour *kneeled* down, fell on His face, and prayed; so did His apostles, and so did the saints of the Old Testament.

I now come to the second reason for stated private prayer. Besides its tending to produce in us lasting impressions, it is also a more direct means of gaining from God an answer to our requests. He has so sanctioned it in the text: "Shut thy door, and pray to thy Father which seeth in secret, and He shall reward thee openly." We do not know *how* it is that prayer receives an answer from God at all. It is strange, indeed, that weak man should have strength to move God; but it is our privilege to know that we *can* do so. The whole system of this world is a history of man's interfering with divine decrees; and if we have the melancholy power of baffling His good will to our own ruin (an awful and incomprehensible truth!) if, when He designs our eternal salvation, we can yet annul our heavenly election, and accomplish our eternal destruction, much more have we the power to move Him (blessed be His name!) when He, the Searcher of hearts, discerns in us the mind of that Holy Spirit which "maketh intercession for the saints according to His will.". . . . .

Stated times of prayer, then, are necessary, first, as a means of making the mind sober and the general temper more religious; secondly, as a means of exercising earnest faith, and therefore of receiving a more certain blessing in answer than we should otherwise obtain. . . . Satan perceives well enough that stated private prayer is the very emblem and safeguard of true devotion to God, as impressing on us and keeping up in us a rule of conduct. He who gives up regularity in prayer has lost a principal means of reminding himself that spiritual life is obedience to a Lawgiver, not a mere feeling or a taste. . . . Be sure, my brethren, whoever of you is persuaded to disuse his morning and evening prayers, is giving up the armour which is to secure him against the wiles of the devil. If you have left off the observance of them, you may fall any day; and you will fall without notice. For a time you will go on, seeming to yourselves to be the same as before; but the Israelites might as well hope to lay in a stock of manna, as you of grace. You pray God for your daily bread, your bread day by day; and if you have not prayed for it this morning, it will profit you little that you prayed for it yesterday. You did then pray, and you obtained—but not a supply for two days. When you have given over the practice of stated prayer, you gradually become weaker without knowing it. Samson did not know he had lost his strength till the Philistines came upon him. You will think yourselves the men you used to be, till suddenly your adversary will come furiously upon you, and you will as suddenly fall. You will be able to make little or no resistance. This is the path which leads to death. . . . Beware then of the subtilty of your enemy, who would fain rob you of your defence. Do not yield to his bad reasonings. Be on your guard especially when you get into novel situations, or circumstances which interest and delight you, lest they throw you out of your regularity in prayer. Anything new or unexpected is dangerous to you. Going much into mixed society, and seeing many strange persons, taking share in any pleasant amusements, reading interesting books, entering into any new line of life, forming some new acquaintance, the prospect of any worldly advantage, travelling; all these things and such like, innocent as they are in themselves, and capable of a religious use, become means of temptation if we are not on our guard. See that you are not *unsettled* by them; this is the danger; fear becoming *unsettled*. Consider that stability of mind is the chief of virtues, for it is faith. "Thou wilt keep him in perfect peace whose mind is stayed on Thee, because he trusteth in Thee;" this is the promise. But "the wicked are like the troubled sea when it cannot rest, whose waters cast up mire and dirt. There is no peace, saith my God, to the wicked." Not to the wicked only, in our common sense of the word "wicked," but to none is there rest who in any way leave their God and rove after the goods of this world. Do not indulge visions of earthly good, fix your hearts on higher things; let your morning and evening thoughts be the points of rest for your mind's eye, and let those thoughts be upon the narrow way and the blessedness of heaven, and the glory and power of Christ your Saviour. Thus will you be kept from unseemly risings and fallings, and steadied in an equable way. Men in general will know nothing of this; they witness not your private prayers, and they will confuse you with the multitude they fall in with. But your friends and acquaintances will gain a light and a comfort from your example; they will see your good works, and be led to trace them to their true secret source, the influences of the Holy Ghost sought and obtained by prayer. Thus they will glorify your heavenly Father, and in emulation of you will seek Him; and He who seeth in secret shall at length reward you openly.

FORMS OF PRIVATE PRAYER.

"Lord, teach us to pray, as John also taught his disciples."—
LUKE xi. 1.

THESE words express the natural feelings of the awakened mind, perceiving its great need of God's help, yet not understanding well what its particular wants are, or how they are to be relieved. The disciples of John the Baptist and the disciples of Christ waited on their respective masters for instruction *how to pray*. *Their* need has been the need of Christians ever since. All of us in childhood, and most men ever after, require direction how to pray; and hence the use of *Forms of prayer*, which have always obtained in the Church. John taught his disciples; Christ gave the apostles the prayer which is distinguished by the name of the *Lord's Prayer;* and after He had ascended on high, the Holy Spirit has given us excellent services of devotion by the mouth of those blessed saints whom from time to time He has raised up to be overseers in the Church. In the words of St. Paul,

"We know not what we should pray for as we ought;" but "the Spirit helpeth our infirmities;" and that not only by guiding our thoughts, but by directing our words.

This, I say, is the origin of *Forms of prayer*, of which I mean to speak to-day; viz., these two undeniable truths: first, that all men have the same spiritual wants, and secondly, that they cannot of themselves express them. . . I suppose no one is in any difficulty about the use of forms of prayer in *public* worship; for common sense almost will tell us that when many are to pray together *as one* man, if their thoughts are to go together, they *must* agree beforehand what is to be the subject of their prayers; nay, what the *words* of their prayers, if there is to be any certainty, composure, ease, and regularity in their united devotions. To be present at extempore prayer, is to *hear prayers*. . . . .

Let us bear in mind the precept of the wise man: "Be not rash with thy mouth, and let not thine heart be hasty to utter anything before God; for God is in heaven, and thou upon earth; therefore let thy words be few." Prayers framed at the moment are likely to become *irreverent*. Let us consider for a few moments before we pray into whose presence we are entering—the presence of God. What need have we of humble, sober, and subdued thoughts, as becomes *creatures* sustained hourly by His bounty; as becomes *lost sinners* who have no right to speak at all, but must submit in silence to Him who is holy; and still more as grateful *servants of Him* who bought us from ruin at the price of His own blood; meekly sitting at His feet like Mary to learn and to do His will, and like the penitent at the great man's feast, quietly adoring Him, and doing Him service without disturbance, washing His feet (as it were) with our tears, and anointing them with precious ointment, as having sinned much and needing a large forgiveness. Therefore, to avoid the irreverence of many or unfit words, and rude half-religious thoughts, it is necessary to pray from book or memory, and not at random. . . .

Again, forms of prayer are necessary to guard us against the irreverence of *wandering* thoughts. If we pray without set words (read or remembered), our minds will stray from the subject; other thoughts will cross us, and we shall pursue them; we shall lose sight of His presence whom we are addressing. This wandering of mind is in good measure prevented, under God's blessing, by forms of prayer. Thus a chief use of them is that of *fixing the attention.*

Next, they are useful in securing us from the irreverence of *excited thoughts.* It is true that in certain times of strong emotion, grief or joy, remorse or fear, our religious feelings outrun and leave behind them any form of words. In such cases not only is there no *need* of forms of prayer, but it is perhaps impossible to write forms of prayer for Christians agitated by such feelings. For each man feels in his own way, perhaps no two men exactly alike; and we can no more write down *how* men ought to pray at such times, than we can give rules how they should weep or be merry. As a general rule, forms of prayer should not be written in strong and impassioned language; but should be calm, composed, and short. Our Saviour's own prayer is our model in this respect. How few are its petitions! how soberly expressed! how reverently! and at the same time how deep they are, and how comprehensive!—I readily grant, then, that there *are* times when the heart outruns any written words; as the jailor cried out, "What shall I do to be saved?" Nay, rather I would maintain that set words should not attempt to imitate the impetuous workings to which all minds are subject at times in this world of change (and therefore religious minds in the number), lest one should seem to encourage them.

Granting that there *are* times when a thankful or a wounded heart bursts through all forms of prayer, yet these are not *frequent*. To be excited is not the ordinary state of the mind, but the extraordinary, the now and then state. Nay, more than this, it *ought not* to be the common state of the mind; and if we are encouraging within us this excitement, this unceasing rush and alternation of feelings, and think that this, and this only, is being in earnest in religion, we are harming our minds, and (in one sense) I may even say, grieving the peaceful Spirit of God, which would silently and tranquilly work His divine work in our hearts. This, then, is an especial *use* of forms of prayer, *when* we are in earnest, as we ought always to be, viz., to keep us from irreverent earnestness, to still emotion, to calm us, to remind us what and where we are, to lead us to a purer and serener temper, and to that deep unruffled love of God and man which is really the fulfilling of the law and the perfection of human nature.

Let us recollect, the power of praying, being a habit, must be acquired like all other habits, by practice. In order at length to pray well, we must begin by praying ill, since ill is all we can do. Is not this plain? Who, in the case of any other work, would wait till he could do it perfectly before he tried it? The idea is absurd. Yet those who object to forms of prayer fall into this strange error. If, indeed, we could pray and praise God like the angels, we might have no need of forms of prayer; but forms are to teach those who pray poorly to pray better. They are helps to our devotion, as teaching us what to pray for, and how, as St. John and our Lord taught their disciples; and doubtless even the *best* of us prays *but* poorly, and *needs* the help of them. . .

Further, forms are useful to *help our memory*, and to set before us at once, completely, and in order, what we have to pray for. It does not follow, when the heart is really full of the thought of God, and alive to the reality of things unseen, that then it is easiest to pray. Rather, the deeper insight we have into His majesty and our innumerable wants, the less we shall be able to draw out our thoughts into words. The publican could only say, "God be merciful to me a sinner." This was enough for his *acceptance;* but to offer such a scanty service was not to exercise the *gift* of prayer, the privilege of a ransomed and exalted son of God. He whom Christ has illuminated with His grace is heir of all things. He has an interest in the world's multitude of matters. He has a boundless sphere of duties within and without him. He has a glorious prospect before him. The saints shall hereafter judge the world, and shall they not *here* take cognizance of its doings? Are they not in one sense counsellors and confidential servants of their Lord, intercessors at the throne of grace, the secret agents by and for whom He guides His high providence, and carries on the nations to their doom? And in their own persons is forgiveness merely and acceptance (extreme blessings as these are) the scope of their desires? else might they be content with the publican's prayer. Are they not rather bidden to go on to perfection, to use the Spirit given them, to enlarge and purify their own hearts, and to draw out the nature of man into the fulness of its capabilities after the image of the Son of God? And for the thought of all these objects at once who is sufficient? Whose mind is not overpowered by the view of its own immense privilege, so as eagerly to seek for words of prayer and intercession carefully composed according to the number and the nature of the various petitions it has to offer? So that he who prays without plan, is in fact losing a great part of the privilege with which his baptism has gifted him.

And further, the use of a form as a help to the memory is still more obvious when we take into account the engagements of this world with which most men are surrounded. The cares and businesses of life press upon us with a reality which we cannot overlook. Shall we trust the matters of the next world to the chance thoughts of our own minds, which come this moment and go the next, and may not be at hand when the time of employing them arrives, like unreal visions, having no substance and no permanence? This world is Satan's efficacious Form, it is the instrument through which he spreads out, in order and attractiveness, his many snares; and these doubtless will engross us, unless we also give form to the spiritual objects towards which we pray and labour. How short are the seasons which most men have to give to prayer. Before they can collect their memories and minds, their leisure is almost over, even if they have the power to dismiss the thoughts of this world which just before engaged them. Now forms of prayer do this *for* them. They keep the ground occupied, that Satan may not encroach upon the seasons of devotion. They are a standing memorial, to which we can recur as to a temple of God, finding everything in order for our worship as soon as we go into it, though the time allotted us at morning and evening be ever so circumscribed. . . . .

Let us recollect for how long a period our prayers have been the standard Forms of devotion in the Church of Christ, and we shall gain a fresh reason for loving them, and a fresh source of comfort in using them. I know different persons will feel differently here according to their different turn of mind; yet surely there are few of us, if we dwelt on the thought, but would feel it a privilege to use (for instance, in the Lord's Prayer) the very petitions which Christ spoke. He gave the prayer, and used it. His apostles used it; all the saints ever since have used it. When we use it we seem to join company with them. Who does not think himself brought nearer to any celebrated man in history, by seeing his house, or his furniture, or his handwriting, or the very books that were his? Thus does the Lord's Prayer bring us near to Christ, and to His disciples in every age. No wonder, then, that in past times good men thought this form of prayer so sacred, that it seemed to them impossible to say it too often, as if some especial grace went with the use of it. Nor *can* we use it too often; it contains in itself a sort of plea for Christ's listening to us; we cannot, so that we keep our minds fixed on its petitions, and use our minds as well as our lips when we repeat it. And what is true of the Lord's Prayer is in its measure true of most of those prayers which our Church teaches us to use. It is true of the Psalms also, and of the Creeds, all of which have become sacred, from the memory of saints departed who have used them, and whom we hope one day to meet in heaven.

One caution I give in conclusion as to using these thoughts. Beware lest your religion be one of feeling merely, not of practice. Men may speak in a high imaginative way of the ancient saints and the Holy Apostolic Church, without making the fervour or the refinement of their devotion bear upon their conduct. Many a man likes to be religious in graceful language; he loves religious tales and hymns, yet is never the better Christian for all this. The works of every day, these are the tests of our glorious contemplations, whether or not they shall be available to our salvation; and he who does one deed of obedience for Christ's sake, let him have no imagination and no fine feeling, is a better man, and returns to his home justified rather than the most eloquent speaker and the most sensitive hearer, if such men do not practise up to their knowledge.

THE END

A LIST OF BOOKS

PUBLISHED BY

STRAHAN AND CO.,

56, LUDGATE HILL, LONDON.

By ALFRED TENNYSON, D.C.L.
POET LAUREATE.

1. POEMS. Small 8vo., 9s.
2. MAUD, and other Poems. Small 8vo., 5s.
3. THE PRINCESS. Small 8vo., 5s.
4. IDYLLS OF THE KING. Small 8vo., 7s.
   ——————————— Collected, small 8vo., 12s.
5. ENOCH ARDEN, etc. Small 8vo., 6s.
6. SELECTIONS FROM THE ABOVE WORKS. Square 8vo., cloth extra, 5s.
7. THE HOLY GRAIL, and other Poems. Small 8vo., 7s.

IN MEMORIAM. Small 8vo., 6s.

POCKET VOLUME EDITION OF MR. TENNYSON'S WORKS. 10 vols., in neat case, 2l. 5s.

CONCORDANCE TO MR. TENNYSON'S WORKS. Crown 8vo., 7s. 6d.

By the DUKE OF ARGYLL.

1. THE REIGN OF LAW. New Edition, with Additions. Crown 8vo., 6s.
2. PRIMEVAL MAN. An Examination of some Recent Speculations. Crown 8vo., 4s. 6d.

A LIST OF BOOKS PUBLISHED BY STRAHAN AND CO.

By HENRY ALFORD, D.D.
DEAN OF CANTERBURY.

1. THE NEW TESTAMENT. Authorised Version Revised. Long Primer Edition, crown 8vo., 6s. Brevier Edition, fcap. 8vo., 3s. 6d. Nonpariel Edition, small 8vo., 1s. 6d.

2. ESSAYS AND ADDRESSES, chiefly on Church Subjects. Demy 8vo., 7s. 6d.

3. THE YEAR OF PRAYER; being Family Prayers for the Christian Year. Crown 8vo., 3s. 6d.; small 8vo., 1s. 6d.

4. THE YEAR OF PRAISE; being Hymns with Tunes for the Sundays and Holidays of the Year. Large type, with music, 3s. 6d.; without music, 1s. Small type, with music, 1s. 6d.; without music, 6d. Tonic Solfa Edition, 1s. 6d.

5. HOW TO STUDY THE NEW TESTAMENT. 3 vols., small 8vo., 3s. 6d. each.

6. EASTERTIDE SERMONS. Small 8vo., 3s. 6d.

7. MEDITATIONS: Advent, Creation, and Providence. Small 8vo., 3s. 6d.

8. LETTERS FROM ABROAD. Crown 8vo., 7s. 6d.

9. THE QUEEN'S ENGLISH: Stray Notes on Speaking and Spelling. Small 8vo., 5s.

By the Rev. SAMUEL COX.

THE RESURRECTION. Crown 8vo., 5s.

By EDWARD GARRETT.

OCCUPATIONS OF A RETIRED LIFE. Popular Edition. Crown 8vo., 6s.

By DORA GREENWELL.

1. ESSAYS. Crown 8vo., 6s.
2. POEMS. Enlarged Edition. Crown 8vo., 6s.
3. THE COVENANT OF LIFE AND PEACE. Small 8vo., 3s. 6d.
4. THE PATIENCE OF HOPE. Small 8vo., 2s. 6d.
5. TWO FRIENDS. Small 8vo., 3s. 6d.

A LIST OF BOOKS PUBLISHED BY

By THOMAS GUTHRIE, D.D.
1. STUDIES OF CHARACTER FROM THE OLD TESTAMENT. Crown 8vo., 3s. 6d.
2. THE PARABLES READ IN THE LIGHT OF THE PRESENT DAY. Crown 8vo., 3s. 6d.
3. MAN AND THE GOSPEL. Crown 8vo., 3s. 6d.
4. OUR FATHER'S BUSINESS. Crown 8vo., 3s. 6d.
5. OUT OF HARNESS. Crown 8vo., 3s. 6d.
6. SPEAKING TO THE HEART. Crown 8vo., 3s. 6d.
7. THE ANGELS' SONG. 18mo, 1s. 6d.
8. EARLY PIETY. 18mo, 1s. 6d.

SAVING KNOWLEDGE. Addressed to Young Men. By THOMAS GUTHRIE, D.D., and W. G. BLAIKIE, D.D. Crown 8vo., 3s. 6d.

By Sir J. F. W. HERSCHEL, Bart.
FAMILIAR LECTURES ON SCIENTIFIC SUBJECTS. Crown 8vo., 6s.

By J. S. HOWSON, D.D.
DEAN OF CHESTER.
THE METAPHORS OF ST. PAUL. Crown 8vo., 3s. 6d.

By the Rev. JOHN HUNT.
RELIGIOUS THOUGHT IN ENGLAND from the Reformation to the End of Last Century. A Contribution to the History of Theology. Vol. I. Demy 8vo., 16s.

By EDWARD IRVING.
1. COLLECTED WRITINGS. 5 vols., demy 8vo., £3.
2. MISCELLANIES FROM THE COLLECTED WRITINGS. Post 8vo., 6s.
3. PROPHETICAL WRITINGS. Vols. I. and II. Demy 8vo., 15s. each.

By JEAN INGELOW.
1. STUDIES FOR STORIES, FROM GIRLS' LIVES. With Illustrations by Millais and others. Crown 8vo., 5s.
2. A SISTER'S BYE HOURS. With Illustrations. Crown 8vo., 5s.
3. STORIES TOLD TO A CHILD. With Illustrations. Square 32mo., 3s. 6d.

STRAHAN AND CO.

By the Rev. HARRY JONES, M.A.

THE REGULAR SWISS ROUND. With Illustrations by WHYMPER. Small 8vo., 3s. 6d.

By J. T. K.

THE LEGENDS OF KING ARTHUR AND HIS KNIGHTS OF THE ROUND TABLE. Compiled and Edited by J. T. K. Small 8vo., 1s. 6d.; or in paper wrapper, 1s.

By GEORGE MAC DONALD, LL.D.

1. ANNALS OF A QUIET NEIGHBOURHOOD. Crown 8vo., 6s.
2. THE SEABOARD PARISH. Crown 8vo., 6s.
3. THE DISCIPLE, and other Poems. Crown 8vo., 6s.
4. UNSPOKEN SERMONS. Crown 8vo., 3s. 6d.
5. DEALINGS WITH THE FAIRIES. With Illustrations by ARTHUR HUGHES. Square 32mo., 2s. 6d.

By NORMAN MACLEOD, D.D.

1. EASTWARD. Travels in Egypt, Syria, and Palestine. With Illustrations. Crown 8vo., 6s.
2. THE STARLING. A Scotch Story. With Illustrations. Crown 8vo., 6s.
3. REMINISCENCES OF A HIGHLAND PARISH. Crown 8vo., 6s.
4. The OLD LIEUTENANT AND HIS SON. With Illustrations. Crown 8vo., 3s. 6d.
5. THE EARNEST STUDENT: being Memorials of John Mackintosh. Crown 8vo., 3s. 6d.
6. THE GOLD THREAD. A Story for the Young. With Illustrations. Square 8vo., 2s. 6d.
7. PARISH PAPERS. Crown 8vo., 3s. 6d.
8. SIMPLE TRUTH SPOKEN TO WORKING PEOPLE. Small 8vo., 2s. 6d.

By H. L. MANSEL, D.D.
DEAN OF ST. PAUL'S.

THE PHILOSOPHY OF THE CONDITIONED: Sir William Hamilton and John Stuart Mill. Post 8vo., 6s.

A LIST OF BOOKS PUBLISHED BY

By GERALD MASSEY.
A TALE OF ETERNITY, and other Poems. Crown 8vo., 7s.

By the Rev. CHARLES MERIVALE, D.C.L.
DEAN OF ELY.
HOMER'S ILIAD in English Rhymed Verse. 2 vols., Demy 8vo., 24s.

By J. E. MILLAIS, R.A.
MILLAIS' ILLUSTRATIONS. A Collection of Drawings on Wood. Demy 4to., cloth gilt extra, 16s.

By E. H. PLUMPTRE, M.A.
1. BIBLICAL STUDIES. Post 8vo., 7s. 6d.
2. CHRIST AND CHRISTENDOM. Being the Boyle Lectures for 1866. Demy 8vo., 12s.
3. THE TRAGEDIES OF ÆSCHYLOS. A New Translation, with a Biographical Essay, and an Appendix of Rhymed Choral Odes. 2 vols., crown 8vo., 12s.
4. THE TRAGEDIES OF SOPHOCLES. A New Translation, with a Biographical Essay, and an Appendix of Rhymed Choruses. Crown 8vo., 7s. 6d.
5. LAZARUS, and other Poems. Crown 8vo., 5s.
6. MASTER AND SCHOLAR, and other Poems. Crown 8vo., 5s.
7. THEOLOGY AND LIFE. Sermons on Special Occasions. Small 8vo., 6s.
8. SUNDAY. Sewed, 6d.

By the AUTHORS of "POEMS WRITTEN FOR A CHILD."
1. POEMS WRITTEN FOR A CHILD, with Illustrations. Square 32mo., 3s. 6d.
2. CHILD-WORLD, with Illustrations. Square 32mo., 3s. 6d.
3. CHILD-NATURE, with Illustrations. Square 32mo., 3s. 6d.

By W. R. S. RALSTON.
KRILOF AND HIS FABLES. With Illustrations. Crown 8vo., 5s.

By the Rev. ADOLPH SAPHIR.
CONVERSION ILLUSTRATED FROM EXAMPLES RECORDED IN THE BIBLE. New Edition. Small 8vo., 3s. 6d.

By G. A. SIMCOX.
POEMS AND ROMANCES. Crown 8vo., 6s.

By M. B. SMEDLEY.
1. POEMS (including "Lady Grace," a Drama in Five Acts). Crown 8vo., 5s.
2. OTHER FOLK'S LIVES. Crown 8vo., 5s.

By ALEXANDER SMITH.
1. ALFRED HAGART'S HOUSEHOLD. Crown 8vo., 6s.
2. A SUMMER IN SKYE. Crown 8vo., 6s.
3. DREAMTHORP: A Book of Essays written in the Country. Crown 8vo., 3s. 6d.

By A. P. STANLEY, D.D.
DEAN OF WESTMINSTER.
SCRIPTURE PORTRAITS, and other Miscellanies. Crown 8vo., 6s.

By ANTHONY TROLLOPE.
1. RALPH THE HEIR. Now appearing in Sixpenny Monthly Parts.
2. PHINEAS FINN. With Illustrations by Millais. 2 vols., demy 8vo., 25s.
3. HE KNEW HE WAS RIGHT. With Illustrations by MARCUS STONE. 2 vols., demy 8vo., 21s.

By SARAH TYTLER.
1. CITOYENNE JACQUELINE. A Woman's Lot in the Great French Revolution. Crown 8vo., 5s.
2. DAYS OF YORE. Crown 8vo., 5s.
3. GIRLHOOD AND WOMANHOOD. Crown 8vo., 5s.
4. PAPERS FOR THOUGHTFUL GIRLS. With Illustrations by MILLAIS. Crown 8vo., 5s.
5. THE DIAMOND ROSE. A Life of Love and Duty. Crown 8vo., 5s.
6. THE HUGUENOT FAMILY IN THE ENGLISH VILLAGE. With Illustrations. Crown 8vo., 6s.

A LIST OF BOOKS PUBLISHED BY STRAHAN AND CO.

By C. J. VAUGHAN, D.D.
MASTER OF THE TEMPLE.

1. LAST WORDS IN THE PARISH CHURCH OF DONCASTER. Crown 8vo., 3s. 6d.
2. EARNEST WORDS FOR EARNEST MEN. Small 8vo., 4s. 6d.
3. PLAIN WORDS ON CHRISTIAN LIVING. Small 8vo., 2s. 6d.
4. CHRIST THE LIGHT OF THE WORLD. Small 8vo., 2s. 6d.
5. CHARACTERISTICS OF CHRIST'S TEACHING. Small 8vo., 2s. 6d.
6. VOICES OF THE PROPHETS ON FAITH, PRAYER, AND HUMAN LIFE. Small 8vo., 2s. 6d.

By SAMUEL WILBERFORCE, D.D.
BISHOP OF WINCHESTER.

HEROES OF HEBREW HISTORY. Post 8vo., 9s.

By JOHN YOUNG, LL.D.

1. THE CHRIST OF HISTORY. New and Enlarged Edition. Crown 8vo., 6s.
2. THE LIFE AND LIGHT OF MEN. Post 8vo., 7s. 6d.
3. THE CREATOR AND THE CREATION, how related. Crown 8vo., 6s.

Edited by the BISHOP OF ARGYLL.

PRESENT DAY PAPERS ON PROMINENT QUESTIONS IN THEOLOGY. One Shilling Monthly.

1. THE ATONEMENT.
2. THE EUCHARIST.
3. THE RULE OF FAITH.
4. PRESENT UNBELIEF.
5. WORDS FOR THINGS.
6. PRAYERS AND MEDITATIONS.
7. JUSTIFICATION BY FAITH.

STRAHAN & CO., 56, LUDGATE HILL, LONDON.

www.ingramcontent.com/pod-product-compliance
Lightning Source LLC
Chambersburg PA
CBHW030601300426
44111CB00009B/1058